Peacebuilding as Politics

A project of the International Peace Academy

Peacebuilding as Politics

Cultivating Peace in Fragile Societies

edited by
Elizabeth M. Cousens
and Chetan Kumar,
with Karin Wermester

BOULDER
LONDON

Published in the United States of America in 2001 by
Lynne Rienner Publishers, Inc.
1800 30th Street, Boulder, Colorado 80301
www.rienner.com

and in the United Kingdom by
Lynne Rienner Publishers, Inc.
3 Henrietta Street, Covent Garden, London WC2E 8LU

Library of Congress Cataloging-in-Publication Data
Peacebuilding as politics : cultivating peace in fragile societies / edited by Elizabeth M. Cousens and Chetan Kumar, with Karin Wermester.
p. cm.
Includes bibliographical references and index.
ISBN 1-55587-921-7 (alk. paper) — ISBN 1-55587-946-2 (pbk. : alk. paper)
1. Humanitarian assistance—Case studies. 2. Economic assistance—Case studies. 3. Civil war—Case studies. 4. Peace—Case studies. I. Cousens, Elizabeth M. II. Kumar, Chetan. III. Wermester, Karin.

HV544.5.P424 2000
327.1'72—dc21

00-034210

British Cataloguing in Publication Data
A Cataloguing in Publication record for this book is available from the British Library.

Printed and bound in the United States of America

The paper used in this publication meets the requirements of the American National Standard for Permanence of Paper for Printed Library Materials Z39.48-1984.

5 4 3 2 1

Contents

Acknowledgments

Many valued colleagues, supporters, and friends have made this volume possible. We wish to pay special thanks to a few without in any way diminishing the contributions of those we will not be able to name here.

We have been fortunate to work with an extraordinary team of colleagues at the International Peace Academy (IPA), all of whom have in some fashion helped us in the course of our research on peacebuilding. Two former colleagues deserve particular thanks: Lt.-Col. Stephen Moffat and Michèle Griffin, both of whom have gone on to engage directly in peacebuilding for, respectively, the Canadian government and the United Nations Development Programme. We also have been lucky to work with several exceptionally qualified research assistants who joined us as interns while we were developing this project. Perhaps most, we have benefited from the inspiration and active support of IPA's recent presidents, Olara A. Otunnu, under whose stewardship IPA's work on peacebuilding began, and David M. Malone, who arrived at IPA as this project was concluding but was no less energetic in his encouragement. Equally, we are grateful for the warm, intellectual support of IPA's vice president, John L. Hirsch.

We wish also to pay a very special tribute to IPA's two most venerable statesmen, F. T. Liu and George L. Sherry, whose guidance, perspective, and stories have been invaluable.

No project about practice, especially one based on case studies, could move forward without the generosity and candor of the many peacebuilding practitioners—international and indigenous, in headquarters and in the field. We owe an enormous debt to those practitioners who were interviewed over the course of this work. Any insights in the pages ahead truly belong to them; any errors in fact or judgment are fully our own.

We have also benefited greatly from exchange and debate with a number of colleagues working on related issues. Particularly deserving of mention are Richard Hooper, Terje Roed-Larsen, and Mark Taylor of the Norwegian Institute for Applied Social Science (Fafo); Donald Rothchild of the University of California at Davis; Stephen John Stedman of the Center for International Security and Cooperation at Stanford University; Matthias Stieffel and Agneta Johansen of the War-torn Societies Project; Susan L. Woodward of King's College, London; Shepard Forman and Stewart Patrick of the Center on International Cooperation at New York University; Therèse Bouchard and colleagues at the Canadian Center for International Studies and Cooperation; and David L. Phillips and Andrea Bartoli of the International Conflict Resolution Program at Columbia University.

We owe a special thanks to Michael Doyle, whose intellectual leadership and thoughtful support has been immeasurably valuable to each of us in our work at IPA, where he served as vice president and now is a member of the board. He is an inspiration in his example of scholarship wedded to practice. He has also become a friend, and we are lucky to have had the chance to work so closely with him.

Finally, though far from least, none of our research or writing would have been possible without the generous financial and intellectual support we received from the Carnegie Corporation of New York, the Ford Foundation, the Friedrich Ebert Stiftung, the John D. and Catherine T. MacArthur Foundation, the Scherman Foundation, and the United States Institute of Peace.

—*The Editors*

1

Introduction

Elizabeth M. Cousens

With the Cold War's end, the international community became newly seized with the phenomenon of civil wars. In turn, the UN, its family of agencies, and member governments perceived a new chance to tackle the organization's founding mission—to protect new generations from the scourge of war—unapologetically and with an unprecedented marshaling of its many political and institutional resources. Initially, opportunities presented themselves for ending conflicts that had been heavily fueled by Cold War patrons (in, for example, Namibia, El Salvador, Angola, Somalia, Mozambique, Cambodia, Nicaragua, and Guatemala) and for developing common strategies to resolve those conflicts less directly affected by the Cold War (in Rwanda, Sudan, Sierra Leone, and Liberia, to name a few). Indeed, a first wave of such conflicts seemed to have been settled, and their respective foundations for peace laid, under confident international stewardship by the early 1990s, including Namibia in 1989, El Salvador and Mozambique in 1992, and Angola, Cambodia, and Rwanda in 1993.[1]

Both the conditions that gave rise to civil wars and those that resulted from them argued for a more holistic approach to keeping peace that went beyond military and security priorities to address issues of governance, democratic legitimacy, social inclusion, and economic equity that, if properly treated, might enable war-torn countries to increase their resilience to new rounds of violence. The particular challenges of civil wars also argued for a longer time frame in which to consider international assistance. Even if peace could be "kept" for one or two years after a civil war ended, peace was unlikely to stabilize, deepen, and become more irreversible rather than less in such a short time frame. For the UN, the operational question was both how to bridge international assistance that usually pooled separately at the ends of what has been called a "continuum between relief and development"[2] and how to leverage the short-term presence of peacekeepers into longer-term peace.

It was in this context that the idea of "postconflict peacebuilding" emerged and appeared to hold great promise. Alongside "preventive diplomacy," "peacemaking," and "peacekeeping," "postconflict peacebuilding" would be the fourth pillar of a comprehensive approach by the UN and other multilateral bodies to peace and security, not only between states but just as important, within them.[3] As described by UN Secretary-General Boutros Boutros-Ghali, postconflict peacebuilding would encourage more deliberate links among the various actors of the UN system, help develop an effective division of labor among their respective forms of assistance—humanitarian, social and economic, as well as political and military—and attend especially to their interrelationship over time.

Within a very few years, however, the opportunities for peacebuilding seemed to pale beside the obstacles to it. Internal wars appeared to be breaking out with alarming frequency and ferocity, particularly in areas previously under Soviet influence or authority (former Yugoslavia, Tajikistan, Chechnya, Georgia, Azerbaijan, and Moldova) and in Africa. Worse, some conflicts that seemed near settlement showed a horrific capacity to reverse course. In Angola and Rwanda, failed peace accords preceded the greatest bloodletting of the 1990s, as well as greater losses than either country had experienced during previous years of civil war.[4] The U.S./UN rout in Somalia, too, seemed to underscore the intractability of internal wars as well as their imperviousness to international intervention. The 1997 coup in Cambodia, in turn, raised questions about the merits of a nearly two billion dollar peace implementation operation that, just four years earlier, had congratulated itself for helping to resolve the country's internal divisions democratically. Peacebuilding, both in concept and operation, evolved accordingly, reflecting the very mixed record of international intervention in its name.

This volume examines five cases of large-scale interventions to build peace: El Salvador, Cambodia, Haiti, Somalia, and Bosnia and Herzegovina. Its aim is fourfold: first, to shed light on the unique conditions for and constraints upon peacebuilding in each case; second, to examine the quality of international efforts to respond to these; third, to bring greater clarity to ongoing debate over the content and purpose of "international peacebuilding"; and fourth, to identify questions that need continuing attention in order to set more nuanced priorities for peacebuilding under different conditions and to better harness the wide range of international activities to address them.[5]

The cases vary significantly. Bosnia's war was comparatively condensed in time, to four years following the declarations of independence from Yugoslavia of the former Yugoslav republics of Croatia, Slovenia, and Bosnia; whereas the other cases had known protracted or episodic violence for much longer periods. El Salvador's government had fought with rebels for twelve years before war ended in 1992; Cambodia was a war zone of some kind for nearly twenty-five years before the peace agreement of 1993; Somalia had experienced bursts of political violence from at least 1988; and Haiti, while never at war, had dealt with generations of internal repression, coups actual and threatened, and political violence against civilians. In Cambodia, El Salvador, and Bosnia, international efforts followed on the heels of comprehensive, laboriously negotiated peace agreements. In Somalia, a flimsy peace accord followed a massive humanitarian intervention and constituted the starting point for further efforts to consolidate a peace by re-creating a national government. In Haiti, an understanding had been reached about restoring a legitimately elected government, but nothing resembling a peace agreement existed, understandably enough since there had never been a war. In Haiti, the United States figured disproportionately in determining the timing, nature, and priorities of multilateral intervention, whereas no single country or even group of countries played as explicit a hegemonic role in the other cases. In Cambodia, the United Nations exercised transitional authority, giving the international community enormous leverage—at least, potentially—not enjoyed in the other cases, although the current operation in Bosnia appears to be trying to acquire the equivalent capacity by degree and over time. Cambodia, Somalia, and Haiti were contending with illegitimate, profoundly weakened, or failed states. Both Bosnia and Cambodia had to deal with a fundamental transition from one system of political authority and administration to another. In Bosnia and Somalia, efforts to build peace were dogged by persistent, unanswered questions about the territorial and administrative boundaries of the unit in which peace was to be built.

Perhaps most dramatically, the cases vary in the crudest measurement often used to characterize such things: did they "succeed" or did they "fail"? International intervention in Somalia has generally been considered one of the international community's most abject failures and El Salvador one of its greater successes. The UN-led operation in Haiti has been viewed as a relative success but one whose ambitions were far more limited. Meanwhile, international engagement in Bosnia after the Dayton Agreement has been a continuing disappointment, and Cambodia, once touted as a success, raises tough questions about long-term effects, given the 1997 coup and subsequent political upheaval three years after the UN operation concluded.

We deliberately chose such a varied set of cases in order to address a common weakness in the literature on peacebuilding: namely, continuing confusion over what constitutes peacebuilding in the first place, what comprise its appropriate objectives, and what are likely to be its most effective methods. Since its first articulation, the concept of peacebuilding has generated a burgeoning literature and a virtual cottage industry of operational activities to be undertaken in its name by a wide range of multilateral organizations, international agencies, governments, and nongovernmental organizations (NGOs).[6] In this volume, we argue that the number and range of peacebuilding initiatives, however commendable in many respects, risk eclipsing the core concerns that led to consideration of peacebuilding in the first place. Instead, peacebuilding needs to sharpen and retain a focus on its original purpose: consolidating whatever degree of peace has been achieved in the short term and, in the longer term, increasing the likelihood that future conflict can be managed without resort to violence. Further, priority should go to the *political* dimension of conflict and its resolution. Although there will be many and various underlying causes of conflict, the proximate cause of internal violence is the fragility or collapse of political processes and institutions.[7] The defining priority of peacebuilding thus becomes *the construction or strengthening of authoritative and, eventually, legitimate mechanisms to resolve internal conflict without violence.* At its base and at best, peacebuilding should bolster the possibility of vibrant, responsive political life in societies where politics have been supplanted by military contest and violence.

When approached with keen sensitivity to context, what could be called "peacebuilding as politics" can best be seen as an organizing principle for determining the appropriate range, timing, and priorities of international action. It also indicates the need for new criteria by which to evaluate both peacebuilding's short-term impact and its long-term efficacy, for more responsive policy mechanisms to reorient peacebuilding assistance in real time when warranted, and for very different benchmarks to govern the entrance and exit of international actors in war-torn societies.

Defining Peacebuilding

Peacebuilding has been variously and often confusingly defined. Some definitions are so general as to include virtually all forms of international assistance to societies that have experienced or are at risk of armed conflict;[8] some are more precise but show greater interest in clarifying international mandates than conditions for peace in a target country; others are more willing to ask tough questions about the comparative value of international efforts vis-à-vis one another and in contrast with domestic initiatives.

Broadly speaking, peacebuilding has been approached along what could be seen as the two axes that circumscribe its possibilities. One describes the peacebuilding tools and capacities available to the organized international community; the other describes the particular conflict in question, its nature, intensity, depth of social support, and so on.[9] These different approaches can usefully be considered as "deductive," where the content of peacebuilding is deduced from the existing capacities and mandates of international agencies and organizations, versus "inductive," where the content of peacebuilding is determined by the particular matrix of needs and capacities in individual cases. Along each dimension—"solution" or "problem"—definitions of peacebuilding have both more and less sophisticated versions that, in turn, are either more or less helpful as guides to effective policymaking.

Deductive Approaches

When peacebuilding debuted in Boutros-Ghali's 1992 *An Agenda for Peace,* the priority was to map the full range of postwar needs and identify those international resources available to help meet them. *An Agenda for Peace* spurred multiple efforts to flesh out the operational content of what it labeled "postconflict peacebuilding": among them, a General Assembly Sub-Group on Post-Conflict Peace-building; a special task force to canvass experts and develop a comprehensive *Inventory of Post-Conflict Peace-building Activities;* and an international colloquium that brought together a comprehensive range of UN agencies and units, Bretton Woods institutions, and major donors to elaborate more precisely what their respective contributions might be to postwar reconstruction and longer-term recovery.[10] This approach treated conflict as linear. Peacebuilding was therefore "postconflict," becoming necessary only *after* preventive diplomacy had failed to avert armed hostilities, *after* peacemaking had established the framework of a negotiated settlement, and *after* peacekeeping had monitored an agreed cease-fire and presumably facilitated the restoration of a threshold of order.

The *Agenda*'s conception of peacebuilding included almost every sector of international assistance, taking its cue from—along with the limits of—the official mandates of UN departments and other agencies, whose resources were to be deployed in the service of an ambitious but strategically undifferentiated set of goals. In the *Agenda*'s terms, peacebuilding ranged from specific tasks that might derive from a comprehensive peace agreement—such as helping to disarm the parties, canton troops, and hold or destroy weapons; monitoring elections; fielding civilian police; and repatriating refugees—through far broader and less tangible objectives: "the restoration of order . . . advancing efforts to protect human rights, reforming or strengthening governmental institutions and promoting formal and informal processes of political participation."[11]

This approach was helpful initially as a road map of the multiple and complex needs of war-ravaged societies, including those that went beyond items provided for in a peace agreement, as well as of the capacities of major international organizations, agencies, and bilateral donors to address them. It remained limited, however, by a lack of critical distinctions and by its starting assumption that peacebuilding would be the final phase of international assistance in conflict resolution. This conception of peacebuilding encouraged a segmented approach to international assistance. It largely avoided questions of priorities among peacebuilding activities or of overlapping or potentially contradictory mandates.[12] Moreover, this approach to peacebuilding gave little indication of how to determine what a particular war-torn society most needed or whether some of its needs might conflict, let alone the precise relationship of various forms of assistance to those needs or how international efforts might be nested in a larger political strategy to help countries reconstruct peacetime political systems. Further, no consideration was given to peacebuilding that might begin before or even in the absence of a formal peace agreement, nor to the challenge of engaging in peacebuilding should a peacekeeping presence be either absent or ineffective. In short, this approach to peacebuilding emphasized the "what" and the "who" of peacebuilding over the "how," "why," or "to what end." It amounted to an inventory of those needs that could be filled by international actors, with the larger purpose of peacebuilding remaining vague.

Once the potential components of international peacebuilding had been reasonably well identified, attention quickly turned to peacebuilding's operational implications. Linking the activities of various organizations and agencies with different mandates, budgets, and operational cultures posed multiple practical challenges, and concerns about coordination began moving toward center stage, picking up where the inventories left off.[13] Within the policy and academic communities, new research emphasized management, organizational handoffs, budgetary gaps,[14] and interoperability among international actors, though it, too, assumed that peacebuilding would take place in the "twilight" of a peacekeeping operation, meaning that debates over peacebuilding largely refrained from their obvious implications for conflict prevention.

Attention to operational coordination added much to early discussions of peacebuilding. Focus on interorganizational coordination, management, and financing has yielded insights for peacebuilding even in the absence of a peacekeeping operation (as well as for international activities other than peacebuilding). It also invites frank consideration of mandates and procedures that might contradict one another, even in the context of shared purposes and good intentions. Moreover, the political dimension of peacebuilding has received increasing attention, with growing recognition that peacebuilding efforts cannot avoid political impact given the volatility of the contexts in which they take place.[15] Changeovers in international assistance can easily and disproportionately upset a fragile peace, for example, either when military assets are being drawn down in anticipation of resumed development assistance or when a civilian mission significantly shifts gears.[16] International assistance has to be adept at anticipating such dynamics and developing ways to target aid accordingly.

Yet even this more operational tack leaves much unexplored. Operational preoccupations tend to remain anchored in the short- to medium-term period in which international assistance is at its most intensive, with minimal attention given to whether shorter-term transitional measures have the capacity to seed long-run capacities for conflict resolution. More, the focus on mechanics and techniques, however important, can displace consideration of strategic priorities or how the international community might go about setting them. Finally, even the most sophisticated efforts to fine-tune international peacebuilding tools cannot answer questions about when and under what conditions those tools can responsibly and effectively be deployed.

Inductive Approaches

Different in emphasis are those definitions that begin with the causes and effects of particular conflicts or conflict in general and that seek to devise peacebuilding strategies accordingly. Peacebuilding, here, implies an analysis of whatever constellation of political, social, and economic forces led to a particular armed conflict. This approach is driven less by the content and form of solutions the international community has to offer than by the problem that wants solving: what caused this particular conflict and how can those causes be redressed? With an appreciation for history, it encourages attention to what may be unique about a given case and invites more holistic assessments of conflict that consider the interrelationship among multiple factors—authoritarian or exclusivist institutions, civil-military relations, economic inequity, urban-rural divides, the impact of regional politics, and so on.

With what could be considered a more problem-driven approach, peacebuilding efforts become an arena for debating the relative importance of different causes of conflict. "Root causes" tend to be favored as such, which usually is shorthand for either long-standing or structural factors, often found within social, economic, or cultural spheres, that are believed to have rendered a particular society vulnerable to armed conflict in the first place. Within the domain of root causes there is further debate about the comparative weight of different factors—skewed or underdevelopment, violations of human rights, and intercommunity tensions, to name just a few—each of which has both academic and organizational advocates. International assistance is then asked to redress chronic inequities or social cleavages in order to build peace effectively.[17]

To the extent that international peacebuilding genuinely targets long-standing root causes and assists populations and new governments in redressing them, it can become a partner in fundamental, sometimes revolutionary change in that society. In Cambodia, such a process was begun by the UN's organization of democratic elections from the ground up and, less directly, by its seeding Cambodia's emerging civil society. In El Salvador, the international community attempted to end criminal impunity and reform the justice system. In Bosnia, international actors have pressed such issues as economic privatization, in its own right and as a perceived precondition for accomplishing other peacebuilding tasks such as reconstruction and return of refugees and displaced persons. International actors can even become drivers of such change, sometimes inadvertently and often problematically. Moreover, the emphasis on deep and chronic contributors to conflict makes more explicit the kinship between peacebuilding and state and nation building.

By placing a premium on diagnosing the problem before offering a solution, an inductive approach invites a more nuanced assessment of what a particular society most needs in order to solidify a fragile peace, without assuming that all war-torn countries will benefit equally from the standard menu of international assistance. It also adds value by emphasizing dimensions of peace and security that have been traditionally neglected but that play a demonstrably consequential role in civil wars.

This approach to peacebuilding is not without weaknesses, however. To begin with, the international policy community has not organized itself in order to answer causal questions. As a result, assertions of the importance of one causal factor over another tend to derive more from advocacy than analysis.[18] More problematic, anchoring peacebuilding in analysis of comparative causes renders peacebuilding vulnerable to the challenge faced by international relations scholarship in general: among the multiple, complex factors contributing to a particular armed conflict, which are demonstrably the most salient? What is the relative contribution between long-standing inequalities and the particular, short-term use made of them by political leaders? Deep, persistent fissures may predispose many societies to conflict, but only some of these impoverished, ethnically divided, or otherwise vulnerable polities suffer protracted political violence. Moreover, what drives armed conflict at the start of a war may cease to be the principal issue by the time the war is over, particularly when wars last for years. Land reform in El Salvador, for instance, was an issue that powerfully mobilized support for rebel forces at the start of the country's war, yet it became far less pressing by the time the war concluded because of agrarian flight to the cities. More than agricultural small holdings, access to small commercial loans and vocational training became newly important for many Salvadorans.[19] Bosnia presents an analogous case, if much more morally troubling, since the imperative of managing rival ethnic claims in a highly intermixed population arguably diminishes once that population has been significantly regrouped into homogeneous enclaves. In each case, conflict may have evolved in ways that make retrospective attention to root causes unnecessary and even counterproductive.

Peacebuilding as Politics

Our conception of peacebuilding draws both on our case experience and on existing approaches in both official and academic circles. Its chief merit lies in identifying critical distinctions on which policy decisions should turn. In our experience, effective peacebuilding requires establishing a strategic framework of objectives for international assistance; a privileging within this framework of conflict resolution over other goals; and in relationship to that objective, setting priorities among international efforts. Especially in this last respect, peacebuilding also requires willingness to make tough trade-offs in a climate of shrinking international commitment to expend material and political resources in societies where needs are perceived to be chronic, if not always so actually.

Revisiting the Goals

Literature on peacebuilding tends to invoke a melange of goals, conservative and ambitious, short- and long-term, that remain relatively undifferentiated, let alone considered in strategic relationship with one another.

Boutros-Ghali's *An Agenda for Peace* set the initial tone in 1992. In its terms, the object of peacebuilding was enormous and included preventing the "recurrence of conflict"; developing structures that would "consolidate peace and advance a sense of confidence and well-being among people"; removing "underlying economic, social, cultural and humanitarian problems"; and enabling "the transformation of deficient national structures and capabilities."[20] Three years later, Boutros-Ghali's *Supplement to An Agenda for Peace* acknowledged the difficulty of reaching most of the goals set out in the *Agenda.* Its conception of goals, however, remained vague, entailing "the creation of structures for the institutionalization of peace." The time frame for judging the effectiveness of peacebuilding was left unspecified.[21]

Yet for peacebuilding to be well designed at the outset and accountable for its achievements when concluded, there needs to be much greater clarity about the goals and benchmarks for success. A failure to differentiate among peacebuilding's goals courts strategic incoherence among the components of international assistance. It also risks holding peacebuilding efforts to an impossibly high standard, overestimating what international engagement can plausibly and constructively deliver while diminishing the importance of more modest achievements.[22]

At least five basic objectives circulate throughout debate over peacebuilding that can be distinguished from one another: first, what could be called "self-enforcing cease-fire," meaning that the armed conflict just settled will not recur, even in the absence of an international presence;[23] second, what can be labeled "self-enforcing peace," meaning that new armed conflicts will not occur; and finally, a trio of the more robust goals of democracy, justice, and equity. In some fashion, policymakers, advocates, and analysts operate within this simple framework of goals. Yet the relationship and relative priority among these goals, however admirable all may be in an ideal world, have yet to be seriously debated among peacebuilding advocates rather than assumed. Disagreements reveal themselves in policy debate—criticism that the Bosnian peace is "only a cease-fire," for instance—but rarely translate into a considered argument about why a cease-fire is an insufficient goal in a particular case or how a cease-fire might relate to more ambitious aspirations such as national unity or democratization. Assertions that "there can be no peace without justice," analogously, mean little unless it is clarified whether peace is being defined robustly, which necessarily includes measures of justice, or whether a causal argument is being made that redress of past grievances is necessary to either a self-enforcing cease-fire or self-enforcing peace.[24]

Beyond clarifying rival goals, we propose that international peacebuilding give priority to the second goal. Self-enforcing peace sets its sights higher than a self-enforcing cease-fire, however considerable an accomplishment the latter may be in societies wracked by war. It is also distinct from democracy, justice, or equity that, for the purposes of peacebuilding, we construe as principally important insofar as each contributes to a society's capacity to resolve conflict without violence. Successful peacebuilding must also recognize that international actors need "exit strategies" or at least what might be termed "reduced commitment strategies." Beyond giving priority to the absence or diminishment of armed conflict, then, effective peacebuilding should define its goals in such a way that they can be self-enforcing, or sustained over time without new international intervention.

In turn, we argue that the most effective means to self-enforcing peace is to cultivate political processes and institutions that can manage group conflict without violence but with authority and, eventually, legitimacy. If war is a continuation of politics by other means, peacebuilding can be seen as an opportunity to channel "war" into manageable forms of competition or to support what I. William Zartman and others characterize as the reinstitution of political life.[25] While multiple and subtle dimensions of postwar recovery are also extrapolitical—cultural, psychological, even spiritual—these are, importantly, domestic processes where international assistance has little comparative advantage and often questionable credibility or legitimacy. International actors should focus scarce resources on only these areas where third parties can play an instrumental role in producing change.

The most effective path to preventing renewed hostilities, then, is for international efforts to help a given society build its political capacity to manage conflict without violence. Moving beyond ceasefire to a deeper, self-enforcing peace depends on the emergence of social, political, and legal mechanisms to resolve conflict authoritatively, though this may not always mean democratically, at least in the conventionally liberal sense. All societies experience conflict, after all. Peacebuilding is not designed to eliminate conflict but to develop effective mechanisms by which a polity can resolve its rival claims, grievances, and competition over common resources.[26] Whether such mechanisms lodge in the state or in society or a productive division of labor between the two will depend on particular histories, cultures, and resources. Societies also need not have all such mechanisms in place in order to be seen as effectively building peace. More important are signs that a commitment to resolving conflicts without violence has begun to emerge among an increasingly inclusive set of national actors at both state and society levels, with an increasing likelihood that mechanisms for conflict resolution will become institutionalized even in the face of continuing violence.[27]

In a sense, we aim to strike a strategic balance between the poles of "negative" and "positive" peace. The objective of peacebuilding thus retains a focus on violent conflict (the central concern when peace is defined as the absence of war) but with an interest in the tools a society can develop to manage such conflict authoritatively and legitimately, which will involve some elements of positive peace. Interestingly, those elements of positive peace that hold the most promise for peacebuilding—effective public institutions, meaningful political inclusion, norms of fairness and access, legal protection for groups and individuals, and so on—are precisely those that create mechanisms for addressing grievances and resolving conflict.

Setting Priorities

By implication, peacebuilding should not be equated to the entire basket of postwar needs, as multiple and complex as they are. Rather, it should be seen as a strategic focus on conflict resolution and opening of political space, *to which these other needs may or may not contribute.* What are frequently conceived as peacebuilding activities, then—demobilization, economic reconstruction, refugee repatriation, human rights monitoring, elections, community reconciliation—are not inherently equivalent to peacebuilding unless they design themselves to be. Progress in some may be a necessary condition for peacebuilding: the complete demobilization of the army in Haiti, for example, along with the creation of a new national police force, established a threshold of public security essential for any more enduring peace. Each of these activities can also be conducive to peacebuilding and ideally will be: the repatriation of 370,000 Cambodian refugees from camps along the Thai border helped restore the semblance of normal life, which strengthened the foundation for further peacebuilding. Each can further become an instrument for peacebuilding, for example, the removal of mines or the rebuilding of a hospital—projects that enable former enemies to work together, as was attempted in multiple projects in Bosnia.[28]

Peacebuilding also becomes an effort that can be pursued at different stages of a conflict. Peacebuilding might take place in the absence of a peace settlement, for instance, as in the Haitian case. Or it might take place despite a peace settlement or an attempted peace process should these be ill conceived or of poor quality, as some argue occurred in Somalia and Bosnia. Furthermore, peacebuilding can occur in advance, alongside, or even in the absence of a peacekeeping operation or a formal peacemaking effort, although it will face different constraints and enjoy fewer resources. As is increasingly recognized by operational actors, the objectives of peacebuilding, peacemaking, and peacekeeping are inseparable, making these three forms of intervention either mutually supportive or mutually corrosive. To be mutually reinforcing, however, the three want more flexible operational linkages based not on sequence but on case-specific needs. Peacebuilding in some cases may need the confidence provided by a peacekeeping presence—any peacebuilding in Bosnia, for instance, depends on the staying power of international peacekeepers—or the organizational expertise of blue-helmet battalions with their extensive logistics and security, both of which were vital in conducting the first Cambodian national elections. In other cases, a particular kind of peacekeeping presence may be an obstacle to developing more effective peacebuilding strategies, as was the mid-course, poorly conceived turn to peace enforcement in Somalia. In contexts where parties are judged truly uncommitted to peace, however, peacebuilding may not even be a prospect without peace enforcement of the most strenuous kind.

It is important to note that certain forms of international assistance and the timing of their delivery can also frustrate peacebuilding.[29] Economic liberalization measures risk, exacerbating perceptions of inequity, for instance, thus eroding confidence in parties' respective stakes in a nascent peace.[30] Postwar elections held before armies have sufficiently demobilized or a threshold of civilian security has been attained can jeopardize even short-term peace, let alone longer-term processes of democratization.[31] Advocates of robust goals, in particular, tend to underestimate the volatility of the process of reaching them, a factor that needs to be appreciated, anticipated, and managed, particularly where economic liberalization or democratization is concerned.

Implications for Policy

The implications of the foregoing for international peacebuilding efforts are several, which our conclusion examines in more detail. For introduction purposes, however, several themes deserve mention.

First, this stance toward peacebuilding places a particular burden on international assistance to be knowledgeable about the unique frailties and strengths of the society it seeks to support. Even the most damaged country is resilient. However shattered the human and institutional resources of war-torn societies, they often possess some capacity for conflict management, though not always the kind easily recognized or accepted by Western institutions.[32] Yet international actors often lack knowledge of local terrain, languages, histories, and habits. War-torn societies need highly context-sensitive approaches to political stabilization, reform and reconstruction, and international efforts that are informed enough to adapt themselves to changing circumstances in real time.

Second, the international community has to develop a greater ability to integrate its various resources—military, civilian, diplomatic, political, economic, humanitarian—with one another functionally and over time. These must be put at the service of a carefully considered set of priorities that leverage the most constructive dynamics within a particular society in order to stabilize peace.

Third, if the ultimate objective of peacebuilding is political, international assistance must be particularly alert to continuing political challenges even after a major settlement has been reached. Until peace is thoroughly stabilized, every arena of assistance becomes an opportunity to consolidate an agreement, mediate outstanding issues, and build confidence; or contrarily, to misunderstand one another, seed distrust, and facilitate obstruction by recalcitrant parties. This is true of all forms of assistance, from food delivery and refugee reintegration through police training. At least in part, all assistance to societies in conflict should be viewed through a political lens focused on internal conflict management.

Fourth, peacebuilding will always encounter multiple challenges. These necessarily vary from conflict to conflict, but peacebuilding efforts will have their best chance when obstacles are anticipated and a flexible range of policy options are generated to manage them. The conclusion to this volume explores several potential pitfalls, including the nature of the settlement, the question of whether parties genuinely want peace, and the complexity of multiple transitions.

Finally, perhaps the greatest challenge for the international community in trying to assist war-torn societies is to be ruthlessly modest about its ambitions. Aspirations to establish positive peace through short- to medium-term intervention fly in the face of historical experience. Especially in the years after a major war has ended, peace needs to be treated as a matter of degree, rarely irreversible, and unlikely to be built in a neat, progressive sequence.[33] In its positive form, peace has never arrived all at once but rather has seen its elements emerge over long periods of time, by fits and starts, and often interspersed with periods of great violence. This is especially the case given that few current candidates for peacebuilding are undergoing only a transition from war to peace. Many are contending with the move from single- to multiple-party political systems, command to market economies, rural to urban social life, and with changing relationships between religious and secular authorities.[34] Some are also attempting to redefine, usually by force, the territorial and administrative boundaries of the prior state to the point of secession or radical decentralization. In other words, in most cases where some form of peacebuilding assistance is under way, states, governments, and societies are also engaged in the complex, multivariate dynamics of what has commonly been called state or nation building. Though one may wish that the resources now available at the turn of the twentieth century, including an unprecedented range of multilateral fora, organizations, and instruments, will enable war-torn societies to jump-start and condense such processes that have historically been long and arduous, the record of multilateral peacebuilding indicates grounds for greater circumspection.

While focusing squarely on a given country's emerging capacity to manage conflict, then, peacebuilding efforts have to go much farther to identify accurately and responsively the unique relationships, mechanisms, processes, institutions, or authorities that hold the greatest promise for ongoing conflict resolution over public issues in a particular country, which may not always look like those in Western states. Every component of international assistance—whether humanitarian, military, social, economic, or political—can then be conscientiously and complementarily harnessed to support and strengthen these capacities. Overall, the "exit goal" for international peacebuilding should be to leave as many essential, mutually reinforcing elements in place for war-torn societies to build their own peace over the unavoidably long run.

Notes

1. In the six years from 1989 to 1994, the UN launched eighteen new peacekeeping missions, most of them "multidimensional" operations mandated to support and even formally implement peace accords in the context of civil

wars. Beginning with the UN Transition Assistance Group (UNTAG) designed to shepherd Namibian independence in 1989, these included: the UN Observer Mission in El Salvador (ONUSAL by its Spanish acronym) and UN Angola Verification Mission (UNAVEM) in 1991; the UN Mission in Mozambique (ONUMOZ) and UN Transitional Authority in Cambodia (UNTAC) in 1992; and the UN Observer Mission in Uganda-Rwanda and UN Military Assistance in Rwanda (UNOMUR and UNAMIR) in 1993.

2. For discussion of evolving ideas about the relationship between relief and development, see Mark Bradbury, "Behind the Rhetoric of the Relief-to-Development Continuum," paper prepared for the NGOs in Complex Emergencies Project (CARE Canada, September 1997).

3. Boutros Boutros-Ghali, *An Agenda for Peace: With the New Supplement and Related UN Documents,* 2nd ed. (New York: United Nations, 1995), para. 46.

4. Close to 400,000 are thought to have been killed following abrogation of the Bicesse Accords in Angola; over one million are thought to have been killed during the Rwandan genocide in 1994. On Angola, see Alex Vines, "One Hand Tied: Angola and the UN," CIIR Briefing Papers (London: Catholic Institute for International Relations, 1993), 10; on Rwanda, see Howard Adelman and Astri Suhrke, eds., *The Path of a Genocide: The Rwanda Crisis from Uganda to Zaire* (Piscataway, NJ: Transaction Publishers, 1999).

5. We use the term *peacebuilding* over *postconflict peacebuilding* for several reasons: it is simpler, it leaves open the possibility that peacebuilding efforts might be worthwhile even before an armed conflict has ended, and it does not imply a linear path from armed conflict to peace.

6. As just a few examples: in 1997, the World Bank established a new Postconflict Unit, and the UN Secretary-General's reform effort recommended setting up a special Postconflict Peacebuilding Unit with the Department of Political Affairs. Earlier, the U.S. Agency for International Development had established an Office of Transition Initiatives (in 1994), and the Canadian government had created a Peacebuilding and Human Security Division within its Department of Foreign Affairs and International Trade and a Peacebuilding Unit within its International Development Agency (in 1995).

7. Several experts reaffirm this point. Recent work by International Institute for Democracy and Electoral Assistance (International IDEA) argues that political mechanisms and processes are the key to lasting peace and must therefore be designed to suit the unique vulnerabilities to violence of particular cases. See Peter Harris and Ben Reilly, eds., *Democracy and Deep-Rooted Conflict: Options for Negotiators* (Stockholm, Sweden: International IDEA, 1998). Michael E. Brown's work on internal conflicts also argues that it is the political manipulation of cleavages, whether social or economic, more than the cleavages themselves that pose the principal threat to peace. See Michael E. Brown, ed., *The International Dimensions of Internal Conflict* (Cambridge, MA: MIT Press, 1996), 23. Increasingly, research on conflict prevention also emphasizes that conflict management is preeminently a political exercise. See Barnett R. Rubin, ed., *Cases and Strategies for Preventive Action* (New York: The Century Foundation Press, 1998), 18.

8. For example, in his 1999 *Report of the Secretary-General on the Work of the Organization,* Kofi Annan describes various UN peacebuilding activities that include government decentralization, fiscal reform, social investment, rural development, human rights, reform of judicial and security institutions, and assistance in nation-building efforts. A/54/1 (August 31, 1999), paras. 101–108.

9. To these, Michael Doyle and Nicholas Sambanis add a third dimension, defined as "local capacity," which they argue defines the effective capacity for building peace. See their unpublished paper, "Strategies of Peacebuilding: A Theoretical and Practical Analysis," (September 29, 1999), 5–7.

10. Task Force on Post-Conflict Peace-Building, *An Inventory of Post-Conflict Peace-building Activities* (New York: UN Department of Humanitarian Affairs, June 1995); United Nations Department for Development Support and Management Services and United Nations Industrial Development Organization, "Post-Conflict Reconstruction Strategies," paper presented at an international colloquium by the Austrian Centre for Peace and Conflict Resolution, (Stadt Schlaining, Austria, June 23–24, 1995). See also Administrative Committee on Coordination, Consultative Committee on Programme and Operational Questions, *Survey of the United Nations System Capabilities in Post-Conflict Reconstruction* (United Nations Office at Vienna, April 1996).

11. Boutros-Ghali, *An Agenda for Peace,* 61.

12. A notable exception is Alvaro de Soto and Graciana del Castillo, "Obstacles to Peacebuilding," *Foreign Policy* 94 (Spring 1994): 69–83.

13. See "Beyond the Emergency: Development Within UN Peace Missions," special issue of *International Peacekeeping,* ed. Jeremy Ginifer, 3, 2 (Summer 1996); Winrich Kühne, *Winning the Peace: Concept and Lessons Learned of Post-conflict Peacebuilding* (Ebenhausen, Germany: Research Institute for International Affairs, July 1996); and Fafo Programme for International Cooperation and Conflict Resolution, "Command from the Saddle: Managing United Nations Peace-Building Missions," Recommendations Report of the Forum on the Special Representative of the Secretary-General: Shaping the UN's Role in Peace Implementation, January 1999.

14. The resource challenge has multiple elements, including the gap between the assessed contributions that fund peacekeeping and the voluntary aid that funds development, and the distance between pledges of assistance and actual disbursement. On this latter point, see Shepard Forman and Stewart Patrick, eds., *Good Intentions: Pledges of Aid for Postconflict Recovery,* Center on International Cooperation Studies in Multilateralism (Boulder, CO: Lynne Rienner Publishers, 2000).

15. See, for example, an unpublished internal report conducted for the UN Under-Secretary-General for Political Affairs by Margaret J. Anstee, "Strengthening the Role of the Department of Political Affairs as Focal Point for Post-Conflict Peace-Building" (October 30, 1998).

16. A dramatic illustration arose in Haiti, when a new General Assembly–mandated International Civilian Support Mission (MICAH) was established in March 2000 to replace the combined efforts of the two missions just ending, the UN Civilian Police Mission in Haiti (MIPONUH) and the joint UN-OAS International Civilian Mission (MICIVIH). Just two months before Haitian elections the new mission was authorized and deployed but within one month had to retrench severely when anticipated voluntary funding failed to materialize.

17. Properly identifying long-term contributors to conflict also creates opportunities for what the Carnegie Commission on Preventing Deadly Conflict refers to as "structural prevention." *Final Report, with Executive Summary* (New York: Carnegie Corporation of New York, December 1997), 37.

18. See, for example, Mary Robinson's remarks that "human rights imperatives can and should be injected into every aspect of the Organization's work [since it is important] . . . to understand that today's human rights violations are the causes of tomorrow's conflicts." Mary Robinson, United Nations High Commissioner for Human Rights, Romanes Lecture at Oxford University, November 11, 1997. (www.unhchr.ch/huricane/huricane.nsf/(Symbol)/OHCHR.STM.97.1.En?Opendocument: p. 6)

19. Graciana del Castillo, "The Arms-for-Land Deal in El Salvador," in *Keeping the Peace: Multidimensional UN Operations in Cambodia and El Salvador*, ed. Michael Doyle, Ian Johnstone, and Robert Orr (New York: Cambridge University Press, 1997).

20. Boutros-Ghali, *An Agenda for Peace,* 55, 59, 57.

21. Boutros-Ghali, *An Agenda for Peace,* 49.

22. Elizabeth Cousens and Stephen John Stedman, "Peace Implementation: Interests, Institutions and Organizations," paper presented at the International Studies Association meeting (Washington, D.C., February 17, 1999).

23. I am grateful to Stephen John Stedman for his emphasis on the quality of being "self-enforcing" as a policy aim for both cease-fires and more robust peace.

24. The exception is the so-called democratic peace theory, which has received enormous attention in recent years and which holds that democracies are more peaceful as international neighbors than nondemocratic regimes. At issue, however, was how such states behaved *internationally* rather than how they maintained peace internally or the processes by which they became democratic in the first place. For a good overview of the democratic peace argument, see Michael E. Brown, Sean Lynn-Jones, and Steven E. Miller, eds., *Debating the Democratic Peace,* International Security Readers Series (Cambridge, MA: MIT Press, 1996).

25. Writes Zartman: "Internal settlements at best provide regimes and mechanisms for handling group grievances, or in other words for reinstituting politics." I. William Zartman, "The Unfinished Agenda: Negotiating Internal Conflicts," in Roy Licklider, ed., *Stopping the Killing: How Civil Wars End* (New York: New York University Press, 1993), 29. Licklider makes essentially the same point: "How people who have been killing one another with considerable skill and enthusiasm can create working political units brings us to the central question of politics: why and under what conditions do people form governments? Creating a government from civil war opponents seems impossible except that practically every current state is the result of one or more such processes." Roy Licklider, "Early Returns: Results of the First Wave of Statistical Studies of Civil War Termination," *The Journal of Civil Wars* 1, 3 (Autumn 1998).

26. In Donald Rothchild's phrasing, the challenge "is not eliminating conflict (since an incompatibility of values and objectives seems ubiquitous) but establishing institutions that reward moderation and encourage compromise among contending interests." See "Conclusion: Responding to Africa's Post–Cold War Conflicts," in *Africa in the New International Order: Rethinking State Sovereignty and Regional Security,* ed. Edmond J. Keller and Donald Rothchild (Boulder, CO: Lynne Rienner Publishers, 1996), 227.

27. Our conception of peacebuilding is analogous to what Nicolaïdis has called "continuous conflict-prevention." Kalypso Nicolaïdis, "International

Preventive Action: Developing a Strategic Framework," in *Vigilance and Vengeance: NGOs Preventing Ethnic Conflict in Divided Societies,"* ed. Robert I. Rotberg (Cambridge, MA: The World Peace Foundation, 1996), 32.

28. Author interview with Jacques Paul Klein, Transitional Administrator for Eastern Slavonia, November 1996. Anticipating that collaborative research might be able to play an analogous role, the War-torn Societies Project (WSP) designed ambitious, in-country "action research projects" in Mozambique, Eritrea, Somalia, and El Salvador. For an overview of WSP's work, see June Kane, *War-torn Societies Project: The First Four Years* (Geneva: WSP, 1999).

29. This is the core of Roland Paris's critique of peacebuilding in "Peacebuilding and the Limits of Liberal Internationalism," *International Security* 22, 2 (Fall 1997): 54–89.

30. De Soto and Castillo made this point in 1994 in their article "Obstacles to Peacebuilding" at an early stage in the international community's experience with peacebuilding, to which others have subsequently returned.

31. See Krishna Kumar, ed., *Postconflict Elections, Democratization, and International Assistance* (Boulder, CO: Lynne Rienner Publishers, 1998). Other commentators on democratization more generally have made similar arguments. Snyder and Mansfield, for example, write that "countries do not become democracies overnight. More typically, they go through a rocky transitional period, where democratic control over foreign policy is partial, where mass politics mixes in a volatile way with authoritarian elite politics, and where democratization suffers reversals. In this transitional phase of democratization countries become more aggressive and war-prone, not less, and they do fight wars with democratic states." See their "Democratization and the Danger of War," in *Debating the Democratic Peace,* 301.

32. See Somalia chapter in this volume; see also Doyle and Sambanis, "Strategies for Peacebuilding."

33. Christopher Coker, "How Wars End," *Millennium: Journal of International Studies* 26, 3 (1997): 615–630.

34. Increasingly, students of postwar societies refer to the problem of "triple transitions," meaning societies moving from war to peace, authoritarian to democratic regimes, and statist to market economies. Here, they are borrowing from studies of transition in Eastern and Central Europe where the triple challenge involved territorial changes as well as political democratization and economic liberalization. See, for example, Claus Offe, "Capitalism by Democratic Design? Democratic Theory Facing the Triple Transition in East Central Europe," *Social Research* 58, 4 (Winter 1991): 865–892.

2

Peacebuilding in Haiti

Chetan Kumar

The Haiti case, perhaps uniquely, exemplifies the full range of approaches to peacebuilding that have been put forward since 1995.

In the first instance, it is a case of "postconflict peacebuilding," where, in the aftermath of protracted violence and in the context of a peacekeeping operation, the international community provides assistance along various dimensions to stabilize the postconflict situation. This assistance has included the repair of infrastructure, the reform of public institutions such as the judicial and police systems, and economic relief and development assistance. In Haiti, the UN has focused on training an effective police force, and the United States, Canada, and France, among others, have provided assistance for building a judicial system. Various national contingents under the UN banner—U.S. army reserves, the Pakistani battalion, the Canadian battalion—have implemented projects to install or rebuild infrastructure, and the United Nations Development Program (UNDP), the World Bank, and the Inter-American Development Bank have focused on putting together specific economic assistance projects.

In the second instance, Haiti offers considerable ammunition for the argument that peacebuilding is essentially about development. Several institutions that the international community has attempted to build in Haiti—an effective police force, an independent judiciary, a capable electoral council—have never existed before, and hence their emergence contributes to Haitian political development. Similarly, many international economic development projects were the first of their kind in a country where the economy has been stillborn from the time of independence almost two centuries ago. These projects have signaled and heralded an accelerated pace of economic development in the country.

In the third instance, peacebuilding in Haiti involves implementation of an accord, in this case the Governors Island Agreement of 1993 between the Haitian government-in-exile of President Jean-Bertrand Aristide and the military junta that ousted him. The accord's key elements included the return of President Aristide, the return of the army to the barracks accompanied by instruction on how to stay there, amnesty for the coup leaders, and the training, through UN assistance, of a police force tasked with respecting human rights and maintaining order. To the extent that the army reneged on elements of the accord by not letting UN trainers land in Haiti during the infamous USS *Harlan County* episode, it had to be ousted from power by a threat of U.S. military action. Other elements of the accord, however, have remained in place. President Aristide did return, no former military officers were brought to trial (even though the army has subsequently been demobilized), and the UN continues to provide assistance and training for Haiti's new police.

In the fourth instance, peacebuilding in Haiti is about conflict management via muscular regional action of the kind witnessed in Liberia, Sierra Leone, Lesotho, or Kosovo. These interventions were prompted in some instances by violence within countries, which spilled beyond their borders either as refugee flows or as itinerant militias. In other instances, these violent episodes challenged established regional norms of good state behavior. Both these factors were operational in Haiti's case, where the gratuitous violence of the military junta aroused the ire of the United States, which had to bear the brunt of the refugees, and of the Organization of American States (OAS), which had committed itself to a rather strict regime of democratic government and nonviolent transfer of power via the Santiago Declaration of 1990. The regional response in Haiti involved using force to restore democracy, first through a punishing sanctions regime and then through the deployment of a U.S.-led multinational force.

Whichever lens one adopts to view international peacebuilding activities in Haiti, a central fact emerges from even a cursory examination of these activities: they were remarkably successful. Contrary to other, previous international interventions, activities of various international organizations and actors in Haiti were particularly well coordinated. Even though still in its infancy, the new police force, which was built from scratch, has managed to maintain civil order. While the work of the elected Haitian government remains paralyzed by fractious political debates, the fact that these debates are no longer being conducted using guns and bullets is momentous. The political deadlock in Haiti is not outside the bounds of newly formed and still weak institutions. And one has to count the successful demobilization of the Haitian armed forces—the bane of Haitian politics until recently—as a success both for the new Haitian government and for the international community that helped in the process. No less significant is the first-ever democratic and peaceful transfer of power in Haitian history, when President Aristide handed the baton to the incumbent President René Preval. In addition, the new development projects currently being implemented by both bilateral and international aid organizations ranging from the U.S. Agency for International Development (USAID) to the UNDP are perhaps the greatest success given their emphasis on participation, decentralization, and access to markets.

Yet despite these achievements, there continues to prevail an overwhelming sense of despair and hopelessness among the majority of Haitians. Electoral participation has declined to the point that in the last parliamentary and municipal elections in 1997, turnout was a mere 5 percent of registered voters. Complaints are frequently heard among the population that they have been left out of the majority of decisionmaking regarding their economic and political future (to the extent that such decisionmaking has taken place at all) and also that the leaders who promised so much in the heady years of the democratic upsurge following the end of Duvalierism have not delivered. While the deadlock in Haiti's political process might be within the bounds of an emerging democracy, it certainly is counterproductive to the country's long-term economic and political health. Most macroeconomic indicators for the country continue to decline, and there has been little improvement in the quality of life of the majority of Haitians. Some observers will argue that the level of frustration and animosity among Haitians has now reached the point where the country is ready for another explosion of violence. While this may be debatable, Haiti is not yet ready to stand on its own after several years of international engagement. In other words, peacebuilding in Haiti has not yet generated sustainable peace.

Some might argue that an even greater commitment of international resources and time is needed before peace in Haiti can become sustainable. This chapter will suggest that while individual steps taken by the international community in Haiti have been correct, they have yet to collectively cohere into a sustainable framework for lasting peace in the country. The missing elements do not involve revisiting what has already been accomplished, but perhaps some additional steps may have to be taken by both the Haitian leadership and the international community. The key to understanding these missing steps lies in knowledge of the highly particular circumstances of Haiti's history and development as a nation and in the manner in which recent turns in its history have altered these circumstances. This chapter will therefore provide a brief exposé of the historical circumstances and certain recent developments, followed by an analysis of international peacebuilding activities in the light of these. It will conclude by offering recommendations that could help recent international successes in Haiti acquire permanence.

The Particularities of Haitian History

Haiti's current plight can be traced partly to the circumstances in which it gained its independence from French rule in 1804. French colonial rule in Haiti had certain unique characteristics. Unlike their English colonial counterparts, the French frequently indulged in conjugal relationships with their slaves, giving rise to a class of mulattoes who were often sent to France to be educated in the French language and mannerisms. These individuals frequently aspired to and sometimes attained the commercial status and properties of their masters.[1] At the other extreme, French plantation owners often treated their slaves with unspeakable brutality, causing many to escape from the plantations into the surrounding tropical wilderness where they lived as *marrons,* constantly on the run from their former masters and seeking little more from life than opportunities to melt into the hilly jungles to practice their animistic religion, popularly known as *vodoun.* This constant dodging of persecution, the constant need to avoid permanence lest one be pinned down, has left a very strong mark on Haitian politics and national culture in the tradition of *marronage,* which involves persistently avoiding one's persecutors until they tire of pursuit. While an effective form of resistance, *marronage* often obstructs the kind of deal making and bargaining that lie at the heart of viable political processes. Haitians still prefer to dodge their opponents rather than deal with them.

The war of independence of 1791–1804, in which the slaves overthrew their French masters, also resulted in certain unique impacts on the course of Haitian history.[2] The war was launched by an alliance of *marrons* and slaves who had overthrown their masters. The exact point of origin of the war remains clouded in myth, but a grand *vodoun* ceremony at Bois Cayman in August 1791 marked the Haitian equivalent of the U.S. Declaration of Independence. A critical consequence of the war of independence was the destruction of the plantation economy and its replacement by subsistence and small commercial farming.[3] Many of the slaves who took over plantation land after overthrowing the former owners subdivided the land among themselves and settled down to agriculture that was targeted primarily at feeding their families and secondarily at producing for the local market. The postindependence elite that formed the first few Haitian governments in the cities, however, still saw plantations as assets.[4] While most freed slaves, as well as *marrons* who had settled on former plantation land, were black, this urban elite consisted largely of mulattoes, who had trading and commercial interests.[5] The first two presidents of Haiti, Jean-Jacques Dessalines and Alexandre Pétion, and also the aborted Christophe monarchy in the north, tried to revive some aspects of the plantation economy. The newly formed peasantry, however, resisted. As Michel-Rolph Trouillot has correctly pointed out, the essence of the nation that the people had created was defined for the rebellious slaves by landownership freed from the yoke of French masters.[6] The slaves were not about to change old masters for new. For its part, the new Haitian elite, having been formed in the crucible of the rebellion, did not want to be in the same position as the former French oppressors and therefore, after a few feeble attempts, gave up trying to force the peasantry into being plantation labor. The result was a curious economic situation best described as stasis.[7]

While the demise of the plantation economy ended existing agricultural opportunities, the urban elite did not actively try to foster new ones.[8] For the most part, the state contented itself with taxing the export of the modest amounts of coffee that Haiti continued to produce. Trade in imports, along with monopolistic and speculative practices, formed the primary sources of income for the mercantile families. Few attempts were made to generate long-term investment or to create productive capital.[9] The entrepreneurial enthusiasm of the elite was partly dampened by the sixty-year embargo imposed on Haiti by the major colonial powers and the United States for daring to be black and free.[10] The primary factor behind this lack of entrepreneurship, however, was internal. While Haiti's elite and its peasantry shared a common sense of nationhood born out of the war of independence, they were also separated by a vast gulf. While the peasants practiced the animistic religions of West Africa and spoke only Creole, the elite also spoke French and practiced Catholicism. Though color was not primary in this distinction, it was generally understood that mixed color went hand in hand with French breeding. The biggest psychological factor in this division was very possibly the role that *vodoun* allegedly played in the defeat of the French. While the difficulties of operating in a malaria-infested tropical environment against a determined guerrilla force are perhaps the most plausible explanation for why a large French army met with considerable grief in Haiti, the aura of French grandeur was so great, and the European and mulatto estimate of the war-fighting capabilities of slaves so low, that much undue credence was given to the slaves' use of black magic. Hence for generations afterwards, Paris-educated mulattoes not only despised African religious traditions but also feared them. The elite in Haitian cities actively sought to promote French education among the city dwellers and suppress the practice of vodoun (even as they secretively sought the services of the neighborhood *houngans*), which acquired the hagiographic trappings of Catholicism in order to survive. Haiti's culture and polity, and consequently its economy, became highly schizophrenic, with a subtle but powerful exclusion of the majority not only from the country's *haute culture* but also from its high politics.[11]

In the absence of any role for the state in creating economic opportunity or growth over the past nineteen decades, Haitian politics has lacked substance and tended to focus on the division of very narrow spoils among a small set of parasitic elites.[12] Outsiders are often taken aback by the extent to which Haitian politics continue to be about form and procedure, lacking deeper economic or social agendas. The mercantile families, as long as their monopolies and freedom from taxation have been assured, have tended to stay aloof from politics. The state apparatus, through practices tantamount to racketeering, has sought to reap personal benefits for those in charge. The line between the private and public sector has been thinly drawn, with both sectors being controlled often by the same monopolistic elements.[13] Even where the political debate has shown substance, as in the current set of disputes over privatization, it has masked narrower factional disputes over parochial control of a few functioning enterprises. The lack of a national development program and of substantive politics has devastated the country during its almost two centuries of independence. Lack of investment and organization in agriculture, for instance, has meant the absence of a system of adjudicating disputes over land titles, and also the absence of any long-term attempts to conserve or renew the soil. Little protection or incentives have been given to the peasantry to enable them to develop their land. The result is a vista of treeless landscapes, desert scrub vegetation, and previously lush hillsides denuded of topsoil, all in a wet, tropical climate that normally fosters an excess of greenery. Even where greenery and topsoil remain, as in the fertile Artibonite Valley, the state provided no rural extension services to enable farmers to capitalize on their natural ability to form instant cooperatives (or *konbite*[14]) to assist one another in times of distress.[15] As a result, Haiti's economy has been in a two-century, quasiperpetual decline since independence.

The last decade of the Duvalier era, from the mid-1970s to the mid-1980s, saw some international efforts to bring Haiti out of stasis and into a regional market economy. These efforts had some important consequences for Haiti's current situation. During the 1960s, the regime of François Duvalier sought forcibly to diminish the more visible presence of the mulatto elite and ostensibly made efforts to promote black leadership in the civil service, military, and commercial sectors. This policy assisted the emergence of a small middle class that was dependent upon the regime but was also open to additional economic activity within Haiti. Hence, Jean-Claude Duvalier, who succeeded François in 1971, sought an understanding with several international organizations in the early 1980s whereby Haiti would receive development assistance under the rubric of the Caribbean Basin Initiative (CBI).

This assistance was predicated on the assumption that Haiti's only remaining comparative economic advantage was the availability of labor at rock-bottom prices for assembling consumer goods destined primarily for the U.S. market. Under this strategy, assembly industries, once established and flourishing, would form the center for growth that would pull up the rest of the economy.[16] International assistance thus aimed to contribute to creating state institutions that could guarantee a stable and free market for the assembly manufacturers and toward providing infrastructure such as power plants and feeder roads for the assembly plants.

While this development strategy was based on sound economic theory, its implementation was problematic.[17] First, to the extent that the strategy was not formulated on the basis of broad popular or even elite consensus, it could not mobilize the energies of the majority of Haitians to make it work. Second, the Duvalier state was as lacking in social and economic roots[18] in the rest of Haitian society as its predecessors, even though it had access to a large and decentralized mechanism for inflicting terror in the form of the *tontons macoutes*.[19] Lacking roots and therefore substance, the state did not attempt to streamline and modernize itself to run a competitive and productive market economy that benefited the majority of Haitians, as the foreign donors had anticipated.[20] Third, Haitian elites who subcontracted and worked for the assembly manufacturers transferred all their earnings abroad and did not reinvest in Haiti to create a sustainable indigenous dynamic of savings, reinvestment, and new production. In the absence of a broader national framework, the elite saw little incentive for keeping their money within the country.[21] Also, while the Duvalier regime had certainly increased the numbers of the black middle class with its policies, it had done little to diminish the stranglehold of a few large mercantile families on the Haitian economy that had little interest in increasing local production.[22] Hence, even assembly manufacturing did not reach its full potential.

An important apparent lapse in these development policies was to not take into account the historic exclusion of the peasantry by the ruling elite. The general assumption was that as the decline of Haitian agriculture continued to produce an outflow of migrants to the cities, they would be absorbed by the new industries. Since the latter did not live up to their full potential, the unabsorbed migrants congregated in large slums in Port-au-Prince. Those peasants who still remained in the rural areas had little contact with the state and little access to services with which to develop their considerable artisanal and productive talents.

A focused effort to marketize this peasantry through devices that have been used elsewhere in the developing world, such as rural cooperatives and microcredit, would have led to some positive engagement between the state and the peasantry. Given the fact that despite years of massive migration, most Haitians still live rural lives, any engagement between the state and the peasantry might have given the latter a more noble reason for existence than parasitism. What was needed was a development strategy that required the fullest possible engagement between the state and its people, even if such a strategy made only partial economic sense in the short run, since such engagement might have prompted a more resilient political process that was better able to deal with internal tensions. A state situated within a more substantial national framework might then have fulfilled international expectations by providing a stable context for a flourishing market that, among other industries, would also have allowed assembly manufacturing to take root.[23] Given the stark divergence of the elite and peasant conceptions of Haitian nationhood shortly after independence, the issue of the peasants' status was significant not just from the economic standpoint but also from the viewpoint of defining the nature and role of the Haitian state in the country's economy and society. Of course, enabling the peasants to acquire sustainable and profitable livelihoods in their localities would also have prevented the rapid growth of slums in the cities during the mid-1970s to mid-1980s.

In the absence of this kind of engagement, large numbers of Haitians who came to cities not only found themselves unemployed but, devoid for the first time in their history of the virtues of rural isolation, discovered that at the heart of a lot of their problems lay a nonfunctioning state. Beginning in the early 1980s, a movement for change grew in both urban and rural areas that sought a sometimes violent overthrow of what was seen as a failed system.[24] This movement was led first by the Haitian version of the liberation theology church, the *ti legliz,* and then increasingly by progressive members of the bourgeoisie.[25] Popular frustrations, accentuated by the massive numbers of Haitians living in slums, often led to violent exchanges between elites and activists. In the four years following Duvalier's departure in 1986, Haiti saw a number of coups and ineffective governments as the elite reacted to the popular upsurge. Clearly, Haiti's wholly inadequate political process could manage neither the economic development program of the 1980s nor the consequences of its failure.

A failed attempt at holding elections in 1987,[26] followed by rigged elections in 1988, prompted the international community, in the form of monitors from the UN, OAS, the Caribbean Community (CARICOM), and the United States, to intervene to guarantee free and fair elections in 1990—the first in Haitian history. Marc Bazin, a former World Bank official with liberal economic views, was expected to win the elections at the head of a coalition of progressive parties. Instead, much to the chagrin of the elite, he lost to a popular priest named Jean-Bertrand Aristide who entered the fray only at the last moment.

With origins in Haiti's lower middle class, Aristide had become a lightning rod for the popular upsurge against the country's rulers during the 1980s. Many mistakenly believed he had created this upsurge. His fiery oratory from the pulpit apparently gave voice to many previously silenced Haitians, who saw in his promise of complete transformation of the corrupt system an answer to their needs in the face of tentative pledges by more conventional political parties. Aristide called this popular upsurge "Lavalas," or "flood," and perhaps incorrectly concluded that it was his destiny to carry this flood to the gates of power in Port-au-Prince. His promise of transformation also attracted many bourgeois intellectuals, and even technocrats, who had fled Haiti during the Duvalier regime and who had upon their return correctly diagnosed Haiti's traditional politics as incapable of bringing the country into the modern era. A coalition of these reformist leaders let Aristide run on their platform at the last minute. Upon his election, they acquired positions of significance in the new government. The more conventional politicians, however, retained control of the parliament.

In 1991, during the nine months of the first Aristide government clashes between the parliament and the presidency were frequent; however, this was not parliamentary politics of a conventional sort. The Lavalas government and its opponents both sent their supporters into the streets to push their positions. This was a frightening time for Haiti's old elite. Many interpreted Aristide's inflamed rhetoric about uprooting the old system as a call for their physical extermination. However, the elite only reacted to this situation and did not challenge Aristide themselves by reaching out to the population or by building progressive agendas and strategies. The technocrats in the Aristide government, on the other hand, came up with an economic plan that won the approval of international financial institutions.[27] The plan sought, for the first time in the country's history, to streamline government,[28] collect taxes efficiently, and redefine the role of the state as a net provider of services, not as a net extractor of value. The great blunder of the government was not calling for public debate of the plan through a series of national forums or symposia, where consensus could have been built around the plan's key tenets. Instead, rowdy demonstrators called for compliance with the Lavalas agenda.[29] For their part, many in the elite saw the plan as little more than a vendetta against their interests. In the absence of broader, more sober consensus, the plan and indeed the progressive agenda of the first government became a victim of Haiti's perennial class conflict. Fearing extinction, Haiti's elite responded with a coup in September 1991.

The military overthrew Aristide and proceeded systematically to slaughter Lavalas activists by the hundreds. The purpose was to preserve the status quo by physically eliminating members of the post-Duvalier popular upsurge. The vicious nature of this reaction and the resulting outflow of refugees prompted concerted international response and action. The OAS and CARICOM were especially vigorous in their rejoinder, spurred by both the former's firm post–Cold War commitment to consolidating democracy in the Western Hemisphere and the crucial role played by both organizations in facilitating and monitoring the election that had won Aristide the presidency.[30] The OAS rapidly suspended all aid to Haiti, except humanitarian assistance. Several days later, when the OAS delegation negotiating with the military regime was ordered to leave the country, the organization called on members to impose a trade embargo.

In the fall of 1992, UN Secretary-General Boutros Boutros-Ghali authorized a joint OAS/UN mission to Haiti to negotiate with the government, and a Special Envoy for Haiti, Dante Caputo, was soon appointed (shortly thereafter, he was also named OAS Special Envoy).[31] The coup leader, General Raoul Cedras, indicated his willingness to cooperate. Writing to Caputo in January 1993, he accepted a proposal to establish a joint OAS/UN civilian mission to monitor human rights. Under the terms of the agreement, the mission would have full freedom of movement, monitor human rights in accordance with the Haitian constitution and relevant international conventions, and make recommendations to Haitian authorities as well as verify their implementation. The Cedras regime also agreed to work under the leadership of the Special Envoy toward rebuilding Haiti's frail institutions. On April 10, 1993, the joint human rights mission, the International Civilian Mission to Haiti (MICIVIH), was authorized by the UN General Assembly;[32] and by early June it submitted its first report.[33]

Caputo's efforts to engage the Haitian military in dialogue, however, made little overall progress. On June 16, 1993, the Security

Council, acting under Chapter VII of the UN Charter, placed an oil and arms embargo upon Haiti.[34] Immediately upon the imposition of the embargo, Cedras again indicated a willingness to negotiate and began talks that resulted in the Governors Island Agreement (named for the location of the talks in New York). The agreement, signed on July 3, 1993, pledged Cedras to retire from government and allow Aristide's return to Haiti by October 30. In the interim, Aristide would work with the Haitian parliament to restore normal functioning in Haiti's institutions, and the United Nations would provide a small force to help modernize the armed forces and create a new civilian police force.

The initial signs regarding implementation were promising, with the Haitian parliament ratifying Aristide's appointment as prime minister and the Security Council lifting the embargo on Haiti and authorizing a United Nations Mission in Haiti (UNMIH).[35] However, the situation quickly turned sour when the UNMIH advance team arrived in the Port-au-Prince harbor on October 11; it was met by hostile demonstrations and turned back (the *Harlan County*[36] episode), prompting the flight of most of MICIVIH's personnel.[37] The ensuing developments demonstrated a downward spiral of tit-for-tat responses between the international community and the Haitian regime. While the Security Council rapidly reimposed the arms and oil embargo, the Haitian junta followed by assassinating Aristide's justice minister, François Guy Malary, on October 15. By early 1994, the few remaining MICIVIH personnel reported an alarming increase in human rights violations. Facing continued intransigence from the military government, the Security Council imposed a comprehensive set of sanctions on Haiti,[38] to which the regime responded by appointing a "provisional" president, Emile Jonassaint, who formally expelled MICIVIH from the country on July 11, 1994.

By 1994, the deteriorating situation in Haiti had caused a surge of refugees onto American shores, putting domestic pressure on the Clinton administration most notably from Florida, which bore the brunt of the refugee wave. Additional pressure for American action came from the Congressional Black Caucus and influential African-American organizations such as TransAfrica. The upshot was the adoption on July 30, 1994, of Security Council Resolution 940, which authorized the formation of a multinational force (MNF) under Chapter VII of the UN Charter:

> to use all necessary means to facilitate the departure from Haiti of the military leadership, consistent with the Governors Island agreement, the prompt return of the legitimately elected President and the restoration of the legitimate authorities of the Government of Haiti, and to establish and maintain a secure and stable environment that will permit implementation of the Governors Island agreement.

The U.S.-led MNF would then be replaced by an expanded UN mission in Haiti (UNMIH), which would be responsible for "(a) sustaining the secure and stable environment established during the multinational phase and protecting international personnel and key installations; and (b) the professionalization of the Haitian armed forces and the creation of a separate police force."

Even with the passage of Resolution 940 and preparations for MNF deployment, it was not until mid-September that President Bill Clinton declared all diplomatic measures exhausted. Faced with impending invasion, the Cedras regime appealed for a last-minute intercession. After skillful negotiation by former President Jimmy Carter, General Colin Powell, and U.S. Senator Sam Nunn,[39] Haiti's military leaders agreed to resign with an amnesty from the Haitian parliament. As a result, the MNF was able to move into Haiti on September 19 without opposition. Operating with flexible rules of engagement, the MNF responded to resistance decisively, which may explain why it was challenged on only one occasion,[40] and implemented its mandate effectively, including collecting large numbers of weapons from the former regime's supporters. The MNF also created an Interim Public Security Force (IPSF) from new recruits and the remnants of the old army to provide security temporarily until a completely new civilian police could be fielded.[41] President Aristide returned to Haiti on October 15, 1994.

Shortly following the MNF's arrival came a new UNMIH advance team (under Lakhdar Brahimi) and the returning core group of MICIVIH (under Colin Granderson). By January 10, 1995, the Security Council declared that a safe and secure environment had been established and that UNMIH could assume the reins from the MNF. On March 31, 1995, command transferred from the MNF to UNMIH under U.S. Major-General Joseph Kinzer.[42] In 1996, UNMIH was succeeded by a scaled-down version called the UN Support Mission in Haiti (UNSMIH),[43] which was followed in the fall of 1997 by a still smaller version called the UN Transition Mission in Haiti (UNTMIH). In 1998, the UN Security Council reduced the UN peacekeeping role in the country essentially to that of supporting the further development of the civilian police and instituted the UN Police Mission in Haiti (MIPONUH).

In early 1999, the UN Secretary-General reported to the Security Council that the civilian Haitian National Police, developed under MNF and UN auspices, had despite tremendous odds displayed a satisfactory level of competence in maintaining public order at a time of great political stress and that it continued to be led by highly capable civil servants with a reputation for integrity.[44] The resilience of this police force and the absence of large-scale political violence testified to the success of the international community's peacekeeping efforts. Despite this accomplishment, however, Haitian democracy continued to stumble.

Haiti's constitution bars two consecutive presidential terms. In accordance with his promise at Governors Island to assist in building Haiti's frail institutions, Aristide agreed to step down as president at the end of his first term in 1996. His supporters, however, argued that since he had spent most of this term in exile, he should be allowed a second term.[45] The international community informally backed the constitutional position.[46] It helped finance and monitor the 1995 presidential elections that led René Preval to succeed Aristide as president[47] and has assisted with subsequent national and local elections.[48] While the transfer of power from Aristide to Preval through elections was a historic accomplishment in that it was the first of its kind in the country's history, Haitian institutions subsequently became deadlocked.

Aristide, who remained Haiti's most popular political figure even after Preval succeeded him as president, argued after the transition that the reform package Preval's government had agreed to implement would benefit a small elite and cause great suffering to the majority of the population. By 1997, opposition had brought key components of the reform process to a halt.[49] Complicating this standoff was a dispute over the elections of April 6, 1997. Aristide's LaFanmi Lavalas group was one of the two primary groups—the other being the Lavalas Political Organization, subsequently renamed Organisation du Peuple en Lutte (OPL)—into which the original Lavalas movement had split over the issue of Aristide having to make way for Preval.[50] In the April elections, the LaFanmi Lavalas supporters emerged ahead of their opponents, who claimed that Haiti's electoral council, allegedly dominated by Aristide sympathizers, had permitted electoral malpractices that had facilitated

Aristide's lead.[51] The international community also lent their support to the opposition's claims of fraud.[52] As of 1999, this contentious issue remained unresolved. It led to the resignation of Prime Minister Rosny Smarth in June 1997, further paralyzing the government. Successive attempts to appoint a prime minister foundered over the differences between the two Lavalas factions. In a hopeful sign, certain opposition parties (not including the OPL) had reached an informal accord with the president in March 1999 for appointing an interim prime minister and a new electoral council and holding new legislative elections to replace the previous legislature, the duration of whose term had also become a matter of dispute between the presidency and members of the legislature.

The most obvious consequence of this political deadlock and wrangling was to hold up hundreds of millions of dollars in international development assistance, further impoverishing an already poor country.[53] More significant, the political deadlock caused an almost complete dissipation of the popular energies and enthusiasm generated by the democracy movement of the late 1980s. Thus despite international peacebuilding efforts, the Haitian political process appeared largely incapable of addressing the issues and tensions arising from the new socioeconomic circumstances facing the country. Peace in Haiti was therefore not sustainable.

International Peacebuilding Activities

Before analyzing the missing elements in international and domestic efforts to build lasting peace in Haiti, a brief reprise of international efforts is in order. Following Aristide's restoration, the international community correctly identified and proceeded to treat several symptoms of Haiti's underlying pathology. The key elements of this strategy involved:

- *Accelerating efforts to develop the Haitian National Police.* Previously, the army had been mandated with the task of maintaining public order, although in practice its only action had been gratuitous violence since its establishment in the early 1930s. The Governors Island accord had called for its retraining, but following his return in 1994, Aristide simply abolished the much hated army, a move welcomed by many in the international community.

- *Providing assistance for the reform and the retraining of the Haitian judiciary.*[54] This was necessary so the judiciary could function as an independent public institution and complement the police force in establishing a rule of law.
- *Providing general public security while Haiti's nascent institutions developed.* Four UN missions—UNMIH, UNSMIH, UNTMIH, and MIPONUH—all successfully assisted in keeping public peace and in helping the new civilian police force stand on its own.[55]
- *Providing assistance in creating a credible record of past human rights violations and monitoring Haitian institutions in order to prevent further violations.*[56] Violent as Haiti's history was, the particularly horrific violence of the past decade had left deep scars on the national psyche. Recognizing the need for reconciliation, the international community repeatedly renewed the mandate of MICIVIH, even after the restoration of democracy.
- *Retraining and reintegrating demobilized soldiers into the civilian workforce.* Recognizing that there was more to demobilizing an army than merely abolishing it and given Haiti's unemployment situation, this was a considerable task.
- *Providing assistance to the peasantry to enable their entry into the market economy and bringing back assembly manufacturers.* Economic underdevelopment was identified as *the* critical Haitian problem. Development schemes included components for restoration and conservation of Haiti's environment, bringing back manufacturers scared off by the recent violence, and several projects to restore or build critically needed infrastructure.
- *Developing a package for fiscal and institutional reform.* Such a plan would allow the Haitian state to identify and unleash the energies of Haitian entrepreneurs in recognition of the fact that an effective economy requires an effective state.
- *Providing electoral assistance.* In the face of the perennial Haitian problem of institutional instability, this was needed for the transition from Aristide to Preval and for various national and local elections.

In short, the international community targeted almost all of the lacunae in Haiti's national life in an attempt to ensure that massive violence did not recur. By and large, all of these projects and initiatives achieved impressive success, despite a few setbacks and disappointments that were to be expected given the severity of Haiti's condition.[57]

The Haitian National Police was a significant achievement. While it came under occasional criticism for the perceived heavy-handedness or corruption of its officers, these lapses were more a set of growing pains than part of a pattern of systematic abuse.[58] The Directorate of the Police included some of the most honest and dedicated civil servants in Haiti. Despite being under considerable pressure from Haiti's emergence as a transshipment point for narcotics, members of the new police did an impressive job of performing basic functions such as guiding traffic, providing general law enforcement services, and preserving public order.[59]

International attempts to assist in the creation of an effective judiciary were somewhat less successful, although this had more to do with Haitian history than with the quality of international efforts. Haitian judges had traditionally seen themselves as enforcers of the dominant local interests rather than as neutral arbitrators. However, international assistance began to change this picture with the critical help of nongovernmental organizations. For instance, a prominent trial of individuals indicted for the Raboteau massacre in 1999 seemed to be proceeding and augured well for the future.

UN peacekeeping in Haiti has received a lot of praise, much of it well deserved. An important lesson has definitely been learned in Haiti regarding different peacekeeping "styles." In a context such as Haiti's where there is no peace to be kept in the traditional sense and where international troops are essentially performing a policing function, a peacekeeping style characterized by a heavy dose of community relations becomes almost compulsory. To the extent that the peacekeepers' security can be threatened by general lawlessness and expressions of public grievance over shortages of basic goods and amenities, effective intelligence-gathering on these matters and a conscious building of good relations with community leaders become essential for the tactical success of the operation. For instance, Pakistani peacekeepers in Haiti, attuned to the limitations and possibilities of patrolling in a developing country, took concrete steps to establish good relations with local officials as well as community leaders and to identify the grievances of the population in their zones of operation. Where possible, they assisted communities with small, low-technology projects that addressed local needs and could be sustained with local resources once the peacekeepers left.[60]

The goodwill generated by these activities among the local population was evident during a visit to Cap-Haitien during February 1996, and again to Cité Soleil in October 1997. A similar approach was also adopted by U.S. civil affairs teams.[61] Significantly, none of these activities were specifically decreed under the mandates of any of the various peacekeeping operations approved in Haiti by the Security Council. However, commanders on the ground creatively interpreted their general mandate to ensure local security and the security of their troops as including better community relations.[62] As a result, much needed local and sustainable infrastructure was built.

The joint OAS/UN mission, MICIVIH, did a heroic job in collecting and recording information on human rights violations under the coup prior to 1994.[63] Following Aristide's return, it collected a large amount of additional data and provided valuable assistance to the Haitian government commission preparing a report on these violations. When released, the report was voluminous; however, the government failed to use it to the fullest effect. It was neither widely or accessibly disseminated nor used as the basis for national debate on issues of justice and reconciliation.[64] MICIVIH's work was more successful in the area of monitoring, where it played the role of unofficial watchdog for the emerging public security institutions.

The joint project of the U.S. Agency for International Development (USAID) and the International Organization for Migration (IOM) to reintegrate demobilized soldiers into society had retrained twenty-four hundred soldiers in civilian professions between its launch in 1994 and January 1996.[65] It had been critiqued on the grounds that soldiers, many of whom had violated the rights of civilians, should not receive priority for employment while many deserving civilians remained unemployed. However, the long-term worth of the project was indisputable. Despite the fact that in the aftermath of this project many former soldiers could not find jobs and some were suspected of resorting to banditry[66] and drug running, the situation would certainly have been much worse in the absence of the USAID effort.

It is perhaps in the area of long-term economic development that some of the most promising international efforts have taken place. Particular credit is due to UNDP and USAID.[67] Both have undertaken projects in recent years, especially outside Port-au-Prince, that have helped integrate previously marginalized sectors into a market economy in a sustainable fashion.[68] The central features of these projects have been participatory decisionmaking, decentralized implementation, and the use of cooperatives, microcredit, and other devices to facilitate market access for small producers. A good example was the USAID project in Fond Jean-Noel, which divided a federation of eighteen thousand farmers into twenty-five cooperatives to grow and market, minus the traditional middlemen, the increasingly popular Haitian Bleu coffee for export to U.S. markets.[69] Given the direct involvement of peasants in this project and the fact that the coffee bush requires the shade of large trees, many project participants took to actively conserving trees instead of felling them.[70]

In the area of economic reform, the international community, led by international financial institutions, assisted the government in preparing a reform package that had the same overall goals as the strategy developed by the first Aristide government: the creation of a leaner and more effective state.[71] The package was largely accepted by the Haitian parliament, and the government began a process of privatization of state-owned industries.[72] The government also continued to show great restraint in spending public money. However, little progress was made in the overall reduction of the budget deficit and in streamlining the bloated state bureaucracy. Also, the central state apparatus appeared incapable of responding to the needs of provinces and localities. The one exception, personally promoted by President Preval, was the land reform program in the Artibonite Valley, where the state was attempting for the first time in the country's history to provide peasants with land titles, market access, and other goods needed to participate in the market economy.[73]

The international community experienced the greatest frustration in the area of building national institutions. The political deadlock between the presidency and the parliament that had paralyzed the government has already been described. Local leaderships, however, were more progressive. With help from international agencies, many mayors and local leaders began to articulate local needs and demands in a rational fashion, emphasizing their communities' requirements for participation in a market economy and the importance of sharing information regarding local solutions to problems in common.[74]

To summarize, the international community's attempts to build peace in Haiti following the restoration of democracy encountered both success and frustration. This was certainly no different from international involvement in other fragile societies. One can argue, however, that international involvement in Haiti was better coordinated and executed than most previous interventions. Seen from the various peacebuilding perspectives identified at the beginning of this chapter, a lot was accomplished. For instance, the development and peacekeeping aspects of the UN presence were brought together under unified leadership by making the UNDP Resident Representative the Deputy to the Special Representative of the Secretary-General.[75] Most provisions of the Governors Island accord were successfully implemented. From the perspective of development, Haiti's problematic development strategy during the 1980s was positively reoriented. From the perspective of postconflict peacebuilding, several medium-term measures—demobilization, election monitoring, infrastructure repair—were successfully undertaken in the context of a multidimensional peacekeeping operation. From the perspective of regional security, the flow of refugees was halted and democracy was restored as a result of regional action. However, as pointed out at the beginning of this chapter, a sense of gloom pervaded Haiti in the late 1990s. Despite many successes, popular hope appeared to have dissipated. To many, nothing appeared to have changed and nothing appeared to move.[76] What was missing?

Factors Sustaining the Political Process

The missing piece of the puzzle is a sustainable political process that could mitigate the tensions arising from the country's social and economic transformation in recent years before these tensions lead to violence. The key to understanding the factors that can sustain Haiti's political process lie in the circumstances leading to the coup of 1991, and in the parameters of the country's current deadlock.

As described earlier, the political process proved largely incapable of dealing with the circumstances created by the migration of large numbers of Haitians from the countryside to the cities in the 1970s and 1980s. The latter's burgeoning demands for political participation and economic well-being were met with repression by the state, which also targeted the emerging organs of civil society that were articulating these demands.[77] Having concluded that the political process was incapable of addressing their demands, many common Haitians sought radical transformation through revolutionary means. This revolutionary quest, however, further deepened the traditional chasm between the country's tiny elite and the population at large.

While this hypothesis remains to be tested empirically, several expert observers have argued that Aristide was catapulted to power in the 1990 elections not on the basis of a popular desire for the institutions and norms of democracy, but as the vanguard of a new regime that would fundamentally and radically transform the polity. These expectations, amply reflected in Aristide's own rhetoric, contradicted the more gradual approach of those members of the Lavalas alliance that belonged to a small but growing middle class, as well as the more progressive elements of the traditional political and economic elite.[78] The elected government of 1990–1991, therefore, suffered from a fundamental contradiction. It sought to address the popular demands for overwhelming social and economic change through the forms and institutions of electoral democracy. The "flood" metaphor was a clear contradiction, however, of the laborious, consensus-building methodology of a parliamentary democracy. It also clearly contradicted the interests and priorities of the established elite. These contradictions led to the collapse of Haiti's political process in the form of an army takeover in mid-1991. The army responded to the growing tensions and violence in the only way it knew: with more violence.

Thus, two main factors can be distinguished as debilitating the Haitian political process:

- The absence of the state from the lives of most Haitians as a provider of basic services, which in turn implies a political process focused on shallow procedural issues; and
- The absence of broad consensus among different sectors of the country concerning the parameters of both a democratic political process and a progressive socioeconomic transformation in Haiti; this lack of consensus reflects the wide geographical and socioeconomic gaps between the urban ruling elites and the vast majority of the country's population.[79]

Clear lessons can be drawn from this episode regarding the factors that will sustain a political process in Haiti capable of managing tensions arising from rapid social change before they lead to violence. The first and minimum factor is a system of security that provides public order in a neutral fashion and allows a vocal civil society and opposition to flourish. The neutrality of this system is of crucial importance, because if various sectors are prevented from using state violence as a tool of political discourse, greater incentives emerge to settle disputes through bargaining and consensus building. Second, Haiti's elected institutions, while characterized by the airing of differences that take place in any democracy, have to address the lack of existing compromise between the country's different sectors concerning fundamental social and economic goals and the means—radical or gradual—for achieving them. It is important to note that key compromises cannot be achieved within the bounds of elected institutions alone; in fact, they may be one of the factors enabling the institutions to function in the first place. In the absence of such compromises, the institutions themselves merely reflect the broader societal standoff.[80] The process of developing such compromises engages many sectors of the society with the state, and this gives the latter some depth and substance.

The country's continued political deadlock supports the hypothesis that although progress has been made in providing basic security, not enough has been done to develop the political capacity for obtaining compromise on key issues. Following the restoration of Haiti's elected government in 1994, the international community invested heavily and successfully in the creation of a viable security system. When the country's ongoing political deadlock came to a peak in early 1999, the new police did an admirable job of remaining neutral and providing security, preventing the parties from taking recourse to violence.

The problem is that providing public security has not been enough to transform the stasis at the political level. When the international community restored Haiti's president and parliament in 1994, they also restored the contradiction that had formerly existed in Haitian democracy: the tendency of Haiti's elected leaders to take their profound differences to the floors of elected institutions, without an ability to compromise despite these differences, thus producing paralysis. The crisis of 1997 manifested this contradiction.

The considerable economic and infrastructure-related assistance provided by the international community has done little to ameliorate this situation. In fact, the political class remains resolutely deadlocked despite constant threats from the international community that once the window of opportunity created by international intervention closes, economic assistance will dry to a trickle. Clearly, in the absence of a political process (characterized by the ability to compromise) to absorb and manage it, economic assistance cannot be a reliable path to building lasting peace.

It should be noted that the international community has provided assistance to Haiti's nascent institutions for democracy building. Many political parties as well as parliamentarians have attended educational programs targeted at building their understanding of democratic political processes. This has been mirrored at the societal level by education programs targeted at inculcating democratic civic virtues. These exhortatory approaches, however, have had little lasting impact. The population, having concluded that neither the international community nor the political elite is interested in a radical redressing of their more immediate needs, has by and large lost interest in the political process. The political elite, as always, has remained focused on acquiring control of the limited state institutions that do exist.

What are some of the steps that could be taken to build the capacity, critical for sustaining the Haitian political process, for obtaining compromise in a participatory fashion?

Recommendations for Peacebuilding

First, the Haitian political process would benefit from implementing specific international initiatives accompanied by broad-based dialogue within affected sectors.[81] These need not be open-ended but could focus on the identification of common interests among different sectors in sustaining a particular initiative in the long run.[82] If certain sectors are likely to benefit more than others in the short run, they should be brought to an understanding that in the long term their benefit would be even greater if they did not try to appropriate the entire initiative right away. Those likely to lose in the short run should receive guarantees and assurances that their short-term sacrifice will also lead to long-term gain. This process of identifying common gains and mutual guarantees can develop rapidly between a pragmatic set of individuals, which Haitians often tend to be. It is also a very powerful tool for building long-term exchange and interaction between different sectors, and iterated interactions often form the basis for larger national frameworks of social and economic action. Additionally, expressing their interests in common projects could provide Haitians with much needed experience in articulating specific political demands instead of expressing their needs through revolutionary spasms. There are several examples of international projects of this kind, such as the USAID project in Fond Jean-Noel discussed above.

Second, the promotion of lasting processes of public dialogue among and between civic and political leaders not only would provide a cathartic balm for grievances of the past but would constitute a genuine, national compromise-building exercise. Such an exercise at the national level would also inspire similar exchanges at the local level. Indeed, experts on Haiti typically point to the fact that many Haitians respond better to exemplary rather than exhortatory forms of instruction. In Guatemala and South Africa, for instance, negotiations to end decades of civil conflict also took the form of public dialogue stretched over several years, which served both as an inspiration and as an example to the populations of these countries. While the South African process focused on building consensus regarding the political institutions that would politically empower all, as opposed to some of its citizens,[83] the Guatemala process, which also involved international financial institutions, focused on a wide range of social and economic issues. Significantly, the Guatemalan dialogue did not emerge as a prelude to launching the country's democratic institutions but as part of a broader process of democratization that also included institution building. In Haiti, the international community should encourage and participate as partners in a series of dialogues that would bring together national and local political and civic leaders from all sectors (government, labor, business, religions, and so on) in order to develop an understanding of each other's positions and interests and to build common agendas on the basis of these interests.[84] As in Guatemala, however, these dialogues would not supplant the existing institutions but supplement their work in critical ways. Their purpose would be to ensure that the state did not simply pay lip service to participation but actively worked to bring it about.

Third, although much has been invested in building so-called political parties in Haiti (many are no more than a few individuals with fax machines seeking a share of the state's spoils), not enough has been done to assist the emergence of a viable civil society. Many civic organizations in recent years initially arose as a component of the popular upsurge that Aristide appropriated under the Lavalas name, and hence they became part of the political equation instead of acting independently. Many of them, however, expressing disillusionment with Haiti's political parties, have adopted more independent positions in recent months. Before political ennui causes them to fade away, they should be strengthened so that they will be able to constitute a vital force in making the political system more responsive and accountable to Haiti's people.

Conclusions from Peacebuilding in Haiti

The primary regional security interest in Haiti remains the stability of the country and the maintenance of democratic government, so that massive refugee outflows do not strain neighbors and regional norms are not violated. Both these objectives will be better served through establishing a political process in Haiti that can sustainably prevent the tensions generated by socioeconomic change from leading to violence. It has been assumed that a number of international initiatives and plans ought to be completed within a short period of time in order to avert the recurrence of disaster. An excessive emphasis on achieving specific objectives within limited time frames without a broader framework of consensus might, however, produce even more acrimony and division. On the other hand, comprehensive dialogue and exchange embedded in a participatory political process, even if open-ended, will create a strong sense of participation and ownership of the future among the majority of Haitians. This could be the salve keeping many Haitians on their own shores, even though all-around prosperity and development might be longer in coming.[85] In the past, Haitians have certainly left their country in order to seek opportunities elsewhere, but the overwhelming majority of Haitians have fled as a result of being persecuted by their own government. Constant engagement with one another and with their government not only will keep hope alive but will keep Haiti stable overall.

External observers have often bemoaned the lack of a Mandela-like figure capable of heralding a process of national reconciliation. Several of Haiti's neighbors—Dominican Republic, El Salvador, and Guatemala—however, have been able to take significant strides in this direction without a charismatic figure. It is quite likely that peace could also be built in Haiti when it is seen as a process rather than as a sum of several end products.

Notes

1. Sidney Mintz, "Can Haiti Change?" *Foreign Affairs* 74, 1 (Jan.-Feb. 1995): 76.

2. For an evocative fictional account of the Haitian war of independence, see Madison Smartt Bell, *All Souls Rising* (New York: Pantheon Books, 1995).

3. Mintz, "Can Haiti Change?" 79–81.

4. See Michel-Rolph Trouillot, *Haiti—State Against Nation: The Origins and Legacy of Duvalierism* (New York: Monthly Review Press, 1990), 44–48.

5. While Haiti's mercantile elite was primarily mulatto, the country's military leadership, which often provided the political leadership, has been primarily black. The latter, however, has often been indirectly manipulated and dominated by the mercantile elite in a system known as *la politique de doublure.* See Ernest H. Preeg, *The Haitian Dilemma: A Case Study in Demographics, Development, and US Foreign Policy* (Washington, D.C.: The Center for Strategic and International Studies, 1996), 13.

6. See Trouillot, *Haiti—State Against Nation,* 49–50.

7. Mintz, "Can Haiti Change?" 79.

8. For an insider's account of the secluded lives of Haiti's elites, see Anthony Schindler-Hattenbach, *Hot Times in Haiti!—A True Story* (Port-au-Prince: JMS Publishings, 1994).

9. Trouillot, *Haiti—State Against Nation;* in particular, see Chapter 2, "A Republic for the Merchants."

10. Mintz, "Can Haiti Change?" 78–79. See also Trouillot, *Haiti—State Against Nation,* 50–58, 64–69.

11. The work of Edwidge Danticat provides powerful accounts of the travails of Haiti's common people. It includes the critically acclaimed novel *Breath, Eyes, Memory* (New York: Random House, 1998), and the short story collection, *Krik!Krak!* (Vintage Contemporaries) (New York: Random House, 1996).

12. Trouillot, *Haiti—State Against Nation,* 85–86.

13. See Jean-Germain Gros, "Haiti's Flagging Transition," *Journal of Democracy* 8, 4 (October 1997): 104.

14. Catholic Institute for International Relations, *Haiti—Building Democracy: Comment* (London: CIIR, 1996), 23.

15. Perhaps the most authentic account of the potential of Haiti's peasantry is provided by the Haitian author Jacques Roumain in his classic novel, *Masters of the Dew* (1944; reprint, London: Heineman, 1978).

16. See Alex Dupuy, "Free Trade and Underdevelopment in Haiti: The World Bank/USAID Agenda for Social Change in the Post-Duvalier Era," in *The Caribbean in the Global Political Economy,* ed. Hilbourne A. Watson (Boulder, CO: Lynne Rienner, 1994), 93–95.

17. For arguments in support of an assembly manufacturing-led growth strategy for Haiti, see Clive Gray, "Alternative Models for Haiti's Economic Reconstruction," and Mats Lundahl, "The Haitian Dilemma Reexamined," in *Haiti Renewed: Political and Economic Prospects,* ed. Robert Rotberg (Washington, D.C.: Brookings Institution Press, 1997).

18. See Robert Maguire et al., "Haiti Held Hostage: International Responses to the Quest for Nationhood, 1986 to 1996," Occasional Paper no. 23 (Providence, RI: Thomas J. Watson Institute for International Studies and United Nations University, 1996), 8.

19. For a brief outline of the thirty-year reign of terror of the *tontons macoutes* and the possibly irreversible scar it has left on Haiti's national psyche, see Michel S. Laguerre, "The Tontons Macoutes," in *The Haiti Files: Decoding the Crisis,* ed. James Ridgeway (Washington, D.C.: Essential Books, 1994).

20. See Dupuy, "Free Trade and Underdevelopment in Haiti," 95–96.

21. Dupuy, "Free Trade and Underdevelopment in Haiti," 97.

22. See Dupuy, "Free Trade and Underdevelopment in Haiti," 98. Also see Trouillot, *Haiti—State Against Nation,* 158. For a detailed account of the role of

big mercantile families in Haiti's economy, see "Haiti's 'Economic Barons': Memo from Congressman Walter E. Fauntroy," in Ridgeway, ed., *The Haiti Files.*

23. An article by Peter M. Lewis, which reviews several recent volumes that draw lessons from the experience of promoting development and economic reform in Africa, points to the nature of governance in a society—the institutions of the state, the relations between these institutions and the people, and the social coalitions that engender these relations—as key variables in determining the path of economic reform. Peter M. Lewis, "Economic Reform and Political Transition in Africa: The Quest for a Politics of Development," *World Politics* 49 (October 1996): 92–129.

24. See Marx V. Aristide and Laurie Richardson, "The Popular Movement," in Ridgeway, eds., *The Haiti Files.* Also see Alex Dupuy, *Haiti in the New World Order: The Limits of the Democratic Revolution* (Boulder, CO: Westview Press, 1997), 97–98.

25. For a summary of *ti legliz* activities, see *Haiti—Building Democracy,* 7.

26. Maguire et al., "Haiti Held Hostage," 16.

27. See Donald E. Schulz and Gabriel Marcella, "Reconciling the Irreconcilable: The Troubled Outlook for U.S. Policy Toward Haiti," Working Paper (Carlisle, PA: U.S. Army War College, Strategic Studies Institute, March 10, 1994), 12.

28. Maguire et al., "Haiti Held Hostage," 18.

29. Schulz and Marcella, "Reconciling the Irreconcilable," 9–11.

30. The increasing vigor of the OAS commitment to democracy was dramatic: in 1985, the Protocol of Cartagena de Indias incorporated democracy promotion in the OAS charter; in 1989, the organization began to observe elections in member states when requested; in 1990, it created a "Unit for Promotion of Democracy" and launched additional programs to bolster democratization; in 1991, its general assembly adopted a mechanism to respond when democratic order is interrupted in any member state; and in 1992, it strengthened its several instruments for promoting democratic government in the Protocol of Washington.

31. David Malone's authoritative and detailed work, *Decision-Making in the UN Security Council: The Case of Haiti, 1990–1997* (Oxford: Clarendon Press, 1998), provides the best available account of the complexities of international decisionmaking on Haiti in the aftermath of the overthrow of President Aristide in 1991.

32. UN Resolution 40/27B (April 10, 1993).

33. See UN/OAS, *Haiti—Learning the Hard Way: The UN/OAS Human Rights Monitoring Operation in Haiti, 1993–94* (New York: United Nations/OAS, 1995), 72.

34. Resolution 841 (1993) (June 16, 1993).

35. Resolution 861 (August 27, 1993) lifted the embargo, and Resolution 867 (September 3, 1993) authorized UNMIH.

36. The USS *Harlan County* was sent to Port-au-Prince with two hundred U.S. Special Forces advisers and Canadian soldiers in October 1993 in order to help ensure the restoration of democracy in Haiti. Embarrassingly, it scuttled back before even docking in the face of a mild but raucous protest demonstration on the dock.

37. Maguire et al., "Haiti Held Hostage," 37.

38. The most comprehensive and critical analysis of these sanctions and their impact is offered by Elizabeth Gibbons in *Sanctions in Haiti: Human Rights and Democracy Under Assault* (Washington D.C.: The CSIS Press, 1999). For

another comprehensive review of the sanctions' initial impact on Haiti, see "Sanctions in Haiti: Crisis in Humanitarian Action," Harvard Center for Population and Development Studies, Program on Human Security Working Paper Series, Boston, MA, November 1993.

39. See Robert A. Pastor, "With Carter in Haiti," *WorldView* (Spring 1995).

40. See Rachel Neild, *Policing Haiti: Preliminary Assessment of the New Civilian Security Force* (Washington D.C.: Washington Office on Latin America, 1995), 33.

41. A more critical assessment of the role of the multinational force in dealing with insecurity in Haiti is provided in Bob Shacochis, *The Immaculate Invasion* (New York: Penguin Books, 1999).

42. The successes of both MNF and UNMIH are detailed in David Bentley, "Operation Uphold Democracy: Military Support for Democracy in Haiti," Strategic Forum no. 78 (Washington, D.C.: Institute for National Strategic Studies, National Defense University, June 1996).

43. Created under SC Resolution 1063 (June 28, 1996).

44. See S/1999/181, *Report of the Secretary-General on the United Nations Police Mission in Haiti* (February 19, 1999), para. 18.

45. See S/1996/112, *Report of the Secretary-General on the United Nations Mission in Haiti* (February 14, 1996), para. 2.

46. *A Report on the Fourth Annual Peacekeeping Mission* (New York: United Nations Association of the USA, 1995), 15.

47. *Report of the Secretary-General on the United Nations Mission in Haiti* (February 14, 1996), paras. 3, 4.

48. See Robert A. Pastor, "Mission to Haiti #3: Elections for Parliament and Municipalities, June 23–26, 1995" (Atlanta, GA: Working Paper Series, The Carter Center of Emory University, July 17, 1995), 7–8.

49. Sandra Marquez Garcia, "Haiti's Ruling Coalition Gets Fractious," *Miami Herald*, February 24, 1997.

50. Don Bohning, "Aristide Comeback? It's Up to the Voters," *Miami Herald*, April 5, 1997.

51. An interesting explanation for disputes among current Haitian politicians, many of whom supported Aristide at one point, has been offered by Andrew Reding, who suggests that Haiti's winner-take-all electoral system, as opposed to the kind of proportional representation system that prevails in South Africa, is putting heavy stress on a nascent democracy. "Exorcising Haiti's Ghosts," *World Policy Journal* 13, 1 (Spring 1996): 21.

52. On August 19, 1997, the United Nations suspended electoral assistance to Haiti until the Provisional Electoral Council could establish that it was capable of holding free and fair elections. Michael Norton, "UN Suspends Election Aid in Haiti," *Associated Press*, August 22, 1997.

53. See Malone, *Decision-Making in the UN Security Council*, 142–143.

54. France and the United States were particularly keen on this strategy and provided considerable assistance to that end. See James F. Dobbins, "Haiti: A Case Study in Post–Cold War Peacekeeping," ISD Reports 2, 1 (Washington, D.C.: Institute for the Study of Diplomacy, Georgetown University, October 1995): 2.

55. Following the restoration of democracy in Haiti, President Aristide had abolished the Forces Armées d'Haiti (FAd'H). The international community had then assisted the government of Haiti in building a new civilian police force, the Haitian National Police (HNP). See David Malone, "Haiti and the International Community: A Case Study," *Survival* 39, 2 (Summer 1997): 134.

56. See William G. O'Neill, "Human Rights Monitoring vs. Political Expediency: The Experience of the OAS/UN Mission in Haiti," *Harvard Human Rights Journal* 8 (Spring 1995): 125–126.

57. For a less positive assessment of international accomplishments in Haiti, see Johanna McGreary, "Did the American Mission Matter?" *Time*, February 19, 1996.

58. See Deputy Secretary of State Strobe Talbott, *From Restoring to Upholding Democracy: A Progress Report on US Policy Toward Haiti*, report prepared for the House International Relations Committee, June 26, 1996.

59. A report released by Human Rights Watch/Americas, in collaboration with National Coalition for Haitian Rights and Washington Office on Latin America, presented a grimmer picture of human rights violations by the police. However, it also complimented the Haitian government and the police leadership on the steps that they had taken to establish accountability within the force. See "Haiti: The Human Rights Record of the Haitian National Police," *Human Rights Watch* 9, 1 (January 1997).

60. For a sample of such activities, see various items in *UNMIH Journal* 1, 15 (December 31, 1995).

61. UNMIH personnel from U.S., personal interviews, Haiti, February 1996. Also see David Bentley and Robert Oakley, "Peace Operations: A Comparison of Somalia and Haiti," Strategic Forum no. 30 (Washington, D.C.: Institute for National Strategic Studies, National Defense University, May 1995).

62. UN commanders, personal interviews, Haiti, February 1996 and October 1997. Also See Leif Ahlquist, *Cooperation, Command and Control in Peace Support Operations: A Case Study of Haiti* (Stockholm: Swedish National Defense College, 1998), 36–37.

63. Maguire et al., "Haiti Held Hostage," 43–44.

64. See Human Rights Watch/Americas, *Thirst for Justice: A Decade of Impunity in Haiti* (New York: Human Rights Watch, 1996), 18–19.

65. See "Communal Governance Programme/Demobilization & Reintegration Programme," *IOM Monthly Report* (Haiti: IOM Documentation Unit, January 1996).

66. See S/1996/813, *Report of the Secretary-General on the United Nations Support Mission in Haiti* (October 1, 1996), paras. 8–9.

67. For outlines of USAID governance programs in Haiti, see USAID Bureau for Humanitarian Response, *Office of Transition Initiatives: The First Two Years, A Report to Congress* (Washington, D.C.: USAID, 1996), 11. Also see USAID/Haiti, *Status Report* (Washington D.C.: USAID, February 7, 1996), 2–3.

68. Several international nongovernmental organizations have taken a different position. See David Briscoe, "Aid Group: US Aid Hurts Haiti," Associated Press, February 12, 1997 (www.washingtonpost.com).

69. So successful was this project in avoiding middlemen that a leading left-wing Haitian journalist, who had taken strong exception to U.S. policies in Haiti in the past, admitted to me in 1998 that he was willing to revise his opinion of the U.S. ability to learn from its mistakes.

70. Some other USAID projects also showed a laudable trend toward more participatory project implementation in Haiti. See Mimi Whitfield, "Clean Water, Garbage Pickup Slated for Cité Soleil Slum," *Miami Herald*, November 3, 1997.

71. The government had created a commission in 1995, headed by Jean-Edouard Baker, to generate ideas for economic modernization. See the

Economist Intelligence Unit, Country Report on Haiti (first quarter 1995), 28, www.eiu.com.

72. See "Haiti—Privatization Measure Passed by Legislature," *Miami Herald* wire services, September 7, 1996.

73. Conversations with Bernard Etheart, director of INARA, the Haitian government's land reform agency, in August 1998.

74. USAID's "Asosye" initiative had provided important assistance for this kind of articulation.

75. Maguire et al., "Haiti Held Hostage," 80.

76. The country's crumbling infrastructure provides the starkest example of this stasis. See Jim Teeple, "Haiti Infrastructure: Correspondent Report," *Voice of America*, February 27, 1997.

77. Haiti missed a remarkable opportunity in 1987, when a congress of national democratic movements was convened to bring together most progressive elements in both the civic and political sectors that had been campaigning for democracy. See Amy Wilentz, *The Rainy Season: Haiti Since Duvalier* (New York: Simon and Schuster, 1989), 210. The agenda set by this congress fell by the wayside, however, as the military heightened its repression in the next few years.

78. Alex Dupuy has described this division in Haiti's democracy movement in *Haiti in the New World Order*, 47–48.

79. The UN Secretary-General recognized that the absence of a consensus on these issues will pose difficulties for Haiti's new institutions in his S/1996/416, *Report of the Secretary-General on the United Nations Mission in Haiti* (June 5, 1996), para. 4.

80. The viewpoint that more than elected institutions is needed to build Haiti's democracy has been supported elsewhere. "The experiences of Suriname and Haiti show that while electoral democracy and stability are necessary, they are not sufficient. One writer makes the important point that 'ending civil conflict, holding relatively free elections, and installing elected civilian regimes [are] not, in and of themselves, sufficient to create democratic systems.'" Ivelaw L. Griffith, "Caribbean Security on the Eve of the 21st Century," McNair Paper 54 (Washington, D.C.: Institute for National Strategic Studies, National Defense University, October 1996).

81. It should also be remembered that building dialogue around specific peacebuilding initiatives is more than just a matter of public relations, since media campaigns are likely to reach only a small audience. The planning and implementation of international initiatives should directly involve the intended beneficiaries, particularly those who stand to accrue concrete gains as a result of the initiative. Participation of these intended beneficiaries in formulating the initiative is the best way to focus their attention and energies in a sustainable fashion. The UN did undertake comprehensive public relations efforts in Haiti in the context of its various peacekeeping missions. See Ingrid Lehman, "Public Information Campaigns in Peacekeeping: The UN Experience in Haiti," The Pearson Papers, Paper no. 1 (Cornwallis Park, Nova Scotia: The Lester B. Pearson Canadian International Peacekeeping Training Centre), 1998.

82. Some pointers toward how more participatory and inclusive planning and implementation of international initiatives would assist in speeding up the judicial reform process are provided in Human Rights Watch/Americas in collaboration with the National Coalition for Haitian Refugees, "Haiti—Human

Rights After President Aristide's Return" (New York: Human Rights Watch/Americas, October 1995), 6–7.

83. For details of the role of civil society and dialogue in the development of South Africa's National Peace Accord, see Peter Gastrow, *Bargaining for Peace: South Africa and the National Peace Accord* (Washington, D.C.: United States Institute for Peace Press, 1995).

84. An experiment of this nature was attempted, with relative success, in Estonia by The Carter Center and the University of Virginia's Center for the Study of Mind and Human Interaction, from 1994 to 1996. A series of six workshops to encourage dialogue among Estonia's various ethnic groups was conducted. For details, see Joyce Neu and Vamik Volkan, "Developing a Methodology for Conflict Prevention: The Case of Estonia," Working Paper Series (Atlanta, GA: The Carter Center of Emory University, 1999).

85. Ricardo Stein, director of the Soros Foundation office in Guatemala City, argued to me in a personal conversation in 1999 that a key factor in ensuring "social patience," or the continued engagement of war-affected populations with nascent postconflict political processes that were hard-pressed to deliver, was the type of participation that has been prescribed in this chapter.

3

Somalia: Building Sovereignty or Restoring Peace?

Ameen Jan

Despite much apprehension within the international community, the withdrawal of the United Nations peacekeeping troops from Somalia in March 1995 did not result in an immediate return to violence in the country. Instead, political dynamics that had been frozen as a consequence of the massive UN presence in the country resumed. Since the termination of the UN peacekeeping operation, the dominant political trend in Somalia has involved a consolidation of divisions of territory along clan lines and the creation of subnational political units that are dominated by one or other of the major Somali clans. These clan-based political authorities have allowed a resumption of civilian social and economic life, notably in the northern regions of the country.

Northern Somalia, which is relatively homogenous in its clan composition, with one or another major clan occupying adjacent portions of territory, appears to be well on its way to recovery. A rough balance of military power now exists among these clans, which is likely to remain unless neighboring states become more deeply involved by providing support to their favored military factions. For the time being, the balance of military power has resulted in a cementing of the frontlines dividing the different territories that they respectively control. Instead of focusing their political and military energies on conquering adjacent territories, the faction leaders from these clans seem inclined to turn their attention inward to consolidate leadership within their zones, thereby transforming themselves from military to civilian leaders.

In southern Somalia, which has a much more heterogeneous clan population and two major port cities, Mogadishu and Kismayu, security remains a problem, and clan-based governance has not taken root. Low-intensity fighting continues in the urban centers of Mogadishu and Kismayu, which historically have had a mixed clan population, and the area populated by the militarily weaker Rahanweyn clan remains under constant threat of invasion from its neighboring clans. Notwithstanding such instability, since 1995 the number of total battle-related deaths (military and civilian) in the country as a whole has been relatively low, between about two hundred and six hundred annually.[1] Economic production, mainly raising livestock and agriculture in the interriverine belt, continues, as does commerce both within Somalia and internationally. Traditional systems of law and order, involving Islamic law or *shari'a,* have been restored in many parts of Somalia.

While large-scale violence no longer plagues the country, Somalia still suffers from poverty, underdevelopment, and the lack of public institutions to facilitate commerce and trade and to provide essential social services. The absence of central government inhibits numerous activities and conveniences, such as international trade agreements and health certification of livestock for export, that are taken for granted in other states. The lack of an effective local or national response to severe flooding of the Juba and Shabelle rivers in late 1997 indicated the continued reliance by Somalis on external support rather than internal mechanisms in times of crisis. International actors, including UN agencies, nongovernmental organizations (NGOs), and various bilateral donor agencies, continue programs in various parts of Somalia to provide health, education, and humanitarian support to vulnerable groups. While the UN continues to monitor political events in the country, the relevance of its political presence to peace efforts in Somalia today is minimal.

The main political efforts undertaken since the end of the second UN Operation in Somalia's (UNOSOM II) mandate were the peace talks among faction leaders initiated by Ethiopia in December 1996, known as the Sodere process, and those held in Cairo in late 1997. The Cairo meeting resulted in the signing on December 22, 1997, of an accord calling for a national reconciliation conference as a first step toward constituting a national transitional government for an initial three years, with a possible subsequent two-year extension. The agreement recognized the need for a federal system of government in Somalia.[2] However, like the previous UN-sponsored efforts, both the Sodere process and the Cairo meeting were unable to bring all the protagonists together, notably Haji Ibrahim Egal's government in "Somaliland." While General Hussein Aidid and Ali Mahdi Mohammed, opposition faction leaders in Mogadishu, both signed the Cairo accord, serious differences remain between them, as well as amongst the other faction leaders, regarding the issues of how power should be shared at the national level and the role of other clan leaders in the proposed national reconciliation conference. The faction leaders' commitment to embark on an inclusive and sustainable process of political reconstruction continues to be minimal. More recently, the escalating border conflict between Ethiopia and Eritrea has resulted in these countries supporting opposing faction leaders in Somalia since 1999. This new "regionalization" of the Somali conflict may signal a return to violence in the country and a new phase in its civil war.

Notwithstanding the recent heightening of tensions due to regional politics and the lack of progress in internationally sponsored peace efforts, two trends of political development occurring within Somalia since 1995 are notable. The first is the growing "civilianization" of clan leaderships, accompanied by diminishing interclan conflict and a de facto partition of the country along clan-controlled zones, particularly in the north, and the restoration of clan-based governance in those zones. The old Barre-era divisions along administrative regional lines no longer hold in many areas, such as the northwest ("Republic of Somaliland"), northeast, and southern regions. Military-civilian authorities continue to perform governance functions in these areas, the earliest example of which was the emergence of the Isaaq clan–based government in "Somaliland" in 1993, followed in 1998 by the formal establishment of "Puntland," an autonomous, although not independent zone governed by the Darod clan. Following the departure of UNOSOM II in 1995, the Rahanweyn clan launched an internal reconciliation process, creating a Supreme Governing Council of Digil-Mirifle in the regions of Bay, Bakool, and parts of Gedo and Lower Shabelle. While this process was soon interrupted by General Aidid's invasion of the area in September 1995, the Rahanweyn have continued to organize against Aidid with the formation of a Rahanweyn Resistance Army (RRA).[3]

The second important development following UNOSOM II's departure is the emergence of Islamic authorities across the country, particularly in Luuq (where they existed even before UNOSOM II), Bulo Hawa, north Mogadishu, Jowhar, Belet Weyn, and Kismayu. While not all of these authorities have lasted, many have responded very effectively to the problem of crime and local security in their areas by instituting courts where accused criminals are judged according to *shari'a*. This process has had a visibly positive effect on crime, which was previously rife in many of these areas. The judges of these courts are typically the religious leaders, or shaikhs, of the community. Some *shari'a* authorities also perform policing and penal functions, as was the case in north Mogadishu.[4]

Islamic politics have historical precedent in Somalia. In the early twentieth century, the Islamic leader Shaikh Mohammed Abdille Hassan—the "mad mullah" according to the British—catalyzed a jihad against colonial rule in Somalia. In the postcolonial period, an Islamic opposition movement joined with the clan-based opposition movements against Barre's rule. Following Barre's defeat, Islamic elements organized efforts to control and govern areas throughout Somalia, including the Medina district in Mogadishu and the city of Luuq in the southern region of Gedo, which remained under Islamic rule during and after the UN intervention. Islamic elements were also present in the Somali National Movement (SNM) in "Somaliland," and a serious uprising in the northeast by Ittihad al-Islami, an Islamic group, was militarily crushed by the Somali Salvation Democratic Front (SSDF) in June–August 1992, when it threatened to take over the major cities and towns in the northeast region.[5]

The relationship between the *shari'a* authorities, faction leaders, and other clan leaders is dynamic. The *shari'a* authorities were, for the most part, established with the consent of the local faction leaders to perform basic governance functions within their area of control. By and large, they have not crossed clan boundaries. However, *shari'a* authorities have rapidly gained popularity because of their ability to deliver basic peace and security to the people. Unlike the centrifugal politics of clan division, the *shari'a* authorities demonstrate a latent political tendency toward integration. While they have not overtly challenged the authority of the factions, several of the shaikhs have correctly indicated that *shari'a* goes beyond clan divisions and is pan-Somali, thus establishing a political platform for themselves that is inherently opposed to the interests of the faction leaders. At the same time, there are internal differences within the various *shari'a* authorities, which include moderate and more radical elements. Assistance from certain external countries to the more radical elements may have wider political implications in Somalia in the future.

Another important development in Somalia recently is the growth of a robust business sector and the emergence of civil society. Thriving business activity in cities such as Bossaso in the northeast, the development of private commercial banking, and a functioning satellite telecommunications system that charges lower rates than most other telecom systems in the developing world, attest to the Somali entrepreneurial spirit.[6] Women's groups have also emerged as important peacemakers in communities, serving to bridge clan-based divisions.[7]

History of the Conflict

Growing Alienation in a Clan-based Society

Somali society has historically been stateless and has conformed primarily to a pastoral mode of economic production. Kinship ties based on clan lines defined political community, and the interplay of traditional codes of conduct (*xeer*) and Islamic law (*shari'a*) provided the backbone for law and order in the society. Following the imposition of colonial rule, a nascent Somali national identity began to emerge as a vehicle for opposition and independence. Independence from colonial rule on July 1, 1960, was accompanied by a voluntary unification of British Somaliland with Italian Somalia. The national ethos of the newly independent Somali Republic was evident in its desire to bring under one national flag the remaining Somali populations living in Djibouti, the Ogaden region of Ethiopia, and northeast Kenya.

Even though a Somali national identity emerged with independence, the traditional clan-based political identities did not recede. Somalia's attempts to institute a democratic political system between 1960 and 1969 became a delicate game of balancing clan interests, which eventually resulted in greater political fractionalization.[8] On October 21, 1969, a bloodless military coup d'état brought Major-General Mohamed Siyaad Barre to power. In the first decade of his military dictatorship, Barre attempted to renew the sense of national identity by denouncing "clanism," espousing the economic philosophy of "scientific socialism," instituting Somali (using the Latin script) as the official national language, and launching a military effort to bring the Ogaden region of Ethiopia under his control.[9]

Notwithstanding these efforts, Barre increasingly reverted to a clan-based system of preferences. His political support derived from his own Darod-Marehan subclan, as well as the Ogaden and Dolbahante clans of his extended family members, which correspondingly benefited from government patronage, to the exclusion of other clans. Following Somalia's defeat by Ethiopia in the Ogaden war of 1976–1977, which increased his paranoia about being challenged by those clans that had been excluded from the benefits of power, Barre accelerated the pattern of pitting clan against clan as part of his strategy of divide-and-rule. With lagging economic growth, continuing poverty and underdevelopment, and a pattern of gross human rights abuses by the regime, one of the most brutal in Africa, divisions in the society rapidly grew and became militarized.[10]

The first faction to emerge was the SSDF, formed by a small group of military officers from the Majerteen subclan who had engineered a failed coup d'état against Barre immediately after his loss to Ethiopia in the Ogaden war. In 1981, leaders of the Isaaq clan, which was suffering massive abuses at the hands of Barre's military forces, formed the SNM with the aim of overthrowing the government. In the 1980s, increasing radicalization of these and other new factions formed along clan and subclan lines as Barre sought to eliminate his opposition by force. Ethiopia, in particular, provided military and economic support to several opposition groups, particularly the SNM, in its efforts to overthrow Barre.

In 1988, in response to a growing rapprochement between Somalia and Ethiopia, which threatened to cut Ethiopian support for the SNM, a serious uprising occurred in northwest Somalia. In response, Barre unleashed the full strength of his military, essentially razing the cities of Hargeisa and Burao and killing thousands of civilians in the bargain. This episode spelled the beginning of the end of Barre's rule. New clan-based factions emerged, including the Hawiye-dominated United Somali Congress (USC) in 1989, with the common agenda of unseating Barre. As these forces gained strength, including through defections from the army, Barre became progressively weakened. Having lost control over increasing parts of Somalia to the different military factions, he was eventually driven out of the capital by the USC in January 1991.

Humanitarian Tragedy and the Initial International Response

Besides the common goal of deposing Barre, there was little that bound the various clan-based factions together. In April 1991, the SNM leadership convened a congress in Burao and decided to restore the legal status of the State of Somaliland as it had existed between independence from British colonial rule on June 26, 1960, and its voluntary reunification with Italian Somalia four days later. The other factions began rapidly consolidating their power over the rest of Somalia. A series of conferences in Djibouti in 1991 resulted in the hasty formation of an interim government, with Ali Mahdi of the USC selected as its president. The chairman of the USC, General Aidid, who had led the final military offensive that drove the Barre forces out of the capital, Mogadishu, challenged this arrangement. Intense fighting between Ali Mahdi and Aidid broke out in November 1991. This demonstration of an unrestrained quest for power resulted in widespread loss of life and destruction of physical infrastructure in the capital.[11]

While the struggle for control of the capital by the various faction leaders played a critical part in the continuing civil war, the struggle over productive land resources was also an important factor. In particular, the interriverine valleys in southern Somalia were contested for several reasons. These areas are the main transit routes from the hinterland to the ports of Mogadishu and Kismayu and comprise fertile agricultural land. In addition, their indigenous population, including the Rahanweyn, the Bantu, and other minority subclans, are militarily weaker than the other clans, such as the Darod and Hawiye that inhabit the more pastoral adjacent areas of the country.[12] These factors increase the temptation of neighboring populations to exert control over the interriverine belt of Somalia.

Interclan fighting soon spread into the southern regions of Somalia, which, combined with the scorched-earth practices of the retreating Barre forces earlier that year, resulted in the local population being unable to farm the land or graze livestock. Increasing malnutrition in these areas rapidly led to the onset of a famine by early 1992. This man-made humanitarian disaster was compounded by the fact that the delivery of humanitarian relief by the International

Committee of the Red Cross (ICRC), various international NGOs, and UN agencies was rendered exceedingly difficult by the prevailing general insecurity, the increased incidence of banditry and theft, and the extortionist practices of the faction militias, whose support was required to guarantee the humanitarian community safe access to the suffering civilians. As a result, several UN agencies withdrew altogether from Somalia during 1991, including the United Nations Development Program (UNDP), which was the Resident Coordinator of all UN agencies in the country.[13] In light of the deteriorating situation, the UN Security Council and the Secretariat, as well as the Organization of African Unity (OAU), the League of Arab States (LAS), and the Organization of the Islamic Conference (OIC), finally began to take increasing interest in the developing situation, dispatching delegations to Somalia to meet with the faction leaders to broker a cease-fire and seek a political resolution to the conflict.

The UN established its first operation in Somalia in May 1992,[14] under the leadership of Algerian diplomat Mohamed Sahnoun. Conceived as a traditional military observer mission, the UN Operation in Somalia (UNOSOM) was mandated to comprise fifty (later increased to five hundred) unarmed military observers in Mogadishu to observe a UN-brokered cease-fire. It soon became evident that this mission was impossible, as the faction leaders continued to hinder the deployment of the observers and as fighting raged in the capital. While Sahnoun untiringly emphasized the need for emergency relief, arguing that its provision would also address in some measure the problems of insecurity in the country, neither the UN agencies nor individual bilateral donors were able to organize a massive relief operation in time.[15]

International Intervention

Operation Restore Hope

As the humanitarian situation worsened in late 1992, images of starving Somalis increasingly began appearing on television screens around the world. Impelled by public opinion to respond to this massive human suffering, and in the absence of serious political constraints following his defeat in the presidential elections in early November 1992, President George Bush decided later that month that the United States would take the lead in dispatching a sizable force to Somalia to assist in the delivery of humanitarian relief. On December 9, 1992, following UN Security Council authorization under Chapter VII of the UN Charter, the Unified Task Force (UNITAF), also known as Operation Restore Hope, was launched.[16] UNITAF's mandate was limited to establishing a secure environment for the delivery of humanitarian relief.

UNITAF's impact in Somalia was immediate and positive. High expectations among the Somali population of what the United States would be able to do to quell the fighting, including disarmament of the factional militias, resulted in a pause in fighting as the faction leaders waited to see how international military intervention would affect their respective military and political fortunes. Delivery of humanitarian assistance was thereby eased, and UNITAF arguably succeeded in saving thousands of human lives in the areas most affected by the famine, mainly the southern regions.[17]

Contrary to the desire of UN Secretary-General Boutros Boutros-Ghali to forcibly disarm the factions while its better-equipped forces were present in Somalia, the United States sought to cooperate with the faction leaders in order to allow the passage of humanitarian relief and the cantonment of heavy weapons. U.S. strategy was based on the assumption that such cooperation would reduce the possibility of confrontation with the faction leaders and thus minimize the risk of casualties to UNITAF forces.[18] The failure to actively disarm the factions of their heavy weapons, which some observers have suggested could have been done by UNITAF with limited resistance from the faction leaders,[19] had a significant psychological effect on both the faction leaders and the Somali population: the faction leaders' sense of invincibility was reinforced while the general expectation that disarmament would occur diminished. This dynamic impaired subsequent efforts at factional reconciliation undertaken by the United Nations.[20]

The Addis Ababa Peace Agreement

The United States intended to rapidly end UNITAF and its own military presence in Somalia by facilitating the quick formation of a new central government in Somalia and providing a broad new mandate to the UN to assist a process of institution building, political reconciliation, and economic rehabilitation. To this end, the United States and the UN launched efforts to convene a major national reconciliation conference, which was held in Addis Ababa in March

1993. Application of strong international pressure resulted in the fifteen factions (not including the SNM, which attended as an observer) signing an agreement on March 27. This agreement committed them, inter alia, to a cease-fire and disarmament within ninety days and the creation of a Transitional National Council (TNC) through a bottom-up, participatory process of forming district and regional councils. Three days later, in a further agreement entitled "Agreements Reached Between the Political Leaders at the Consultations Held in Addis Ababa, 30 March 1993" (which the UN decided to ignore), the same faction leaders explicitly indicated that they themselves would nominate the members of the TNC and that it would be created within forty-five days, a period that was clearly insufficient for effective grassroots participation in the creation of the councils.[21] This second agreement reflected the faction leaders' lack of serious commitment to broad political participation that might erode their own authority.

The international approach of securing a peace accord among the faction leaders was a pragmatic if short-sighted response to the prevailing situation of insecurity in Somalia. The factions and their militias were the principal arbiters of power and had to be contended with. However, in order to obtain a broad and sustainable political agreement, a preceding peace process that recognized the sources of the conflict, addressed the basic insecurities of the different clans, and helped build confidence among them would have been needed. This process would have been long and included a broad range of clan leadership, and it would not necessarily have led to the formation of a central government in the short term.

In contrast, the Addis Ababa agreement was signed in the absence of any peace *process,* which was akin to placing the cart before the horse. The peace effort, based on international mediation to secure a peace agreement among factions, was driven by the U.S. desire to terminate its military involvement in Somalia. This primary concern dictated both the haste with which matters proceeded and the scant attention paid to the basic problems affecting Somalia that had resulted in the humanitarian emergency. Viewed through this narrow lens, the indisputable prerequisites for normalizing the political situation called for rapid creation of a central government in Somalia and reestablishment of a Somali police force to maintain internal security. These state-centric preconceptions revealed an insufficient appreciation of the roots of Somali conflict and the depth of societal divisions along clan and subclan lines that had occurred during the two decades of Barre's rule, particularly since 1988.

Factional reconciliation faced many fundamental obstacles. Most significant, the faction leaders had a vested interest in the continuation of conflict and instability because their power derived from defending their clan interests, including control of territory, against those of other clans. Reconciliation would have meant the erosion of many faction leaders' power, as civilian clan leaders would emerge to lead efforts at reconstruction and governance once peace was achieved. One possible way to overcome this marginalization was for the factions to transform themselves into political parties, taking their cue from the SNM in "Somaliland." The international community, however, made no effort to support such transformations within the existing military factions. Instead, it emphasized reconciliation among faction leaders—an approach focused narrowly on existing power brokers—which effectively further strengthened their position within Somali society, so much so that by the time the second UN operation in Somalia was established they were the main political players.

Moreover, this focus on faction leaders as the principal political class in Somalia was also maintained by the UN operations' leadership throughout the duration of UNOSOM II's mandate. UN-sponsored national reconciliation conferences that were held in Addis Ababa (1993) and Nairobi (1994) further distanced the faction leaders from the larger clan constituents they ostensibly represented. The UN did not seek to centrally involve a wider segment of Somali society, such as clan and religious leaders, elders, and other authority figures, in the negotiation process, focusing instead solely on the leaders of the fifteen factions. Had these constituents been involved, the absolute authority enjoyed by the faction leaders as spokesmen for their clans' interests may have been tempered; new voices, less wedded to military solutions, could have been amplified. Instead, UN peace conferences became a vehicle for enhancing the faction leaders' personal prestige within their own clans rather than for seeking a genuine agreement.

Locally based clan reconciliation conferences that for the most part did not involve UNOSOM II were in fact much more conducive to peacebuilding efforts.[22] These included, among others, the Galkayo conference in May 1993, which resulted in the peaceful division of the Mudug region among three clans; the Boroma conference from January to May 1993, which led to a national charter, or constitution, for the "Republic of Somaliland"; and the Jubaland conference from June to August 1993, which allowed for a six-month cease-fire in Kismayu. These were always conducted in the local area, included a much wider segment of the local population than just the faction leaders, and were of minuscule cost in proportion to the international extravagances that were the UN-sponsored peace conferences. More traditional methods of reconciliation were applied, involving elders, religious leaders, and the educated classes, and sufficient time was allowed for agreements to be reached, which resulted in more lasting and grounded peace settlements.

The result of the internationally sponsored agreements reached by the faction leaders, in contrast, were for the most part worth little more than the paper they were printed on. The Nairobi agreement of March 24, 1994, in particular, had little chance of succeeding, as it was immediately followed by the mobilization of forces by several of the faction leaders and renewed interclan fighting.[23] These agreements served instead as a means by which the faction leaders could demonstrate to the international community that they were not the main obstacles to peace, and for UNOSOM II to assert its continued relevance as an agent for peace in war-torn Somalia.

UNOSOM II

Virtually concurrent with the signing of the Addis Ababa agreement, the UN Security Council adopted Resolution 814, crafted largely by the United States,[24] which laid out in detail the tasks—including disarmament—that were required to establish longer-term peace and stability. This resolution mandated the UN to undertake the following activities:

> (a) assistance in the provision of relief and economic rehabilitation; (b) assistance in the repatriation of refugees and displaced persons; (c) assistance to promote and advance political reconciliation through broad participation by all sectors of Somali society, and the re-establishment of national and regional institutions and civil administrations in the entire country; (d) assistance in the re-establishment of Somali police; (e) assistance in development of a coherent program for demining; (f) development of public information activities in support of UN activities in Somalia; and, (g) creation of conditions for civil society participation in the political reconciliation process.[25]

Madeleine Albright, U.S. Permanent Representative to the UN at the time, remarked that "with this resolution, we will embark on an unprecedented enterprise aimed at nothing less than the restoration of an entire country as a proud, functioning and viable member of the community of nations."[26] UNOSOM II was established to undertake this gargantuan task of peacebuilding, although expectations within the U.S. administration about its ability to successfully perform the tasks at hand were very low.[27]

Many elements of this broad mandate for UNOSOM II were in fact appropriate, as they correctly identified the political, military, economic, and social changes necessary to restore longer-term peace and stability in any war-torn society. Observers both within and outside the United Nations have pointed out that UNOSOM II was not provided with the means to fulfill this broad mandate, including adequately equipped military and civilian personnel, sufficient finances, and time.[28] UNOSOM II's failure should therefore be seen in light of the very limited resources it had.

However, UNOSOM II's failure was a result of more than merely insufficient means. The mandate was handicapped by an initial lack of strategic vision and thus suffered from the ensuing ad hoc manner in which it was implemented. The provisions read like a broad laundry list of issues to be addressed; they were never translated into a strategic plan that took into account the specificities of the Somali problem or devised an appropriate approach to address them. The operation on the ground could have developed a strategic plan, in consultation with the political decisionmakers at UN headquarters and national capitals, as well as Somali and foreign experts with a deeper understanding of the conflict. Following Sahnoun's resignation as the Secretary-General's Special Representative (SRSG), little serious effort was made to develop a strategy of international engagement that would pay attention to local Somali political dynamics and capacities. As a result, UNOSOM II's implementation was not only cursory and ad hoc, but at times counterproductive, serving merely to compound the initial absence of strategic thought and leading to both intended and unintended consequences in Somalia.

Intended Consequences of UNOSOM II

UNOSOM II's various programs had an intentional effect on the Somali political environment in three main areas of grassroots political development, institution building, and economic rehabilitation.

Political efforts. UNOSOM II's political efforts continued to be preoccupied with factional reconciliation, while simultaneously initiating a process of grassroots political development as called for in the Addis Ababa agreement and in Security Council Resolution 814. However, the grassroots political development process suffered from several significant problems. First of all, the faction leaders' commitment to the idea of constructing a national government from the bottom up was highly questionable. Hence, UNOSOM II chose to ignore these leaders' intentions, proceeding instead to assist in the creation of civilian structures of governance at the district and regional levels. It thereby embarked on a process that was destined to result in conflict with many of those faction leaders when they saw alternate authorities being created that posed a potential threat to their own power.

The method of formation of district and regional councils was also imposed by UNOSOM II rather than being locally generated. UNOSOM II political officers traveled to the districts and informed the local population, primarily the community elders, of the Addis Ababa agreement that called for the formation of such councils. They would then issue the formal guidelines for councilors, which, inter alia, included equitable clan representation and seats for women. These officers then returned to each district in several weeks' time to witness the formation of the council and to certify its authenticity. If in UNOSOM II's estimation all the clans of the area had not been adequately represented, the UN would refuse to certify the council. Instead of engaging in a process of dialogue with these communities about the appropriate manner of implementing the provisions of the Addis Ababa agreement concerning local governance, UNOSOM II provided a rigid framework with formalized structures and time frames for their establishment. Somali political authority at the community level resides in a large measure with the elders, who perform the roles of peacemakers and arbitrators through an informal consultative process. The process of formation of the councils ignored this local dynamic and set about to establish modern, recognizable institutions that could provide administrative functions and be the local counterparts to the international community.

The emphasis on the factional reconciliation process itself also undercut the effectiveness of the district and regional councils for two closely linked reasons. First, some authoritative local leaders thought that by going to the councils they would miss their chance at the national reconciliation process, which was for the "big players." Second, those who were not the big players and were therefore unable to participate in the factional process sought instead to enhance their political future by becoming councilors. Few of them were motivated by a desire to make local government work. For these reasons many of the district and regional councils varied in their quality and capacity to govern.[29]

In addition, the design of district and regional boundaries was antiquated, corresponding to old administrative regions that no longer represented the real territorial divisions among clans. A more effective approach than replicating the formal regional boundaries as the basis for political units would have been to help strengthen civilian authorities in areas that were controlled by a unified clan. In this way, indigenous and more authoritative clan-based civilian authorities could have been fostered.

In homogenous districts and regions, such as Nugal and Bakool, there were few problems in creating local councils. Even districts that UNOSOM II did not visit for political reasons—for instance, Haradere that was populated by the Habr-Gedir subclan to which Aidid belonged—formed their own local governance structures. The district and regional councils that worked effectively would very likely have done so even without UN support. In areas of mixed clan composition, the worst impact of UNOSOM II's efforts to form councils was a disruption of local reconciliation processes that resulted in the clans having to quantify in a short period of time their relative importance so that council seats could be allocated accordingly. This disruptive impact became evident in districts such as Qorioley, where UNOSOM II political officers found themselves being physically threatened by the factional militias of those clans whose immediate political standing would be adversely affected by the arrangement advocated by UNOSOM II.

Yet another reason for the councils' lack of effectiveness was their inability to collect tax revenues and provide basic social services for the population, which was defined by UNOSOM II as one of their primary functions. This inability was a result of both the very limited revenue base and the unwillingness of the local population to pay taxes, a factor that was linked at least partially to the lack of political authority, or authenticity, of the councils. In addition, many of the international NGOs, who were the principal providers of social services in large parts of Somalia, were unwilling to work in cooperation with the nascent local administrations. A partnership between the NGOs and the local administrations could have helped to build the capacity of those authorities and given them greater legitimacy within their communities. At the same time, the international NGOs argued correctly that "reporting" to the so-called local authorities would unnecessarily bureaucratize their work and provide legitimacy to institutions that were not genuinely authoritative.

Following UNOSOM II's departure, the district and regional councils—where they existed—became increasingly subsumed by wider clan-based civilian authorities. Basic technical training for such authorities continued to be provided by the Swedish Life and Peace Institute and the UN Development Office for Somalia (UNDOS), which was useful in a limited way in assisting the more authentic of such institutions to perform basic governance tasks, such as planning, budgeting, generating revenue, and providing basic social services.

Institution-building efforts. UNOSOM II's institution-building efforts were aimed at providing assistance to local governance structures, namely district and regional councils, and establishing a Somali justice sector and police force. The reestablishment of a Somali justice sector, comprising a judicial, police, and penal system, was a significant undertaking. Proper and sustainable functioning of these institutions requires the framework of a domestic political authority that can provide legitimacy and direction. Rather than using the existing political authorities—namely the factions—to provide this local framework or, alternately, allowing the emergence of civilian political structures to oversee the police and penal institutions, UNOSOM II set up a justice sector in what was essentially a political and institutional vacuum.

The nucleus of UNOSOM II's efforts in this respect was the establishment by UNITAF of an interim auxiliary force of former Somali police officers tasked with overseeing traffic control and providing security around feeding centers. Subsequently, following the March 1993 Addis Ababa agreement that called for the creation of district, regional, and national police forces as part of the effort to reestablish security in Somalia, UNOSOM II embarked on an extensive program to reconstruct the Somali police along the lines of the former Barre-era police force.[30]

At the strategic level, UNOSOM II's plans in this regard suffered from a serious contradiction. On the one hand, the establishment of the Somali police was tied into the military concept of UNOSOM II's operations, which required a functioning Somali national police force before the withdrawal of peacekeeping forces.[31] On the other hand, the police force was supposed to report to district and regional councils until a transitional national council was established.[32] Not surprisingly, the imperative of quick withdrawal prevailed, causing UNOSOM II to hastily embark on the establishment of approximately five thousand police in Mogadishu and the rest of UNITAF's area of deployment in the absence of local political structures. At the same time, the funding required for creating the initially recommended police strength of eighteen to twenty thousand never materialized.[33]

In the absence of the factions being disarmed, either voluntarily or through force, the Somali police force was destined to remain relatively weak. While petty criminal activity might be addressed by such a police force, its ability to ensure internal security against the well-armed faction militias that often reverted to banditry (the *mooryaan* phenomenon) was very limited.[34] Neither would a focus on establishing police in the relatively secure areas of Somalia, such as the northeast regions, address the issue of reestablishing security in the contested areas of Somalia, which by definition was where the problem resided.[35]

The manner in which police forces and judges were selected, notably with little consultation between UNOSOM II and either the faction leaders or the existing local authorities, was also problematic. The 1962 Somali Penal Code was chosen as the body of law that would apply until a future national authority decided otherwise. This decision undermined whatever local tendencies there were to establish an alternate legal framework, such as *shari'a.* UNOSOM II appointed judges through the recommendations of a thirteen-member judicial committee that was based in Mogadishu and traveled very infrequently to regions where they were supposed to operate. In some instances where the clan balance was sensitive, UNOSOM II's judicial appointments generated considerable opposition and violence, since they upset this balance by vesting formal authority in persons with particular clan affiliations.

Having established, armed, and paid the police, UNOSOM II became the natural authority to which the police reported. Salaries for police superseded the levels established during the Barre era and were far in excess of what the local economy could sustain. These factors, combined with the requirement that police officers must have served at least two years prior to January 1991, resulted in an unsustainable and somewhat aged police force. Not surprisingly, the UNOSOM II–supported justice and police systems disappeared rapidly with its departure. Alternate institutions, notably the *shari'a* authorities, emerged indigenously to perform policing and judicial functions in numerous parts of the country.

Economic rehabilitation efforts. By mid-1993, the humanitarian emergency in Somalia had largely ended, although vast numbers of internally displaced persons remained in camps throughout the country that required ongoing humanitarian assistance.[36] UNOSOM II's inability to shift its emphasis to rehabilitation was compounded by the fact that the international development agencies, particularly UNDP and the World Bank, were not sufficiently engaged in Somalia. The World Bank remained aloof to Somalia's predicament, arguing that it could not engage in a country without having a national government as its interlocutor. At the same time, rather than seeking to incorporate the efforts and harness the expertise of the wider UN system that was involved in Somalia, to assist in the longer-term planning for institution building and economic rehabilitation, UNOSOM II sought to carry out that part of its mandate independently. Two of UNOSOM II's divisions that dealt with economic issues—the Division for Humanitarian Relief and Rehabilitation (DHRR) and the Disarmament, Demobilization, and Demining (3D) Division—in fact could not themselves undertake any rehabilitation efforts, the former because it was mandated to coordinate efforts of other operational agencies and NGOs and the latter because it never received the required funding for demobilization activities. The rehabilitation activities that were undertaken by various UN agencies and NGOs related to supporting education, health, and water and sanitation in different parts of Somalia. While important, these activities remained ad hoc and responsive to immediate needs rather than being part of a broader international approach that could serve to reinforce peace efforts in Somalia.

UNOSOM II did, however, enter into an important partnership with the UN Conference on Trade and Development (UNCTAD) operating in the Somali ports, particularly Mogadishu port, which was under UNOSOM II's military control. This partnership, whereby UNOSOM II protected and UNCTAD managed the port, facilitated Somali trade activities and also enabled the continued delivery of relief supplies. But until the eve of its departure, UNOSOM II did not seek to create a local port authority in Mogadishu that could eventually take over UNCTAD's functions. A gradual process of forming such a port authority could have served as a confidence-building measure between Aidid's and Ali Mahdi's factions, which controlled different parts of the capital city, and might have ensured a smoother transition from international to Somali control of the port when UNOSOM II left. A joint port authority did in fact form independently immediately following UNOSOM II's withdrawal in March 1995, but a few months later a split in Aidid's faction resulted in its collapse and the closure of Mogadishu port.

By the end of 1993, with the ill-conceived and foiled hunt for Aidid over, the bilateral donors for Somalia had clearly lost confidence in UNOSOM II. This was demonstrated unequivocally at the Fourth Coordination Meeting for Humanitarian Assistance to Somalia, where the major donors decided to create the Somalia Aid Coordination Body (SACB) to serve as a common donor platform for coordinating their rehabilitation assistance to Somalia. The SACB adopted a regional approach to development and established two cardinal conditions for providing rehabilitation assistance: security and the existence of local counterparts. Like UNOSOM II, however, the bilateral aid donors also did not seek to develop an overall review of the prevailing situation in Somalia so as to design an economic assistance program in support of a peacebuilding strategy. Their approach focused instead on strengthening the already secure parts of the country by providing funding for reconstruction and institutional strengthening. The idea behind this approach was that the promise of international assistance might provide an incentive to factional leaders in contested areas to resolve their differences so that they too could avail of foreign largesse. But the sums of money potentially available from donors' coffers were paltry compared to what was possible by gaining control of or having a key position in a national government.

While the donors clearly emphasized they did not wish their programs to be associated with UNOSOM II, the regional approach they adopted suffered from two of the same flaws as UNOSOM II. First, they continued to deal with administrative regions rather than territories that were controlled more coherently by a single clan. Second, the SACB asked the regions to create new structures called Regional Development Committees (RDCs), rather than working with the existing but in their view discredited regional councils. However, they did not engage the local and regional leaderships further on how these RDCs should be formed and who should compose them. As a result, the RDCs simply retained the composition of the regional councils but assumed a different name. A third problem was that as soon as money started to flow to more secure regions, resentment grew among other faction leaders who saw their areas not being favored. Therefore, rather than serving as an incentive for the more troubled regions, the regional approach resulted in certain factions attempting to subvert the regions that were being favored. An example was Aidid's invasion of the Bay and Bakool regions in September 1995, which had recently received some donor support.[37]

Unintended Consequences of UNOSOM II

UNOSOM II had an unintended, structural impact on Somali society that was arguably more detrimental than its flawed programmatic intervention. At the height of the operation, UNOSOM II comprised approximately twenty-eight thousand troops in addition to a large civilian presence, deployed primarily in the southern regions of Somalia. In addition, the United States maintained an independent military presence in the form of a quick reaction force (QRF). Both the QRF and UNOSOM II were headquartered in the southern part of Mogadishu, which was controlled by Aidid's faction.

The first unintended impact of UNOSOM II was its own transformation from impartial interlocutor (albeit with enforcement powers) to interested party in the Somali conflict. This occurred as a result of the launching, in conjunction with the QRF, of the hunt for Aidid following the killing of twenty-three Pakistani peacekeepers on June 5, 1993, outside the Aidid-controlled Radio Mogadishu compound. All civilian international efforts were thereafter subsumed by the military objective of marginalizing and eliminating Aidid. A clandestine military operation, including psychological warfare, was launched against Aidid, with "Wanted" posters displaying his picture being posted and dropped all over south Mogadishu and a price of U.S. $25,000 placed on his head. UNOSOM II's "hunt and kill" mission went so far as to bomb the house of a Habr-Gedir elder on July 12 (Abdi House) when it learned that a meeting of clan elders, including Aidid, would be taking place. Aidid did not attend, but according to the ICRC at least fifty-four Habr-Gedir clan members, mainly civilians, were killed without any provocation.[38] These activities clearly transformed the perception of UNOSOM II among Somalis to the extent that it came to be seen as the "sixteenth Somali faction." By the time its military objectives changed, following the killing of eighteen U.S. troops in October 1993, UNOSOM II had become too discredited to be regarded as an honest broker in the Somali political process.

Clearly, the UN had to act in the face of an assault on its peacekeepers in June 1993, but its response should have been preceded by a thorough and impartial investigation into the event and been transparent, measured, judicious, and supportive of the investigation's recommendations for action. An investigation of the events of June fifth was in fact launched by the UN, but its results were not awaited before the faction that was supposedly to blame was targeted.[39] This targeting was largely through the use of force, with no serious consideration of "softer" tools such as a warrant for Aidid's arrest under Somali or international law once an indictment was made. Other options might have included a public relations campaign focused on appealing to the people's sense of honor and justice; Aidid's forces had attacked fellow Muslims who had come to help the Somali people. Such a popular appeal may have helped erode support for Aidid, even if not resulting in his capture.

The second unintended, structural distortion was economic in nature and emerged as a result of the massive presence of UNOSOM II and the concomitant potential for significant economic opportunity it represented. Indigenous political processes became effectively frozen because Somalis wanted to see what benefits UNOSOM II would provide. This expectation was generated by the economic incentive packages it offered to various faction leaders in order to win their support and compliance, and to a lesser degree to the district and regional councils and the police it was helping to establish. The factional reconciliation process sponsored by UNOSOM II most visibly demonstrated the inherent disincentives for reconciliation. Such reconciliation would have meant an end to the financial assistance that UNOSOM II was providing various factions in exchange for their reaching certain agreements, and to their free international trips and treatment as statesmen.

Large amounts of foreign currency were suddenly pumped into the Somali economy with the arrival of UNITAF, a practice that continued with UNOSOM II. The effect of this distortion was most evident in the rising value of the Somali shilling, which appreciated 100 percent, from a rate of approximately SoSh 4000 to SoSh 8000 for one U.S. dollar. UNOSOM II's presence, primarily in south Mogadishu where it was headquartered, fueled the local economy with its rental of houses and vehicles. Rather than helping to create conditions that would generate sustainable employment in Somalia and contribute to long-term peacebuilding, UNOSOM II itself became the single largest employer, engaging approximately three thousand Somalis, primarily in Mogadishu. Salaries for these employees were exceedingly high, particularly for security guards, many of whom also moonlighted as part of the militias. Aside from sustainability considerations, high salaries made continued insecurity lucrative for the factions that provided security guards. Indeed, a bizarre contradiction emerged when UNOSOM II started an offensive against Aidid at the same time its physical presence continued to enrich Aidid and his supporters.

In an economy that could not support basic rehabilitation, considerable resentment was generated among clans that did not benefit equally from UNOSOM II's role as an employer. UNOSOM II rapidly became embroiled in labor-related problems that involved ensuring clan balance in hiring and firing decisions, a task that consumed an increasing amount of its time and energy. In more than one case, UNOSOM II or its subcontracting agents received death threats, and several international staff were in fact killed for employment-related reasons.

Significant distortions arose in the local economy. Indigenous and sustainable Somali employment declined, while a service sector grew around UNOSOM II to provide such items as spare parts for vehicles. At the same time, UNOSOM II preferred to limit its commercial activities with Somalis, importing many items that were in fact available in the local markets. On the one hand, this dampened the local economy's reliance on UNOSOM II; however, it also stifled local production and trade in basic commodities such as oil or grains, which both Somalis and expatriates consumed. A mushrooming of Somali "NGOs," which in fact were Somali entrepreneurs attempting to take advantage of what they perceived as a penchant of UNOSOM II and international NGOs to contract with local humanitarian civil society entities rather than the local business sector, was another social distortion that emerged during this period. In fact, such philanthropic entities were very rare in Somalia, as they are in most underdeveloped countries. Rather than working with the existing Somali private sector in its relief and rehabilitation efforts, thereby generating local employment, the international community's emphasis on local NGOs created a myriad of inauthentic Somali "NGOs," most of which were unable to effectively undertake the functions they purported and were expected to perform.

The final, but no less important, unintended but structural consequence of UNOSOM II was resentment generated among Somalis by the culture of arrogance that pervaded the mission. The underpinnings of this arrogance was UNOSOM II's enforcement mandate, its massive size, and the absence of a Somali government, which de facto provided the UN operation with authority akin to that of a national government. Accompanying this mindset was the general disdain with which Somalis were treated. One small example of this attitude was the difficulty of Somalis to access the U.S. embassy compound in Mogadishu where UNOSOM II was headquartered; for security purposes they had to go through a thorough and somewhat demeaning search process before being allowed in.[40] In general, while much lip service was paid to the phrase "Somali ownership," in practice most political reconstruction efforts were externally led, with little if any advice from Somalis who had to live with its consequences.

UNOSOM II's hiring practices and the salary discrepancies between its international and Somali staff of equivalent levels was another factor contributing to these resentments. Many of the international employees were young, inexperienced, and possessed little knowledge of Somalia. Nevertheless, they drew daily allowances of $100 in addition to their regular salaries, while Somali employees who were sometimes more qualified earned far less. These "internationals" came to be seen as being in Somalia for the principal purpose of enriching themselves. The view of a Somali professional succinctly encapsulated this perception: "UNOSOM has changed what I thought of the UN. Now I think that UN people are no different from businessmen." Equally significant was the fact that very few qualified Somalis were in fact hired by UNOSOM II, understandably vexing to those with valuable expertise, who watched UNOSOM II—and all the opportunity and potential it represented for Somalia—falter for lack of knowledge about Somali culture and politics.

Revisiting Intervention: Could It Have Been Done Better?

The combination of UNITAF's and then UNOSOM II's intended and unintended structural impact—the massive military and economic presence, a continued emphasis on power sharing among the faction leaders, and ill-conceived and unsustainable grassroots political development and institution-building efforts—resulted in a freezing of indigenous political processes in many parts of Somalia. Because of the potential for largesse that the UN promised, local Somali political processes of accommodation among conflicting subclans and clans and the development of indigenous local authorities were effectively halted during its presence. Instead, Somalis waited to see what UNOSOM II, which one Somali UN employee described as "the goose that lays the golden egg," would do to help them.[41] This pattern was particularly acute in the areas where UNOSOM II's presence was concentrated, namely in Mogadishu and the southern regions. Indeed, northeast Somalia and "Somaliland," where UNOSOM II had a minimal presence, went much further than the other parts of the country in reestablishing basic governance and a return to normal life.

Of course, the relative stability in northern Somalia had to do with other factors besides the lack of an international presence, most important being the fact that fighting was concentrated in the southern one-third of the country by the time of the international intervention. Nor should the continuing instability in the southern regions be blamed on UNOSOM II. But the acceleration of local political dynamics in even the southern regions of Somalia following UNOSOM II's departure suggests its role in freezing potential changes that might have led to more lasting political settlements. These local dynamics in the south include the Digil-Mirifle reconciliation process in the Rahanweyn populated regions, the growth of Islamic authorities in many parts of southern Somalia, and the resumption of robust business activity in the contested city of Mogadishu.[42]

The broad mandate and serious resources provided to UNOSOM II suggest the degree of international commitment, at least initially, to helping Somalia emerge from chaos. Yet the international community's underlying assumption of re-creating a central government to restore sovereignty to Somalia, its commitment of resources primarily for military purposes, and its bungled attempts at factional reconciliation, political development, and institution building all stymied efforts to build peace. International engagement in Somalia should, first of all, have sought to better understand the local social and political context, which meant recognizing the fact that the country was deeply divided along clan lines and that it would take a lengthy, internally generated process to heal those divisions.

Approach Adopted by UNOSOM II

The conceptions of peacebuilding that informed UNOSOM II's actions were largely limited either to a preferred sequence of events (as in peacemaking followed by peacekeeping and peacebuilding) or to the performance of specific sets of functions (demobilization, development, policing, judiciary, and so on). During 1993 and 1994, international action emphasized achieving a political resolution to the conflict, which included enforcement action. A political settlement was viewed as a prerequisite to peacebuilding activities that could follow; it was assumed that until an effective cease-fire and power-sharing arrangement at the apex of the Somali political system was established, other efforts such as demobilization or reconstruction would not be effective. In this light, it was entirely appropriate to expend the bulk of international attention and resources on a political and military strategy that aimed to achieve a settlement among faction leaders.

A developmental perspective also applied to international activities in Somalia, albeit to a lesser extent, notably in UNOSOM II's efforts at grassroots political development, resurrecting the Somali judicial system, and the donor community's emphasis on supporting reconstruction in peaceful regions. However, these activities often were poorly conceived and implemented as well as disjointed in nature.

Some saw peacebuilding in Somalia as a transition, focusing on the handoff from military and relief efforts to reconstruction and development activities. However, while much lip service was paid to transitioning from an emergency to a developmental phase, this was informed more by the U.S. desire for a clear and rapid exit strategy and UNOSOM II's time-limited mandate than by real changes in Somali politics that would make such a transition meaningful. The quest to rapidly establish a central government, which was viewed as the precondition for a successful exit of UNOSOM II, overrode any measured assessment of the state of Somali politics and society. Such an analysis would have suggested that establishing an effective central government in Somalia was simply not possible given the time constraint built into UNOSOM II's mandate.

Alternative Approach

Putting the domestic context first. A peacebuilding strategy for Somalia should have considered, as a central element, how to demilitarize or "civilianize" clan politics. The factions were a product of the clans in Somalia, and the faction leaders initially derived authority from their clans' support during the development of the Somali civil war. UNOSOM II's efforts should therefore have concentrated on supporting internal, clan-based political reconciliation processes rather than efforts to reconcile the factions, which served as the military arm of the clans. This did not necessarily mean marginalizing the faction leaders, but it did require involving them within a larger envelope of clan leadership that included other civilian elements such as elders, religious leaders, and educated professionals. Whether they retained their leadership positions would then be determined by their respective clans rather than by the international community.

This type of effort would have had to be internally generated and to take place in Somalia itself, at the clan rather than national level, as was the case with the northwest and the northeast zones. The UN's strategy should have aimed at supporting these internally generated processes rather than embarking on two separate processes—factional reconciliation at the national level and grassroots political development at the district and regional levels—both of which had their own problems. In the short term, this type of support would have facilitated the development of effective governance at the intraclan level, albeit at the cost of strengthening the existing territorial divisions among the various Somali clans.

The key problem with this approach is that it may have been viewed as ostensibly supporting the country's partition. Indeed, what complicated the UN's willingness to assist "Somaliland" was its claim of secession, raising red flags for the international community, which wanted to avoid any suggestion of tacit support for or recognition of its independent status. In fact, there are strong reasons for maintaining a unitary state and reconstituting an effective central government in Somalia. Somalia exists in a modern international system of nation-states and international institutions that conduct commercial and political interactions primarily with other nation-states rather than with substate entities. A united country can better defend its borders and more effectively promote its collective interests internationally than small, independent pieces of it. Additionally, there are economic advantages to maintaining a unitary state, such as access of populations in the country's hinterland to its ports. Finally, notwithstanding the divisions wrought by the civil war, there remains a sense of Somali national identity.[43]

A second problem relates to the economic viability of clan-based political units. In this regard, clearly some clan areas are more economically feasible than others. The northeast, for example, which has the strategic assets of Bossaso port, a section of the Hargeisa-

Mogadishu highway, and an economy based on livestock, fisheries, and frankincense production, can be economically self-sufficient.[44] The southern regions populated by the Rahanweyn clan, in contrast, are in a much more difficult position, with no direct access to the country's ports through which they can engage in essential trade and commerce, including sending livestock and frankincense to overseas markets.

Notwithstanding these problems, the experience of a centralized state in Somalia has been appalling and has led to the divisive tendencies along clan lines that are evident today. A pragmatic strategy for political reconstruction ought to approach peacebuilding from the standpoint of existing circumstances. While the immediate needs were for clan-based political reconstruction, longer-term efforts to help reconstitute a Somali state could also have been initiated. The balance of these efforts, however, should have been very different, with the bulk of international political and economic assistance in the short term being committed to inclusive, intraclan reconciliation processes instead of hasty attempts to form a central government. International support for reconstituting a unitary state would involve helping the emerging clan-based entities to recognize the benefits of reestablishing linkages with one another to create some form of federation based on common economic and other interests.[45]

An effective strategy for peacebuilding in Somalia would recognize that the critical need is to reconstitute governance at various levels, from local to clan-based and eventually to national. The chief responsibility for reconstituting governance necessarily lies with Somalis, with international support only reinforcing and supporting civilian-oriented efforts in that direction. The timing for undertaking these various levels of political reconstruction must also be determined by Somalis and not the international community. In this light, the international community's efforts in various areas should have been reconfigured, as suggested below.

Political and institution building. Instead of two parallel processes—of factional reconciliation and grassroots political development—the international community's political efforts should have been integrated, aiming at political reconciliation within clans followed by a national power-sharing arrangement among the major clans. These efforts should have been initiated at the political "center" of each of the clan-controlled areas. For example, the Rahanweyn clan leadership in Baidoa—including the Somali Democratic Movement (SDM) faction and its two subdivisions; elders; educated civilians; and other important civil society elements—should have been encouraged to support creating local government structures in more distant Rahanweyn-populated areas such as Hoddur. This approach could have been inclusive, involving important leaders from all the Rahanweyn-populated districts, and would have resulted in the creation of more authoritative governance structures than those created by UNOSOM II's district and regional councils. Training and other assistance to these authorities then could have formed an important element of UNOSOM II's efforts to bolster civilian-led politics in Somalia.

UNOSOM II's support for reestablishing a judicial system, including police, should also have been tied to the formation and improvement of governance structures at the clan level, and the express involvement of the clan and local leaderships should have been sought. Political guidance for creating such institutions should have come from authentic, civilian-oriented Somali leadership. In the absence of such leadership, UNOSOM II should have refrained from any efforts at institution building. This approach would have resulted in a staggered series of initiatives, beginning with institution-building assistance to "Somaliland," which had formed its own civilian government, followed perhaps by efforts in the northeast and other coherent, clan-controlled zones.

Undoubtedly, supporting such processes would be far easier in those areas of the country that had already achieved some measure of stability, such as the northwest and northeast. The contested cities in the south, namely Mogadishu and Kismayu, and the central regions populated by the divided Hawiye clan were not ready for such internally driven efforts at political reconstruction. In addition, while the southern regions populated by the Rahanweyn clan could embark on an intraclan political reconstruction effort with international support, its militarily weak status meant that it would remain under threat from neighboring factions, which could undermine any such efforts.

The best the international community could do in the case of the Hawiye clan, which was divided among the factions of Aidid and Ali Mahdi, was to help create conditions whereby they and other Hawiye subclans would be encouraged to seek internal agreement. Most important in this regard was to separate the internal Hawiye contest from the overall national political contest. The Hawiye subclans' control of Mogadishu made them believe that they would naturally inherit the national leadership. The international community should have countered this assumption by de-emphasizing the link between control of Mogadishu and the recognition of claims to national leadership. This could have been done in a variety of ways, including a resolve not to recognize any one faction leader's ambition to form the government of Somalia until all the major clans were internally reconciled and agreeable to a power-sharing arrangement. Only then would the concept of a national capital become meaningful.

Economic support. Economic support from the international community could have been effectively linked with progress toward "civilianization" of clan politics. A key program in this regard should have been demobilization, which would have corresponded with an overall strategy of demilitarization. Demobilization, first of all, would have to be carried out within clan-controlled zones and would be only partially undertaken until sufficient confidence was built among the different clans. Hence, even though many clans would very likely choose to maintain sufficient military strength to defend themselves against any real or imagined threat from other clans, they might also have agreed to partial demobilization. An incentive to demobilize could have been the availability of international assistance programs to create alternative employment for the ex-militia members. Concurrent demobilization of several factions could thus serve as an important confidence-building measure among rival clans.

At the same time, UNOSOM II and the international NGOs present in Somalia should have continued to provide emergency humanitarian assistance wherever needed. The UNITAF intervention had created new networks and channels for such assistance. Besides alleviating human suffering, continued provision of emergency assistance helped to avoid re-creating a situation of political instability that attended a humanitarian emergency.

Military mandate.[46] The situation in Somalia changed dramatically from the time that UNITAF was deployed in December 1992 to when UNOSOM II assumed military control in May 1993. The situation at the end of 1992 required enforcement provisions to establish a secure environment for the delivery of humanitarian relief, which was UNITAF's mandate. An implicit threshold of human suffering had been crossed in late 1992 that required forcible international action. In mid-1993, the limited number of interclan skirmishes, while resulting in some civilian casualties, arguably did not cross the threshold that was commensurate with the costs, including the loss of neutrality attendant with the use of force by the international community.

UNOSOM II should have interpreted its military mandate as assisting in the implementation of the mission's overall mandate and, more specifically, of the peacebuilding activities set out in Resolution 814. The peacebuilding mandate given to UNOSOM II did not require the same type of enforcement capability as UNITAF, especially if coercive disarmament was not to be attempted. In this environment, UNOSOM II should have interpreted its Chapter VII mandate, in the first instance, to justify its presence in Somalia without the consent of a national government (since none existed) and, in the second instance, to protect the continuing humanitarian relief and other civilian efforts it was to undertake. UNOSOM II's military strength should therefore have been calibrated with the need to support international humanitarian and civilian efforts and been a function of the size of these efforts in Somalia. Most important, UNOSOM II should have maintained impartiality among the various factions, which UNITAF did not need to do. This meant that UNOSOM II would not become involved in interclan skirmishes (which in fact it did not, although criticized by both Somalis and international agencies, who could not understand the purpose of UNOSOM II's military presence), but would instead encourage the clans to resolve differences themselves and lend its political support for this purpose when required. However, its Chapter VII mandate would leave open the possibility of undertaking enforcement action if another humanitarian emergency were to arise.[47]

An impartial UNOSOM II military presence could also have been used to monitor demobilization efforts. This task would require military observers, as opposed to peacekeeping troops, to monitor demobilization processes where they were occurring, with the express consent of the clan and faction leaders concerned. Such monitoring could have been used as a confidence-building measure among various clans by providing a degree of transparency in their respective demobilization efforts. As the political situation improved across Somalia, the military presence of UNOSOM II could slowly have been phased out.

Pressure for troop withdrawal would have been unavoidable given the presence of national military contingents in Somalia and would have remained the most charged political issue for the UN Security Council and troop-contributing countries operating under a time-bound mandate. Such pressures would have been exacerbated if the political situation in Somalia remained static or if there were unprovoked attacks on peacekeepers. UNOSOM II would have to address these political calculations and decisions and ultimately consider being prematurely phased out. Notwithstanding this limitation, the restricted (albeit important) role of the military in an overall peacebuilding strategy would have allowed UNOSOM II to continue effectively with the political and economic aspects of its mandate even in the absence of a supporting military role.

Organizational structure. Finally, at the organizational level UNOSOM II's civilian components should have been considerably smaller. The core staff should have been a political team around the SRSG, including Somali experts, supported by professional coordination and liaison staff and logistics personnel. Other UN agencies, and particularly UNDP, should have been structurally linked to UNOSOM II, for example, by appointing the UNDP Resident Representative to a senior position such as Deputy SRSG in UNOSOM II. These organizational linkages would have provided the necessary expertise and civilian orientation that UNOSOM II required to plan and implement peacebuilding efforts. The involvement of other UN agencies and programs in UNOSOM II should have been supplemented by close and effective coordination with bilateral aid agency representatives in Somalia and with other multilateral lending institutions, including the World Bank. UNOSOM II itself should have been decentralized, with strengthened offices in the various clan-controlled areas; this decentralized structure may not have required establishing a headquarters in Mogadishu or elsewhere at all. This type of light, flexible structure could have prevented UNOSOM II from becoming hostage to events in any particular part of the country and would have diffused the structural economic impact of its presence.

The approach suggested above would have had several advantages for sustaining a longer-term international presence in Somalia. First, it would likely have required a much smaller military presence. The military's reduced role—to protect international personnel and monitor demobilization efforts—may have limited opposition from recalcitrant faction leaders. Second, this lower-profile military role would have also reduced pressures for an exit strategy from troop-contributing countries. And finally but perhaps most significantly, it would have resulted in international emphasis being placed on civilian, political efforts rather than military solutions where the political will to sustain those was lacking.

UNOSOM II has a sad legacy in Somalia. It is viewed today by many Somalis as having encouraged divisions between and within the major Somali clans. This unfortunate result arose from the UN's design for political efforts and by the intended and unintended economic and social consequences of its presence. Instead of helping to build peace, UNOSOM II bred further divisions among Somalis, strengthened those elements that were least likely to bring peace, and inhibited most local dynamics toward self-governance. While restoring peace and stability to Somalia was no easy task for the international community, the chances of success could have been significantly improved by taking steps toward better understanding the conflict. Instead, the international community's approach resembled that of a bull in a china shop, with predictable consequences.

Notes

1. See *SIPRI Yearbook: Armaments, Disarmament and International Security* (New York: Oxford University Press, 1996); ibid., 1997. The 1998 edition, which lists the major armed conflicts in the world in 1997, does not include Somalia.

2. S/1997/1000 (December 22, 1997) and annex.

3. Following General Muhammad Farah Aidid's death in a Mogadishu battle on August 1, 1996, his son Hussein Aidid assumed the leadership of the United Somali Congress–Somali National Alliance (USC–SNA), continuing his father's policy of occupation of the Rahanweyn areas and a quest for power in all Somalia.

4. See Ameen Jan, "Warlords on the Wane—Will Islam Fill the Political Void?" *Africa Today* 2, 6 (November/December 1996): 47–48. In 1997, the penal functions practiced by the *shari'a* authorities in north Mogadishu were terminated. Hussein Adam and Richard Ford, with Ali Jimale Ahmed, Abdinasir Osman Isse, Nur Weheliye, and David Smock, "Removing Barricades in Somalia: Options for Peace and Rehabilitation," *Peaceworks*, no. 24 (October 1998).

5. For an excellent historical analysis of Islam in Somalia, see Hussein M. Adam, "Islam and Politics in Somalia," *Journal of Islamic Studies* 6, 2 (July 1995): 189–221.

6. See "Online Service Comes to Somalia," *Associated Press*, September 29, 1999.

7. See Adam and Ford, "Removing Barricades in Somalia."

8. David D. Laitin and Said S. Samatar, *Somalia: Nation in Search of a State* (Boulder, CO: Westview Press; London, Engl.: Gower, 1987), 69–77; Ahmed I. Samatar, "The Curse of Allah: Civic Disembowelment and the Collapse of the

State in Somalia," in *The Somali Challenge: From Catastrophe to Renewal?* ed. Ahmed I. Samatar (Boulder, CO: Lynne Rienner, 1994), 113–115.

9. For a political history of Barre's rule, see Laitin and Samatar, *Somalia,* 77–99.

10. Samuel M. Makinda, "Seeking Peace from Chaos: Humanitarian Intervention in Somalia," International Peace Academy Occasional Paper Series (Boulder, CO: Lynne Rienner, 1993), 17–28, provides a brief analysis of the alienation wrought by Barre's rule and the formation of clan-based factions in Somalia.

11. For an account of this period, see John Drysdale, *Whatever Happened to Somalia?* (London: Haan Associates, 1994); Mohamed Sahnoun, *Somalia: The Missed Opportunities* (Washington, D.C.: United States Institute of Peace, 1994); and Africa Watch, "Somalia: A Fight to the Death? Leaving Civilians at the Mercy of Terror and Starvation," *Africa Watch Report,* February 13, 1992.

12. Lee V. Cassanelli, "Somali Land Resource Issues in Historical Perspective," in *Learning from Somalia: The Lessons of Armed Humanitarian Intervention,* ed. Walter Clarke and Jeffrey Herbst (Boulder, CO: Westview, 1997), 67–76.

13. See Refugee Policy Group, "Hope Restored? Humanitarian Aid in Somalia 1990–1994" (November 1994): 14–15.

14. S/Res/751 (April 24, 1992).

15. Sahnoun, *Missed Opportunities.*

16. S/Res/794 (December 3, 1992).

17. Several commentators have drawn a distinction between the limited and successful, initial U.S.-led humanitarian intervention in Somalia and the much broader UN operation, which is criticized for having taken on the thorny task of "nation building." See, for example, John Bolton, "Wrong Turn in Somalia," *Foreign Affairs* 73, 1 (Jan./Feb. 1994): 56–66. However, a number of other observers, including several humanitarian NGO representatives, have argued that estimates of UNITAF's positive impact were exaggerated because by October–November 1992, prior to the UNITAF intervention, the famine was in fact easing. See Refugee Policy Group, "Hope Restored," 27–28, and African Rights, "Operation Restore Hope: A Preliminary Assessment" (May 1993).

18. John L. Hirsch and Robert B. Oakley, *Somalia and Operation Restore Hope: Reflections on Peacemaking and Peacekeeping* (Washington, D.C.: United States Institute of Peace, 1995), 104. Also see *Disarmament and Conflict Resolution Project: Managing Arms in Peace Processes: Somalia* (Geneva: UNIDIR, 1995), 73–79. The report correctly points out that UNITAF did in fact undertake limited disarmament, first through a "food for guns" program and then a weapons confiscation policy. Two fundamental problems with these disarmament approaches were that they were geographically limited to UNITAF's area of deployment and were therefore unequal, and they were inconsistent and lacked an overall strategy, which resulted in the most compliant segments of the population being disarmed.

19. UNIDR, "Managing Arms in Peace Processes: Somalia," argues that "the organization which desired the vigorous implementation of a disarmament programme in Somalia [the UN] lacked the capability necessary to back it up, whereas the body with the capability to disarm Somali units and irregulars [UNITAF, led by the U.S.] lacked the will to do so" (Geneva: UNIDR, 1995), 69.

20. Also see Walter Clarke and Jeffrey Herbst, "Somalia and the Future of Humanitarian Intervention," *Foreign Affairs* 75, 2 (March/April 1996), for an

analysis of the broader impact of what was considered solely a humanitarian intervention.

21. For an account of this period, see Drysdale, *Whatever Happened to Somalia?* 115–128; and Terence Lyons and Ahmed I. Samatar, *Somalia: State Collapse, Multilateral Intervention, and Strategies for Political Reconstruction* (Washington, D.C.: The Brookings Institution, 1995), 49–52. The Addis Ababa agreement is reproduced in *The United Nations in Somalia, 1992–1996* (New York: United Nations Department of Public Information, 1996), 264–266. Notably, the agreement of March 30, 1993, is not included in the publication.

22. For a cogent analysis of the different types of peace and reconciliation processes undertaken in Somalia during the period of UN intervention, with their relative successes and failures, see Ken Menkhaus, "International Peacebuilding and the Dynamics of Local and National Reconciliation in Somalia," in *Learning from Somalia,* 42–63.

23. See "Muddled Alliances," *Somalia News Update/Voice of America,* Uppsala/Nairobi, 3, 10 (April 1, 1994), and "From Kiev to Merca with Arms?" *Somalia News Update,* Uppsala, 3, 11 (April 18, 1994).

24. Senior official in UN Department of Peacekeeping Operations, confidential personal interview, March 1, 1996. Also see Bolton, "Wrong Turn in Somalia," 62.

25. S/Res/814 (March 26, 1993), para. 4.

26. Quoted in Bolton, "Wrong Turn in Somalia," 62.

27. Walter Clarke, in reference to the expectations placed on the UN with Resolution 814, quotes a senior U.S. official who claimed that "no one expected [the UN] to be able to do it!" See Walter Clarke, "Failed Visions and Uncertain Mandates," in *Learning from Somalia,* 18 n. 19.

28. See, for example, Friedrich Ebert Stiftung (Germany), Life and Peace Institute (Sweden), Norwegian Institute of International Affairs, in cooperation with the Lessons Learned Unit of the Department of Peacekeeping Operations, United Nations, "Comprehensive Report on Lessons-Learned from United Nations Operation in Somalia, April 1992–March 1995" (December 1995).

29. See Lyons and Samatar, *Somalia,* in which they argue that pursuing either one of the two strategies—factional reconciliation or grassroots political development—would have had a greater possibility of success than pursuing both simultaneously.

30. An account of efforts to rebuild the Somali justice sector is provided in Martin R. Ganzglass, "The Restoration of the Somali Justice System," in *Learning from Somalia,* 20–41.

31. See S/25354 (March 3, 1993) and *Further Report of the Secretary-General Submitted in Pursuance of Paragraphs 18 and 19 of Resolution 794* (December 3, 1992), para. 86.

32. S/26317 (August 17, 1993). *Further Report of the Secretary-General Submitted in Pursuance of Paragraph 18 of Resolution 814 with Annex on the Re-establishment of Police, Judicial and Penal Systems* (March 26, 1993).

33. Ganzglass, "Restoration of the Somali Justice System," 24–26.

34. See Ronald Marshal, "Les *Mooryaan* de Mogadishu: Formes de la violence dans un espace urbain en guerre," *Cahiers d'Etudes Africaines* 33-2, no. 130 (1993): 295–320.

35. Ganzglass, by contrast, argues that investment in the justice sector should have been prioritized in "those regions where UNOSOM was likely to

succeed in a short time." Ganzglass, "Restoration of the Somali Justice System," 29.

36. See Refugee Policy Group, "Hope Restored," 44.

37. A number of other reasons, including his own weakened position within his subclan, also influenced Aidid's decision to invade these regions.

38. *African Rights,* "Somalia: Human Rights Abuses by the United Nations Forces" (July 1993).

39. See Tom Farer, draft report submitted to the Secretary-General regarding the attack on UN peacekeepers in Somalia on June 5, 1993 (New York, United Nations, August 1993)

40. While the situation of insecurity placed responsibility on the UN to guard its facilities, it nonetheless was viewed by Somali employees of the UN as being a symbol of the two classes—international and local—that worked for the UN.

41. I wish to credit Abdi Salad Hasan for this quote.

42. In a visit to north Mogadishu in March 1996, one year after UNOSOM II's withdrawal, I was struck by the brisk and efficient business in telecommunications, private banking, and currency trading, as well as the bustling trade in consumer goods that filled the marketplace. A similar pattern was noted by Michael Maren later that year (see Michael Maren, "Progress in Mogadishu Is Endangered by Foreign Interference" [http://www.users.interport.net/~mmaren/somarchive.html]), and by a group of Somali experts in 1997 (see Adam and Ford, "Removing Barricades in Somalia").

43. One analyst has argued that Somalia lacks a history of an "autonomist tradition," since it shifted from a society that was completely decentralized to a nation with a strong central government. In his view, supporting regional autonomy is dangerous because it will empower those individuals who have politicized tribalism only to enhance their own power. See Ahmed Ashkir Botan, "Somalia: Regional State or Cantonization of Clans?" in *Mending Rips in the Sky: Options for Somali Communities in the 21st Century,* ed. Hussein M. Adam and Richard Ford (Lawrenceville, NJ: The Red Sea Press, Inc., 1997), 255–270.

44. See War-torn Societies Project, "Rebuilding Somalia: The Northeast Somalia Zonal Note" (Geneva: United Nations Research Institute for Social Development, June 1998).

45. In mid-1994, even as the discredited UN peace operation continued, a modest initiative was proposed by the UN Development Office for Somalia (UNDOS) for a study detailing a series of options for federal governance in Somalia. A study was subsequently commissioned by the European Union's Somalia Unit with the assistance of UNDOS and undertaken by consultants from the London School of Economics and Political Science. The report, entitled "A Study of Decentralized Political Structures for Somalia: A Menu of Options," which was produced in August 1995, injected a new, substantive element in the ongoing political debate in Somalia. While political discussions among Somali leaders had revolved around the implicit understanding that a decentralized form of government was necessary, the study provided for the first time a set of concrete alternatives that could form the basis for practical discussions. The study is a modest but critical contribution to helping define the parameters of political debate, including depersonalizing the issue of government succession, and it is an example of the kind of strategic input that the international community can make with a small but targeted commitment of resources.

46. I wish to thank Lt. Col. Stephen Moffat (Senior Associate, IPA), who served with the Canadian military contingent in UNITAF, for sharing his insights on the UN's military role in Somalia.

47. See S/25354 (March 3, 1993) for the military mandate proposed by the UN Secretary-General for UNOSOM II and later adopted in S/Res/814. This mandate included, inter alia, covering the entire territory of Somalia to consolidate and expand security (by contrast, UNITAF was deployed in 40 percent of the country), taking "appropriate" action against any faction that violated the cessation of hostilities, seizing small arms of "unauthorized elements," *undertaking disarmament by force if the factions did not voluntarily relinquish their weapons*, and protecting civilian UN and other international personnel and property [emphasis added].

4

Peacebuilding in Cambodia: Legitimacy and Power

Michael W. Doyle

On July 5–6, 1997, Cambodia experienced a coup that erased many of the political gains made during and after the 1992–1993 United Nations Transitional Authority in Cambodia (UNTAC). After an expenditure of more than $1.8 billion for UNTAC, the death of seventy-eight UNTAC soldiers and civilians (and many more Cambodians), and more than a billion dollars in foreign aid, Cambodia found itself in almost the same condition as it was at the beginning of the decade, before the UN peace operation began. Second co-Prime Minister Hun Sen's forces clamped down on the center of Cambodia, and once again, a government lacking in legitimacy faced an internal insurgency on its border. Forces from First co-Prime Minister Prince Norodom Ranariddh's opposition party resumed armed opposition, joining but not aligning with the Khmer Rouge (which had dropped out of the peace process in 1993). In 1998, following considerable international pressure and another election, the Hun Sen–Ranariddh coalition was patched together, and the government struggled on to confront the deep challenges of national development that years of war and autogenocide under the Khmer Rouge had inflicted on a troubled land.

It was not supposed to turn out this way. The peace operation in Cambodia that culminated in the June 1993 elections was widely hailed as one of the UN's "peacekeeping" successes. But it has become increasingly clear that Cambodia also needed "peacebuilding"—the institutional, social, and economic reforms that can serve to defuse or peacefully resolve conflict. Failure to build on a peace treaty can unravel a peacekeeping success. Only concerted action by the government, the donor community, nongovernmental organizations, and the UN—both during and following UNTAC—could have kept a peace on track and have ensured a continued effort at reconstruction and reconciliation.

This chapter assesses how a peacekeeping operation that went relatively well turned into a peacebuilding experience that wasted the political opening created by the former. The main peacebuilding gap was between factions that had legitimacy without power and factions that had power without legitimacy. Some of the roots of the erosion lay in opportunities missed during UNTAC and in ones neglected during the almost four years that followed the peace operation. The deeper roots of the crisis lay in the social, economic, and political structure of Cambodia itself and its unfortunate history during the past fifty years.

From Coalition to Coup to Coalition

During the four years preceding the coup, Cambodia teetered between hope for a deepening peace and fear of deepening violence. A coalition government combined the two leading political parties: the Cambodian Peoples Party (CPP) and the United Front for a Cooperative, Independent, Peaceful, and Neutral Cambodia (FUNCINPEC). CPP was a former communist party led by Hun Sen and installed in the Vietnamese invasion of 1978. FUNCINPEC was led by King Norodom Sihanouk's son, Prince Ranariddh, representing Cambodia's traditional legitimacy and its aristocratic elite. Despite the formation of a coalition government (the often prescribed remedy for peacebuilding), Cambodia experienced little progress in building peace beyond that achieved by the Paris Peace Agreement (1991) and the UNTAC peace process (1992–1993).[1] The urban economy was booming, but the continuing counterinsurgency war against the Khmer Rouge, the uncertain pace of revival of the rural economy, and a dangerous polarization within the government plagued the fragile peace.

In 1995–1996, tension mounted between CPP and FUNCINPEC. The parties' two leaders had combined as co-prime ministers in a "shotgun marriage" blessed by the international community following the UNTAC election of June 1993. Although FUNCINPEC won the plurality of the vote, the CPP controlled the bulk of the army, all the lower-level bureaucracy, the judiciary, and the police. Four coups were attempted between 1993 and 1997; the fifth, that of Hun Sen on July 5, 1997, was successful.[2]

Starting with reports of an attempted coup in the spring of 1996, the escalation of tensions was marked by violent confrontations. On March 30, a grenade attack on a political rally of opposition leader Sam Rainsy, head of the Sam Rainsy Party (allied with Ranariddh), caused sixteen deaths and more than a hundred wounded. In May, bodyguards for FUNCINPEC (Ranariddh's party) and CPP (Hun Sen's party) battled in the streets, and on May 29, Hun Sen's bodyguards announced he had been the target of an assassination attempt. In June, a pitched battle was fought in the streets of the capital, and a rocket landed in the U.S. embassy compound.

Constitutional procedures and effective government ground to a halt; neither the cabinet nor the National Assembly met. Essential legislation for Cambodia's planned entry into the Association of Southeast Asian Nations (ASEAN) and for the national election announced for May 1998 was stymied. The nation's forests were still being illegally harvested, resulting in revenue losses of $100 to $300 million a year. Moreover, almost half the government income derived from foreign aid and half of all government expenditures went to support the military. Millions of mines, still littered throughout the countryside, continued to maim and kill. Corruption was rife and international drug trafficking grew. All this in a country with an average real income per capita of about one-twentieth that of the United States, an adult literacy rate of 38 percent, and a life expectancy of fifty-two years.

Given the weakness of the Cambodian state, the underdevelopment of the economy, and the "thinness" of Cambodian civil society, a coup was hardly surprising.[3] But in retrospect, the timing of the July coup appears to have been triggered by two unpredicted events.

The first was the surprising breakup of the Khmer Rouge in 1996–1997. In September 1996, Ieng Sary, former foreign minister during the Pol Pot regime, defected with three "divisions" and control of the timber and gem-rich region around Pailin. After strenuous bargaining between Hun Sen and Ranariddh, Hun Sen won over Ieng Sary, whose cohorts then received a royal pardon and Pailin to rule as a nearly independent fiefdom.

In the following summer of 1997, reports of the capture of Pol Pot were hailed as the end to Cambodia's persisting malaise. Instead, they marked a sign of escalation. The one thousand or so of the once fearsome guerrillas holed up along the northwest Cambodian border finally turned on their founder in June 1997, when he summarily executed and then photographed vehicles crushing the bodies of Son Sen (Pol Pot's deputy) and his family. In Cambodia, amidst genuine popular anticipation of long-delayed justice, the possibility of a trial of Pol Pot fanned the flames of CPP-FUNCINPEC discord. Handing him over became a bargaining chip for the amnesty of remaining Khmer Rouge leaders, as Prince Ranariddh and Hun Sen competed for the allegiance of the Khmer Rouge. The Khmer Rouge offered disciplined cadres, effective guerrilla soldiers, and up to $200 million secreted in Southeast Asian bank accounts. As word of a deal between Khieu Samphan—a top Khmer Rouge leader—and Ranariddh began to circulate, a deal that would bring all the Khmer Rouge remnants over to FUNCINPEC, Hun Sen struck.

The other unexpected trigger of the coup was the growing competition—the increased premium on allies—stimulated by the scheduled 1998 elections. The problem was not the elections per se, which, as will be discussed further below, were necessary to maintain legitimacy and establish a two-way connection between the Cambodian state and the people it ruled.[4] The problem was the unraveling of the governing coalition. Tension escalated in 1996, when FUNCINPEC, alarmed that it had little influence in the administration of the countryside, demanded a share of the district-level offices. Control of districts was decisive in determining effective access to the voters. CPP stalled and FUNCINPEC failed to provide a plausible, comprehensive list of candidates. The real source of concern was that the elections presented the threat that the winner would have the authority to rule alone, should it win an absolute majority. This was a threat for the CPP especially, which according to an early 1997 public opinion poll was deeply unpopular in the country as a whole: only 20 percent said they supported Hun Sen's party.[5]

The state officials who were members of Hun Sen's party had high stakes in the elections, as their livelihood depended on their bureaucratic position. Many had joined the Khmer Rouge in the early 1970s, fled to Vietnam in 1977 or 1978, returned with the Vietnamese invasion in December 1978, and had held government office as the State of Cambodia (SOC) since then. In addition, Hun Sen's apprehension was doubtless deepened by rumors that King Sihanouk, the one political leader with wide rural legitimacy, might abdicate and run for election. For Ranariddh, the prospect of an election became an opportunity to escape from the paper coalition that rendered FUNCINPEC powerless. He thus formed an electoral alliance with Sam Rainsy, who was widely popular among the urban young. As tension mounted, Ranariddh began to arm a bodyguard, allegedly with smuggled arms shipments, to match the much larger guard already surrounding Hun Sen.

Hun Sen struck with a coup overthrowing the existing regime on July 5, 1997. Hundreds of FUNCINPEC supporters were rounded up, and by the estimates of human rights groups, up to forty were summarily executed. The former opposition was intimidated; civil society ran for cover. The UN General Assembly refused to recognize the coup government and ASEAN membership was put on hold. U.S., Australian, World Bank, International Monetary Fund (IMF) and European Union aid to the government was frozen. The exchange rate depreciated; tourism sagged. Private investors began an informal freeze on new investments. Fifty thousand Cambodians became refugees on the Thai border.[6] General Niek Bun Chhay led a military resistance in FUNCINPEC's name, joined by the few remnants of the Khmer Rouge. The new coalition (an unfortunate revival of the 1980s' joint resistance to CPP) operated uneasily on the Thai-Cambodian border in late 1997.

In 1998, the country began another turnaround, but few expect that Cambodia's political tensions are resolved for the long term. Responding to international pressure and a Japanese-brokered assistance plan, Hun Sen authorized new elections for July 1998. Following Ranariddh's "conviction" and royal pardon, the election campaign got under way with widespread accusations of manipulation of the electoral commission and campaign intimidation. Nonetheless, the vote count appeared to be fair and was certified as such by international observers. Indeed, had it not been for a split between FUNCINPEC and the Sam Rainsy Party opposition forces (who were united in 1993), FUNCINPEC might again have won a plurality. In the event, the CPP won, and Hun Sen emerged as the sole prime minister in a new coalition government (November 1998) in which Prince Ranariddh accepted the chairmanship of the National Assembly.[7]

Earlier, in April, Pol Pot, responsible for the death of 1.7 million Cambodians in the autogenocide of 1975–1978, had died. By the end of the year, all the remaining Khmer Rouge leaders (including Ieng Sary, Khieu Samphan, and Nuon Chea, among others) had defected to the government and were comfortably housed in the

Pailin, the province they continued to rule, although now under government auspices. The military commander Ta Mok (known as "the butcher") and the former head of the torture center, Kang Khek Iev (known as "Duch"), were in custody awaiting trial. How they would be tried produced new controversy. International observers familiar with the political character of the Cambodian judiciary demanded an international trial of the entire Khmer Rouge leadership. Hun Sen held firm for local justice and—further annoying the international community—suggested that various Western and Chinese heads of states and ministers would have to be called to testify before the tribunal to determine the full scope of their support for the Khmer Rouge in the 1970s.[8]

The condition of Cambodia today confirms that the peace process was only begun with international intervention, when the parties signed the Paris Peace Agreement in October 1991 and when UNTAC arrived in March 1992 to help implement it. Nonetheless, peacebuilding was stillborn, and the parties remained in a state of considerable and unstable tension. The roots of the peacebuilding crisis lie in Cambodia's past and especially in victimization by its neighbors, near and far; in the concentrated underdevelopment of the Cambodian economy and polity; and in UNTAC's inability to jump-start the process of civic reform and economic rehabilitation.

Burden of the Past

For much of its recent postwar history Cambodia found itself in a dangerous neighborhood. Bombing by the United States during the Vietnam War radicalized the intellectuals and peasantry. In 1975, it fell prey to the Khmer Rouge, the worst fanatics in the second half of the twentieth century. Cambodia was rescued by its historic enemy Vietnam in 1978, only to be occupied by the latter for a decade. As a result, Cambodia lacked the space in which to address the key challenges of modern development. It has faced crisis after crisis, and each before it had time to adjust to or resolve the previous one. Cambodia is now—at last—simultaneously trying to recover from a combination of trials.

- Cambodia is still seeking to overcome the legacies of colonialism. Indeed, the first generation of postcolonial leadership is still in place—King Sihanouk was first enthroned by the French in 1941. During his rule, huge inequalities between city and countryside persisted, inequalities typical of export-oriented, metropolitan-based, colonial economic development. Before these inequalities and dependencies had been overcome, the 1978 Vietnamese invasion imposed a new kind of colonialism. The SOC regime ruled from the "knapsack" of Vietnam in 1979, and Vietnam continued to govern from behind the scenes until 1989.[9]

- Cambodia is still recovering from the destruction inflicted by wars, beginning with the U.S. bombing and devastations inflicted by the Khmer Rouge and continuing into the civil wars of the 1990s. All left deep rehabilitation needs, similar to those of countries such as Vietnam and Eritrea.
- Cambodia suffers from a postholocaust syndrome. The Khmer Rouge massacres left a desperate need for social reconstruction. Only a handful of monks, intellectuals, medical doctors, and trained lawyers survived the Khmer Rouge massacres. A massive social capital deficit resulted, and many survivors face deep psychological burdens that discourage reconstruction.
- Cambodia is also a post–civil war survivor from the pitched battles of 1979–1991 between SOC and the unified resistance on the Thai border. As in Mozambique and Angola, the reconciliation and reintegration of 370,000 refugees challenge all the country's efforts to rebuild.
- Like Eastern Europe, Cambodia is undergoing a postcommunist transition to a market economy, begun by the SOC in 1991.

Any one of these challenges would have been sufficient to overwhelm one of the poorest countries in the world. Cambodia is unique in facing all of them at once. All its efforts should be judged in light of this exceptional burden.

Underdevelopment and Dependence

The difficult and deep-rooted tasks of state and economy building are thus still pending. Cambodia is fortunate in having a profound sense of nationhood and a revered national religion in Buddhism, but it lacks a capable modern state and integrated modern economy. Suffering from unintegrated underdevelopment, it needs integrated development. Most important, the productive base must spread beyond cities to the countryside. (See Table 4.1.)

Table 4.1 Estimates of GDP and Shares by Sector, 1995–1996 (GDP is 349 billion riels)

Sector	Amount of GDP	Population (percent)	Share per Population
Agriculture	152 billion	75	.57
Rice	51 billion		
Rubber	36 billion		
Total % of GDP	43 percent		
Industry	68 billion	4.5	4.22
Construction	35 billion		
Total % of GDP	19 percent		
Services	129 billion	20	1.85
Trade	52 billion		
Total % of GDP	37 percent		

Source: Ministry of Planning, *First Socioeconomic Development Plan: 1996–2000* (Phnom Penh: Ministry of Planning, February 1996), 103, 20.

Note: The share per population of Industry is 7.4 times as much as in the Agriculture sector, and the share per population in the Services sector is 3.25 times as much as in Agriculture.

Unfortunately, current trends suggest that these inequalities will worsen before they improve. With population growth at 3.5 percent, Phnom Penh is likely to become overwhelmed by jobseekers. The overall GDP grew at 5.9 percent from 1990 to 1995, dropped to 2 percent in 1997, and began to recover in 1999.[10] However, while the urban and hotel sector grew at 20 percent per year and construction at 15.2 percent, the rural sector stagnated as rice production declined at –0.1 percent and livestock grew at 3.8 percent.[11] Expenditure patterns reveal similar discrepancies. Average households in rural areas have only 33 percent of the average household expenditure per day of Phnom Penh households, and they have only 14 percent of the discretionary expenditure of Phnom Penh.[12]

Poverty and inequality both undermine peace. These large and growing gaps breed rural discontent and anger against the government. Discontent in turn undermines government incentives to democratize and increases the prospect of predatory human rights abuses. Poverty and inequality not only once contributed to support for the Khmer Rouge; more important, they waste the development potential of the vast bulk of the population.

Further complicating efforts to spur development and establish the rule of law is the state's weakness and lack of autonomy. The

Khmer Rouge destroyed the postcolonial state that Cambodia inherited from the French and replaced it with a regime that abandoned all normal state functions and created a national prison camp in its place. Although sovereign authority was in the hands of the Vietnamese until 1989, some capacity building was accomplished by the SOC during the 1980s. It assisted in training officials but only in very small numbers. Technical training in Eastern Europe often involved rote learning of weak technology—and in Bulgarian or German at that. Although many able individuals made the most of the East bloc training, it was not that useful in coping with modern capitalist management and the dynamic development standards of contemporary East Asia. One official in his late forties who had already learned Khmer, French, Vietnamese, and Bulgarian was now taking English—all in the process of furthering his technical education.

Nonetheless, despite the initiative and patience of officials such as this one, the Cambodian civil service is not ready to supervise modern economic development. Too few of the SOC or newly returned expatriates have experienced the responsibility of modern management. In one famous case at the Cambodian Development Council (the elite unit charged with the overall coordination of investment and foreign aid in the development plan), an approved "Soybean investment response letter" was sent out for six months to every request for information on Cambodian investments, irrespective of the sector, before the problem was identified.[13]

In addition to these, state capacity building is retarded by the politicization and underpayment of the bureaucracy. In the 1980s, anyone who was literate (and politically reliable) could be considered for a judgeship or other government post under SOC. In 1993–1994, the coalition government brought in thousands of new FUNCINPEC officials to share the spoils enjoyed by CPP officials. While the CPP continued to monopolize the lower, operational levels, every major ministry acquired a double administration at the top—two interior ministers, two deputies, and so on—and every provincial governorship was also divided. In order to construct the latest (1998) coalition between the CPP and FUNCINPEC, two hundred ministerial, secretary, and undersecretary of state positions had to be filled.[14] As a result, the civil service is highly partisan, reflecting their affiliations with the CPP or, in much smaller numbers, FUNCINPEC. Moreover, with salaries that are clearly too low at $20 per month for the lower civil service and $1,000 per month for a minister, practically all the lower-level civil servants irrespective of party depend on a second job in the private sector, while many of the higher-level state officials rely on corruption. Income at those levels invites inefficiency and corruption and a consequent loss of national revenue. Logging revenue is $15 million (1998), but illegal logging alone results in $100 million per annum in lost revenue when contracts do not go through the ministry of finance and instead swell personal, party, and military coffers.[15]

Reflecting a similar politicization, the army is bloated far beyond national security needs. With the formation of the coalition government, FUNCINPEC soldiers were incorporated en masse into what was previously the SOC-CPP military force. In 1999, the military budget consumed a full 45 percent of total spending, not counting the lost revenue from illegal logging by military officers. Demobilizing soldiers is thus high on the reform agenda but is costly in the short run. If it is attempted without a comprehensive plan to resettle former soldiers on land of their own or without another form of transitional assistance to productive work, they are likely to turn into marauders. In Uganda, one careful study found that dismissed soldiers were 100 times more likely to commit crimes than those with land or other transitional assistance.[16]

Problems such as these are no excuse for despair. Rapid economic development can be achieved with a small and lean civil service, such as the one that led Thailand to economic growth in the 1950s.[17] The real lesson for Cambodia is the importance of, on the one hand, marketization in order to reduce the overall level of demand on public management and, on the other hand, capacity building for the civil service in order to create a genuinely national state.[18] An effective state should play a key role in developing the rule of law by ensuring the state police and judiciary have the means to implement the law impartially. Incentives for military predation can only be reduced by military demobilization and improving the training and logistics of the remaining forces. And the state needs to play a key role in further democratization by planning and organizing the upcoming elections.

Yet the current Cambodian state is in a very weak position. Budgetary dependence is significant: 85 percent of all public investment is foreign financed as is 18 percent of private investment. Almost one-half of the total government budget (46 percent) was foreign financed in 1995.[19] Between 1992 and 1994, aid commitments stagnated. Actual project aid and assistance commitments declined, but technical assistance from foreign experts grew by 20 to

30 percent and direct assistance to the government budget from 0.5 to 27 percent.[20] In light of the extensive destruction in Cambodia in the past thirty years, technical assistance is both necessary and welcome, but current practices may prevent capacity building.

The current development strategy of the World Bank is to bypass the state. The Bank and many bilateral donors contract much of the implementation of their projects directly with international and some domestic NGOs. This may have been necessary in order to impose sanctions on the July 1997 coup, but over the longer run, a reformed state will need to obtain the opportunities it requires in order to build capacity.[21]

A vicious circle has been drawn around reform. Lacking an effective civil service, international donors cannot entrust projects to the Cambodian state; but without experience, the state cannot build capacity. The requirements of technical education and attempts to institute more rigorous selection processes for civil servants pose significant management problems. They pose even greater political challenges, since the civil service is politically chosen and is the major source of patronage and security (with the army) for the two parties. Broader measures of trust building are also necessary, including reform of the judiciary and the police. Short of these broader reforms, Cambodia will remain in a developmental crisis even after the restoration of constitutional legitimacy in the July 1998 elections.

UNTAC's Legacy

Some of Cambodia's current problems are the product of peacebuilding that ideally should have taken place during the period in which UNTAC was serving as the transitional authority. During this time, UNTAC achieved many successes, but it also missed some significant opportunities to reform and assist the Cambodian state and economy.

UNTAC achieved significant successes in restoring key features of Cambodian civil society. It facilitated the return of refugees, encouraged the formation of Cambodian NGOs, engaged in human rights education, and most significant, helped give Cambodian society a sense of participation in politics through national elections, thereby helping secure legitimacy for the state. But it failed to demobilize the armies and control the SOC civil service. In 1993, the

Royal Government of Cambodia (RGC) inherited the continuing war with the Khmer Rouge, still well armed and ready to fight, and the RGC had to accommodate both the existing SOC (CPP) civil service and add to them the newly enrolled FUNCINPEC officials. The result was a bureaucratic stalemate in which the two parties blocked each other at the price of overall government effectiveness.

Looking back, a senior FUNCINPEC official now complains that UNTAC failed to demobilize both the armies and the civil service.[22] Former UNTAC officials reply that demobilizing the civil service was never in the UNTAC mandate and that the SOC never agreed to it in the Paris agreements.[23] But then, UNTAC neither "controlled" the civil service nor did it launch the rehabilitation (except in very minor ways) of the Cambodian economy, which it was supposed to do under the terms of the UNTAC mandate.[24]

Both SOC and the Khmer Rouge undermined the key bargain of the Paris Peace Agreements, and each blamed the other. SOC denied its cooperation to UNTAC for the purpose of effecting neutralizing control when the Khmer Rouge refused to demobilize. The Khmer Rouge refused to demobilize when UNTAC failed to neutralize SOC. Both charges appear to have been correct. But it should also be noted that the Khmer Rouge denied UNTAC access to its zone, while SOC did allow UNTAC to deploy in its territory, which was 85 percent of Cambodia. Some observers have suggested that control might have been more effective had it been combined with training and capacity building. The UNTAC customs service experienced some success in this role, as did the Australian police in Banteay Meanchey province in 1993. Control/training might then have handed over a more stable, responsive, and effective bureaucracy. Training both CPP and FUNCINPEC cadres could have transferred desired skills and job security, opening up the way for a more neutral, national public civil service.[25]

A mandate to modernize the bureaucracy was not out of the question in the late spring of 1993. No one knew who would pay the factional armies after the national election occurred in May-June and before the formation of a sovereign government. Prince (soon-to-be King) Sihanouk offered General John Sanderson, an Australian general and the UNTAC Force Commander, the command of Cambodia's armies in a new peacebuilding effort designed to integrate and create a genuinely Cambodian army out of the two factional armies (Cambodia People's Armed Forces [CPAF] and National Army of Independent Cambodia [ANKI], military forces respectively of the CPP and FUNCINPEC). With wisdom of hindsight, one could add that the police, the judiciary, and the bureaucracy as a whole would have benefited from a newly negotiated peacebuilding initiative at the uncertain time of the national election, as a quid pro quo for a prenegotiated coalition regime. But in May 1993, the UN was all too ready to leave Cambodia in order to shoulder the increasing burdens in Somalia and Bosnia. Instead, the UN wanted an official "success" to mark against the increasing crises elsewhere—a parade, not a renewed campaign.

The other UNTAC peacebuilding gap lay in the failure to jump-start the rehabilitation of the economy. As Elisabeth Uphoff has explained, the "Rehabilitation Component," a separate unit of UNTAC, was responsible for assessing needs, ensuring efficient and effective coordination, and raising resources.[26] Further complicating a slow start, one of the first two coordinators resigned, and the other was dismissed, within months. The component was not fully operational until January 1993. The unit focused on coordinating international aid and providing technical assistance. UNTAC did no rehabilitation work itself until the very end of the mission, when the needs of refugee resettlement required a more active role.

What did UNTAC rehabilitation actually contribute? Aid flowed into the country, and the Rehabilitation Component kept track of it. Important financial and administrative reforms were put into place, and several major disasters were averted, including hyperinflation, rice shortages, and government bankruptcy. Yet between 30 and 40 percent of returnees continued to live hand-to-mouth. Only a fraction of the millions of mines littering the country were cleared, and with the war continuing, more were laid. Major roads and bridges were repaired, but security problems still limit their use.

Aid did not, however, "benefit all areas of Cambodia, especially the more disadvantaged, and reach all levels of society," as the Declaration on the Reconstruction of Cambodia required. Aid, in fact, showed a strong urban-returnee relief bias, in contrast to the declaration's plan for developing rural areas and local capacity building. Instead, urban bias expanded the service sector (including prostitution) and fostered high rates of consumer imports and growing inequality.

Peacekeeping does not establish long-term peace without training for peacebuilding, and Cambodia is a prime example of this lesson. Furthermore, a new regime requires a new bureaucracy in order to be fully sovereign or effective as a reformer and national "peacebuilder." The politics of peacebuilding are crucial, and it is essential that political processes inform all aspects of peacebuilding. Without it, transitional control will not provide neutrality, and the peacekeepers will not be able to promote a transition to effective, national, legitimate power.

In Cambodia, the peace process left behind contradiction, not reconciliation, in the political arena. All the factions lacked either legitimacy, or power, or both. Both the more powerful factions—the CPP's SOC and the Khmer Rouge—had substantial bureaucratic cadres and effective military battalions. However, they lacked international recognition and popular support. SOC had been established following Vietnam's 1978–1979 intervention and, after ten years of counterinsurgency warfare, had a disciplined bureaucracy and well-honed army. But only the Soviet bloc recognized the regime; neither the UN nor its Southeast Asian neighbors recognized its legitimacy. The Khmer Rouge had a highly disciplined army but was recognized only by China. On the other hand, the more legitimate, internationally recognized, and popular faction, the followers of Prince Sihanouk in FUNCINPEC, lacked bureaucracy and military force. Relegitimization was begun by UNTAC's successful organization of democratic elections from the ground up. The problem for the winner, FUNCINPEC, was that although they won democratic legitimacy, they were not offered a real opportunity to control the state. The bureaucracy, the police, the judges, and the bulk of the army remained in the hands of the CPP party, the followers of Hun Sen.

Resuming Peacebuilding

After UNTAC, Cambodia was left with a continuing war and an unreconciled bureaucracy. The counterinsurgency war with the remaining six thousand or so Khmer Rouge, holed up along the western border with Thailand, produced a thousand military casualties in addition to uncounted civilian casualties. Each year government forces pushed the Khmer Rouge guerrillas back into the jungle during the dry season, and each year guerrillas infiltrated back during the wet season. The war absorbed 40 percent or more of the government budget and led to more mines being laid in a country already suffering some of the worst rates of mine casualties in the world. Government forces were not able to inflict decisive defeats on the guerrillas, and the guerrillas posed no military threat to the population centers. In 1996 and 1997, Khmer Rouge defections served instead to whet factional strife.

Meanwhile, the state neglected the two key peacebuilding components: improving the capacity of the civilian bureaucracy and bringing economic development to the countryside. While the capital, Phnom Penh, experienced a gold rush–style boom during the UNTAC period, fueled by UN spending, the countryside experienced the added burden of inflation on top of the devastation wreaked during the previous twenty years. Urban-rural inequality continued to increase, producing rural anger with ominous overtones.

Long-term peacebuilding requires a coherent and dedicated government prepared to fulfill its commitments to develop an impartial judicial system, respect the rule of law, manage the bureaucracy effectively, and promote economic development. Instead, the CPP-FUNCINPEC rivalry created a bureaucratic stalemate. The stalemate tempted both parties to purge leading dissidents and reformers. Partisan financial corruption disrupted the development process.

The coup rolled back much of the slight progress that Cambodia had achieved since 1993. In response to the coup and continuing budgetary irregularities resulting in large part from the lack of transparency, the United States, Australia, the European Union, the World Bank, and the IMF suspended all nonhumanitarian assistance. The United Nations General Assembly and ASEAN refused to seat either the Hun Sen/Ung Huot delegation or the Ranariddh delegation until the coalition government was formed in November 1998. The peacebuilding deficit continues to shape and misshape the process of Cambodian development. The question is, can peacebuilding be put back on track?

Many international actors now question whether there should be further involvement and investment in Cambodian peacebuilding. Cambodia has already received the more than $2 billion spent on the UNTAC peace effort and $1.3 billion pledged in aid since then. Other countries, these critics argue, are more deserving and more capable of using the aid effectively. By abandoning Cambodia, the international community neglects the fact that the vast majority of Cambodians are still on the list of the world's neediest individuals. Moreover, the international community still has a stake in the success of one its major peace operations. Cambodia's factions made commitments in the Paris agreements that the international community, represented by the UN, agreed to monitor and guarantee for all the people of Cambodia. Moreover, Cambodia's regional neighbors have an especially strong incentive to keep their neighborhood productive and secure. An unstable, crime-dominated Cambodia would be very costly for Thailand, Laos, Vietnam, and Malaysia.[27] Finally, thousands of Cambodians have jeopardized their careers by returning from abroad to join the state. Others have undertaken new and hazardous professions as human rights activists and journalists at home. Millions of Cambodians risked their lives to vote in May 1993. They should not and need not be abandoned.

Cambodia's experience from 1991 to 1998 is a hard lesson in peacebuilding, and it demonstrates that establishing internal peace is a distinct and difficult task. Someone or something must be sovereign, guaranteeing law and order by force if need be, in order to ensure the discontinuation of civil war and a self-enforcing peace. Victory by one side (as in the July coup), partition among the contending factions, subordination to foreign rule, and national peacebuilding are the alternatives. In Cambodia, national peacebuilding is and must be the critical step toward long-term peace and development.

Peacebuilding Challenges

The challenges of building peace for the new coalition government are threefold. First, there is a need to restore legitimacy by conducting the new national coalition government in a way that builds the rule of law and democratic participation. Second, the government needs to enhance the effectiveness of the state bureaucracy by reforming civilian and military institutions, thereby creating a state capable of governing on a national rather than a partisan basis. In this way, legitimacy and power can reinforce one another: the government will gain legitimacy, and the legitimate government will control the resources of a national impartial state. And third, Cambodia needs to continue to develop a civil society, including a market economy that reaches and benefits the ordinary citizen, especially in underdeveloped rural regions. Achieving all three is needed to put peacebuilding back on track, a feat that will require international assistance and considerable good fortune.

Building legitimacy. Major progress toward the first goal was made when the coalition between Hun Sen's and Ranariddh's followers was formed in November 1998. Nonetheless, a series of political crises revealed the fragility of the arrangement. The exclusion of Sam Rainsy and his party; the many disputes over political favoritism in judicial proceedings (e.g., the purported judicial cover-ups concerning alleged attacks by Hun Sen's wife and another minister's wife on their husbands' putative mistresses); and political amnesties for Khmer Rouge leaders in Pailin, in addition to the dispute with the United Nations over the organization of a fair tribunal for the Khmer Rouge—all indicated a continuing crisis in the rule of law.

The second election in 1998 was an important step in Cambodia, because participation in local decisionmaking mechanisms is crucial to establish a responsive connection between the state and the people. International human rights sanctions by multilateral donors also serve this purpose, but inauthentically and sporadically. A commitment to electoral legitimacy creates an indigenous connection as legislators provide a locally chosen voice for protest of and protection from arbitrary and corrupt state policy. It need not destabilize the state nor preclude a national coalition government, which can assist in establishing a stable state. But no coalition should be a permanent government. Five (as in South Africa) to ten years of power sharing appears to be the best duration.[28]

Broader measures of trust building are also necessary, if only to help hold the coalition together. They include, for example, a greater role for the National Assembly, the implementation of the Constitutional Council, and the promise of truly free and fair elections. The National Assembly needs to play a more independent role in the legislative process. In a parliamentary system, party leaderships naturally exert considerable discipline. But the legislature, like the bureaucracy, needs capacity building. It needs to serve as a better watchdog over the government, a better provider for the constituencies, and a better representative of the diversity of the popular will. One good step could be modeled on USAID's provision of assistance—everything from desks and equipment to workshops on legislative procedures and duties—for the fledgling Cambodian legislature. The RGC should also establish a genuinely neutral electoral commission composed of eminent Cambodians from civil society and experts from the region and abroad to monitor the work of the ministry of the interior. Charges of manipulation of the commission from 1998 will need to be addressed and its legitimacy buttressed if the electoral process is going to continue to be the key to a legitimate Cambodian government.

Creating a state that works. With the time a coalition can offer, political stability and economic development can be achieved. The lesson for Cambodia is the importance of a bureaucracy with the technical education and political authority to make and implement governmental decisions, as well as reliance on open markets and transparent protection for contracts and private property.[29]

Incentives for military predation can only be reduced by military demobilization and improving the training and logistics of the remaining forces. The government should also introduce transparency in all contracts. The Cambodia Development Council thus should make all its investment contracts and concessions public, and the government should publish all private and public investment and aid contracts. Cambodia today faces no external threats sufficiently serious to justify secrecy. Nor does secrecy allow Cambodia to exercise monopoly bargaining power to improve its contract terms. Secrecy today merely serves to cover corruption. Transparency works to the advantage of all reformers and may enhance Cambodia's bargaining power by limiting the ability of foreign investors to play Cambodian officials and ministries against each other. Donors can require that all foreign assistance projects be made public. Indeed, the terms of every project can be nailed on a nearby tree—who will do what for how much. The IMF set the standard when it sanctioned the RGC for a failure of transparency in the sale of state assets. The so-called million meter logging deal with twenty Thai companies was the last straw that led IMF Director Michel Camdessus to cut off $20 million in budgetary assistance planned to be disbursed in June 1996. His action sent an appropriate signal directly to the responsible officials because it sanctioned the government budget.[30]

Developing civil society. Civil socialization works by reducing demands on the managerial capacity of the state and improving a society's capacity to articulate and meet public needs. It also generates employment and careers outside the bureaucracy and the army. UNTAC helped open a space for hundreds of new, indigenous Cambodian NGOs. In step with the moderating of civil war, traditional Buddhist organizations began to reestablish their role as spiritual guides and community organizers in the countryside.

Marketization has created new sources of livelihood in Cambodia's cities and towns. Having international donors require transparent investment contracts can limit corruption and encourage broad-based economic development that takes advantage of

Cambodia's low wages and access to booming ASEAN and international markets. Apparel and other light manufacturing are currently experiencing a boom around the cities. Well-meaning foreign activists are protesting child labor. A better focus for the international protection of labor is establishing the right to unionize and promoting basic health and safety standards. Working in a clean, safe factory near their parents is a step up for the many Cambodian children who toil on the rice farms and for the unfortunate thousands who work in the brothel villages that surround Phnom Penh.

The UN Development Program (UNDP) developed the single most promising model for combined market and democratic development in the countryside. The Cambodia Area Rehabilitation and Regeneration Project (CARERE 2) or SEILA (the word means "foundation stone" in Khmer) combined rural infrastructure, local participatory decisionmaking, and state capacity building. Designed as a pilot for five provinces, SEILA established a chain of elected committees beginning with the village development committee, which elected a commune committee, which in turn elected district and then provincial development committees. The provinces were given independent budgets (as were the districts) to allocate to worthy projects proposed by the villages and communes. This was designed to be bottom-up, not top-down democratization. It embodied the potential of building participatory, responsible, local self-determination and accountability. UNDP assisted the provincial committee with technical advice designed to build planning capacity and responsible budgetary control at the provincial level. SEILA won the support of the national government and five provincial governors. It was scheduled to go into expanded operation in fifty villages.[31] The autocratic structure of the Cambodian village will not be changed overnight, but even first steps toward consultation and accountability, when joined to real investments, can begin to mobilize rural effort.

International facilitation. Outsiders are needed to provide temporary glue. They control the international legitimacy, the capital, and the markets that the CPP needs. In September 1997, the Permanent Five members of the Security Council and ASEAN wisely combined forces in a "Friends of Cambodia" group to focus diplomatic efforts.[32] The result was ASEAN's decision to postpone Cambodia's membership until May 1999 and the UN's decision not to seat the coup delegation until the coalition was formed in November 1998. Confidential yet concerned, this diplomacy sent a clear signal of international and regional interest in the continued progress toward peace in Cambodia.

A new international mandate, UNTAC II, was out of the question while the coup was in place, since no one in the international community was prepared to invest the officials, troops, and budget. Nonetheless, Cambodia, like many post–civil war and postpeace operation governments, continues to need more than the monitoring of human rights and development assistance. Monitoring will be too late to correct most human rights abuses.

Cambodia continues to require the attention of a World Bank Consultative Group that matches heightened financial attention with political sensitivity. With an annual per capita income of $280, among the lowest in the world according to the World Bank, Cambodia depends on Bank financing. Its reforms of the military and public sectors will be highly controversial, dangerous, and difficult, and international support is likely to be decisive in mobilizing domestic reformers.[33] Cambodia also would benefit from a continuation of the UN Human Rights Center established there. The UN Human Rights Center assists the government in a variety of ways, including human rights education and training, but it is urgent that it retain its active and outspoken reporting of abuses. The center's rigorous monitoring is a valuable source of information. Without the cover and umbrella of transparency it provides, local human rights activists believe that they would soon be forced into silence.[34]

Conclusion

Cambodia is "running out" of its single most important political asset, King Sihanouk. The man who led Cambodia to independence from France in 1941, balanced the country precariously between the North Vietnamese and the United States in the 1960s, orchestrated the Paris Peace Agreement of 1991, and engineered the November 1998 coalition is straining the conventional actuarial tables. The coalition will need to become viable, capable of building legitimacy and effectiveness for the Cambodian state, before he passes on.

Peacebuilding in Cambodia tests whether the antagonists of civil wars can be turned into the protagonists of party politics. The Paris Peace Agreement was comprehensively negotiated among the factions over ten years and received the full support of the international community, together with the deployment of twenty-three thousand peacekeepers in 1992–1993 and an expenditure of about $4 billion in peacekeeping and foreign aid. Smaller efforts in less divided countries have contributed to sustainable peace and development in Namibia, El Salvador, and Mozambique. Will this larger, more difficult test be passed? And if not, what are the prospects for peacebuilding where the divisions are even more severe?

Notes

This chapter builds on my *UN Peacekeeping in Cambodia: UNTAC's Civil Mandate* (Boulder, CO: Lynne Rienner Publishers, 1995). It also draws on interviews conducted in Cambodia in May–June 1996. I would especially like to thank Mr. James Gibney and Ms. Laura Thornton for their many valuable suggestions. I also benefited from the advice of Mr. Benny Widyono, the Secretary-General Representative in Cambodia, Ms. Genevieve Merceur and Ambassador Dato Deva Mohd. Ridzam and Mr. Din Merican of the Malaysian Embassy in Cambodia; Mr. Suparidh Hy; Mr. David Ashley, Mr. David Timberman, and the participants at an IPA seminar on Cambodian peacebuilding, June 19, 1996.

1. For example, a U.S. Government Accounting Office report suggested that little or no progress had been made toward free elections, human rights, or mine clearing following UNTAC, in *Cambodia: Limited Progress on Free Elections, Human Rights, and Mine Clearing* (Washington, D.C.: GAO, February 29, 1996); David Ashley arrived at similar skeptical conclusions in "The Failure of Conflict Resolution in Cambodia," in *Cambodia and the International Community,* ed. Frederick Z. Brown and David Timberman (New York: Asia Society, 1998), 49–78.

2. Previous coup attempts had been foiled when the parties united against dissidents, or the two senior generals, Ke Kim Yan for CPP and Niek Bunh Chhay for FUNCINPEC, stopped them.

3. In *UN Peacekeeping in Cambodia* (1), I reported that a near consensus existed among Cambodia experts that the chances of a coup in the near future were about 50 percent.

4. For a criticism of electoral strategies for peace, see Jack Snyder and Karen Ballentine, "Nationalism and the Marketplace of Ideas," *International Security* 21, 2 (Fall 1996): 5–40.

5. Keith Richburg and R. Jeffrey Smith, "Cambodian Chaos," *International Herald Tribune,* July 14, 1997, 4.

6. "Cambodian Villagers Continue to Flee War Zones," *Reuters World Service,* October 7, 1997.

7. Sorpong Peou, "Cambodia in 1998: From Despair to Hope?" *Asian Survey* 39, 1 (Jan./Feb. 1999): 20–26.

8. As of December 1999, the current compromise appears to be a trial of the top five or so leaders before a Cambodian tribunal, with international judges participating in a minority role. For a discussion of genocide trial issues, see Steven Ratner and Jason Abrams, *Accountability for Human Rights Atrocities in International Law: Beyond the Nuremberg Legacy* (New York: Oxford University Press, 1997).

9. For a thoughtful discussion of Cambodia's political legacy, see Aun Porn Moniroth, "Democracy in Cambodia: Theories and Realities," trans. Khieu Mealy (Phnom Penh: Cambodian Institute for Cooperation Peace [CICP], 1995); and Lao Mong Hay, "Building Democracy in Cambodia," in *Cambodia and the International Community,* 169–186. For background on the Cambodian conflict, see Ben Kiernan and Chantou Boua, eds., *Peasants and Politics in Kampuchea 1942–1981* (London: Zed Press, 1982); Michael Vickery, *Kampuchea: Politics, Economics and Society* (Boulder, CO: Lynne Rienner Publishers, 1986); and David Chandler, "Three Visions of Politics in Cambodia," in *Keeping the Peace: Multidimensional UN Operations in Cambodia and El Salvador,* ed. Michael W. Doyle, Ian Johnstone, and Robert C. Orr (New York: Cambridge University Press, 1997): 25–52.

10. "Cambodia Gets $81.6 Million IMF Loan," *Bloomberg Press,* October 22, 1999, in CAMNEWS, October 23, 1999.

11. *First Socioeconomic Development Plan,* 85.

12. *First Socioeconomic Development Plan,* 17, table 2.3.

13. Cambodian Development Council, author interview, May 1996.

14. Peou, "Cambodia in 1998."

15. One lower-level development official complained to me that "every stump in the country has been sold at least once."

16. J. P. Azam, "Some Economic Consequences of the Transition from Civil War to Peace" (Washington, D.C.: World Bank, 1994).

17. Robert J. Muscat, "Rebuilding Cambodia: Problems of Governance and Human Resources," in *Rebuilding Cambodia: Human Resources, Human Rights and Law,* ed. Dolores Donovan et al. (Washington, D.C.: Foreign Policy Institute, 1993), 13–42.

18. The general case for marketization is made in *From Plan to Market: World Development Report 1996* (Washington, D.C.: World Bank, 1996). See also Mancur Olson, "Disorder, Cooperation and Development: A Way of Thinking About Cambodian Development" (Phnom Penh: CICP, February 1996); and Naranhkiri Tith, "The Challenge of Sustainable Economic Growth in Cambodia," in *Cambodia and the International Community,* ed. Brown and Timberman, 101–125.

19. *First Socioeconomic Development Plan,* 90.

20. John P. McAndrew, "Aid Infusions, Aid Illusions," Working Paper no. 2 (Phnom Penh: Cambodian Development Resource Institute, January 1996).

21. "Recommendation to the International Committee on the Rehabilitation and Reconstruction of Cambodia [ICORC] 1995," in *Cambodia Rehabilitation Program: Implementation and Outlook: A World Bank Report for the 1995 ICORC Conference* (Washington, D.C.: World Bank, 1995). See also Benny Widyono, "Reconstruction of the Post-conflict Public Administrative Machinery in Cambodia," paper prepared for the interregional seminar "On Restoring Government Administrative Machinery in Situations of Conflict" (Rome, Italy, March 13–15, 1996); and Royal Government of Cambodia, *The Administrative Reform: An Overview Prepared for the Donor's Meeting* (Phnom Penh: RGC, May 10, 1996).

22. Phnom Penh, Cambodia, author interview, May 1996.

23. The UNTAC mandate specifically requires UNTAC to exercise supervision over "agencies, bodies and other offices [that] could continue to operate in order to ensure normal day-to-day life." For background on the new features of the UN mandate in Cambodia, see Steven R. Ratner, *The New UN Peacekeeping: Building Peace in Lands of Conflict After the Cold War* (New York: St. Martin's Press,

1995); Trevor Findlay, *The UN in Cambodia* (Stockholm, Sweden: SIPRI, 1995); Janet Heininger, *Peacekeeping in Transition: The United Nations in Cambodia* (New York: Twentieth Century Fund, 1994); and Nishkala Suntharalingam, "The Cambodian Settlement Agreements," in *Keeping the Peace,* 83–106. For additional valuable assessments of the successes and failures of UNTAC, see Steven Heder and Judy Ledgerwood, eds., *Propaganda, Politics and Violence in Cambodia* (Armonk, NY: M.E. Sharpe, 1996), and William Shawcross, *Cambodia's New Deal* (Washington, D.C.: Carnegie Endowment for Peace, 1994).

24. On the control function, see Article 6 of the "Agreement on a Comprehensive Political Settlement of the Cambodia Conflict" and UNTAC Mandate Annex 1, Section B, both in A/46/608–S/23177 (October 30, 1991).

25. Former senior officials of UNTAC disagree, arguing in response that the parties would not have accepted so proactive a mandate at the Paris peace negotiations. All agree that a training function, if widely implemented, would have required an increase in the UNTAC budget.

26. Elisabeth Uphoff, "Quick Impacts, Slow Rehabilitation in Cambodia," in *Keeping the Peace,* 186–205.

27. The press has been suggesting a connection between the coup and Teng Bunma, who is said to have bankrolled the coup and to be involved himself, according to U.S. officials, in the transshipment of drugs in Southeast Asia. Teng Bunma recently received a timber concession of one million acres (see "Cambodian Tycoon Acquires Major Timber Concession," Reuters World Serve, October 2, 1997).

28. For examples, see Tim Sisk, *Powersharing and International Mediation in Ethnic Conflicts* (Washington, D.C.: U.S. Institute for Peace, 1996).

29. The general case for marketization is made in *From Plan to Market: World Development Report 1996* (Washington, D.C.: World Bank, 1996). See also Olson, "Disorder, Cooperation and Development: A Way of Thinking About Cambodia Development."

30. Mathew Grainger, "IMF Freezes Funding," *Phnom Penh Post,* May 31–June 13, 1996, 1.

31. UNDP and RGC, Project Document, CMB/95/011/01/31, CARERE 2 (Phnom Penh: February 1996) and Scott Leiper, UNDP, author interviews, May 1996. For background, see Royal Government of Cambodia, UNDP, and UN Office for Project Services, *Building the Foundation of the SEILA Programme: The 1996 Work Plan of the Cambodia Area Rehabilitation and Regeneration (CARERE) Project* (Phnom Penh, March 1996).

32. Robert Birsel, "Cambodia Meeting Seen Focusing on Poll, Prince," Reuters World Serve, September 28, 1997.

33. See the concluding chapter to this volume where peacebuilding as a politically sensitive, international catalyst is discussed.

34. UNCHR, author interviews; Phnom Penh, author interviews, May 1996.

5

Building Peace in Bosnia

Elizabeth M. Cousens

When Bosnian fire ceased in November 1995, two questions loomed. First, was war really over or might it resume? Second, even if war did not recur, on whose terms would Bosnia construct peace? Neither question had been conclusively answered by 1999. Massive hostilities are unlikely to resume, but violent conflict over more targeted objectives remains a real concern should international peacekeepers leave. More troubling, the parties to Bosnia's peace have resisted committing themselves credibly to a common political design for the country, leaving it a still-open question whether the country rebuilds itself as one state, two, or three.

Meanwhile, the international community has tried to adapt the nature and scale of its own continuing involvement in Bosnia accordingly. Since 1995, two NATO-led multinational military forces have been deployed to Bosnia, the sixty-thousand-strong Implementation Force (IFOR) and its thirty-thousand-strong successor mission, the Stabilization Force (SFOR), whose mandate has been renewed and is likely to be extended for some years to come.[1] Parallel to the international military presence are thousands of international civilian personnel working through numerous organizations and agencies—the United Nations, the Organization for Security and Cooperation in Europe (OSCE), the European Union, the United Nations High Commissioner for Refugees (UNHCR), the World Bank, and an international civilian "High Representative," among others—on issues ranging from elections, economic reconstruction and institution building to civilian policing, human rights, and the return of the displaced. International actors can count multiple achievements from their engagement in Bosnia's cease-fire, but all are fragile. Moreover, interpretations made, priorities set, and decisions taken during implementation have heavily and needlessly contributed to consolidation of the tripartite division of Bosnia. International implementation efforts have also exerted a contradictory impact on Bosnia's democratic development, consistently calling for democratization but with programs that alternately foster or undermine democratic capacities in Bosnian political society. Despite apparent intentions to the contrary, the cumulative impact of implementation has made it a much harder task to "implement Dayton" and build peace today than when the war ended.

The Bosnian war ended with a particularly precarious negotiated settlement. Under intense international pressure, from the United States in particular, its parties committed themselves to the terms of a compromise that deeply dissatisfied all of them but that was sufficiently ambiguous on key points that each party believed it could be turned to their respective aims during implementation. This agreement, forged during twenty-one days of proximity talks in Dayton, Ohio, was not atypical of negotiated settlements, though it was a particularly thorny example: ambiguous, at times contradictory, comprehensive in some respects, while incomplete in others. Predictably, such qualities placed a unique burden on the period of implementation, which would unavoidably be treated by the parties as an opportunity to obstruct, revise, and sabotage the agreement to which they had pledged themselves.[2] In Bosnia, as in comparable cases, the period of implementation has also become the dumping ground for all issues left unresolved by the agreement, which will be settled by default if not by conscious design. Where the Dayton Agreement is concerned, these issues go to the heart of why and how the war was fought; as a result, their cumulative resolution by Bosnian and international implementers will decide the nature of whatever peace is built.

My argument is straightforward. First, the Dayton Agreement that ended Bosnia's war presented serious, if not insuperable, obstacles to peacebuilding, notably: an implausibly short timetable for national elections; a postwar constitution that privileged the leading mononational parties; a settlement overly dependent on the continuing commitment of a narrow set of elites whose interest in either peace or broader political liberalization was, as it remains, debatable; and a framework for international engagement that excessively segregated military from civilian efforts. Second, the agreement provided negligible strategic guidance to either the parties or international peacebuilders. As soon as the parties and major implementing agencies set up shop on the ground to begin turning the agreement into reality, they faced an immediate and constant need to make sensitive judgments about events, set priorities among the agreement's provisions, and develop strategies to make their own work maximally effective. On none of these did the agreement itself give much assistance. Third, international third parties enjoyed great potential influence in this context and, therefore, over the successful implementation and long-term sustainability of the settlement. They would also have to be willing to exercise it. Bosnia's experience demonstrates that implementing a complex peace agreement is a highly creative enterprise, in which interpretations and decisions by implementers have enormous practical consequence. The judgments and actions of third parties will be decisive in such a setting, either enabling spoilers or curbing them, either giving robust support to those genuinely committed to peace or weakening them with inadequate assistance. Finally, the confluence of factors that brought the Bosnian parties to Dayton and enabled them to emerge with a comprehensive peace agreement—even one laced with unwieldy compromises—desperately needed to be sustained during implementation, both to ensure that agreed-upon provisions were fully implemented and to move toward final settlement of those issues left unresolved. Instead, the diplomatic and military commitment that produced the Dayton Agreement was abandoned during the first eighteen months of implementation. Now, Bosnia faces continuing obstacles to peace that arguably derive from mistakes made and opportunities missed, which international implementers could have both predicted and avoided.

History of the Conflict

Bosnia and Herzegovina found itself fully at war in the spring of 1992, after a year in which the Yugoslav federal state it belonged to had come sequentially and violently apart. The Bosnian war was the third and most destructive stage of Yugoslavia's disintegration, following a short scuffle over Slovenia's departure and a serious war over Croatia's. How one explains the breakup of Yugoslavia bears heavily on how one assesses Bosnia's current prospects for peace, particularly since this former republic uniquely replicated Yugoslavia's mix of nationalities and its power-sharing formulas for managing them.

From at least the late 1980s, Yugoslavia's complex balance of powers among its six republics, two autonomous provinces, and six constituent nationalities had become increasingly unable to function as an effective state, as well as increasingly fertile ground for competition among political leaders emerging in Yugoslavia's republics.[3] Long before it would have seemed plausible that Yugoslavia would literally dissolve, the political center of gravity had shifted significantly from the country's federal institutions to its republics and provinces. Yugoslavia's third constitution, adopted in 1974, devolved authority along virtually every axis of institutional power: each republic now had its own central bank, its own Communist Party, its own educational system, its own judiciary, and very important, its own police. The only institution that still operated exclusively at the federal level was Yugoslavia's national army (the JNA), though it now acquired as commander-in-chief an eight-member, rotating federal presidency.[4] In theory, the 1974 constitutional amendments were a progressive response to demands for local autonomy; in practice, they gave each republic an institutional tool kit to become a powerful rival to the central state and to one another.

This unwieldy institutional framework was a godsend to any politician interested in building a personal power base, and Yugoslavia had several. The most ambitious of these appealed to national loyalties, grievance, and fears, particularly as the Yugoslav state's capacity to deliver basic goods shriveled and as Yugoslavia's economic and strategic status was called into question with the end of the Cold War.[5] By the end of the 1980s, conditions in Yugoslavia closely resembled those described by scholars as at high risk for ethnic conflict: declining socioeconomic standards, weakening state institutions, social uncertainty, and anxiety about "plausible futures," along with such longer-term attributes as a history of intergroup violence and affinities with groups on other sides of political or administrative boundaries.[6] Moreover, nationalism had long been the primary language of political opposition in Yugoslavia. National sentiment was also generally on the rise as the Cold War drew to a close, which Western governments and institutions greeted with a degree of careless acceptance.

By 1990, when the first democratic elections were held in all six republics, nationalist politicians and parties were clear winners.

Serbian president Slobodan Milosevic had emerged as a champion of the Serb people, whose rights he encouraged them to believe were under assault everywhere from the province of Kosovo—which was 90 percent Albanian Muslim to 10 percent Serb—to the republic of Croatia, whose draft constitution in June appeared to grant rights only to Croats and not to the 12 percent of its population that was Serb. Slovenian leaders had openly declared their desire for national independence, directly challenging Milosevic in particular, who expressed a fierce commitment to keeping Yugoslavia together.[7] Croatia was meanwhile experiencing its own nationalist revival, electing the well-credentialed nationalist Franjo Tudjman as its first president of the postcommunist era, and its new ruling party—the Croatian Democratic Union (HDZ)—replacing the emblems of Yugoslavia with Croatian symbols last seen during Croatia's collaboration with Nazi Germany. At the same time, hard-line Croatian Serbs had begun a militant autonomy movement, whose core became the new Serbian Democratic Party (SDS). Bosnian politics had also turned in nationalist directions. The Muslim-dominated Party of Democratic Action (SDA) was founded in the spring, with Alija Izetbegovic as president, and sister parties of the Croat HDZ and the Serb SDS were founded shortly thereafter.

More ominous, segments of the political population in Croatia and Bosnia had already begun to prepare for armed confrontation, both at the boundaries of the republics and within them. Within Croatia, the SDS, with support from Serbia proper, was building its own village-to-village military capacity in pursuit of what would soon be declared an independent "Republic of Serb Krajina."[8] By early fall, the Croatian government was secretly arming police and territorial defense forces and purging its security forces of Serbs in anticipation of JNA resistance to its secession. In Bosnia, Serb communities also began setting up village patrols that were increasingly militarized over the course of 1991 and 1992, when the JNA began discreetly transferring its Bosnian Serb troops back to Bosnia.

The immediate sequence of events that culminated in full-scale war in Bosnia was swift and brutal. Slovenia declared its independence on June 25, 1991, which it effectively won after an extremely short "war" with the JNA—more of a halfhearted police action conducted by military troops. Croatia simultaneously declared independence but met far more serious resistance from the JNA, Serb paramilitary units, and its own autonomy-seeking Serbs. As war in Croatia continued through late 1991, Bosnia's Serb and, to a lesser extent, Croat communities also began to mobilize for conflict. Serb leaders very vocally declared their intention to remain within the Yugoslav federation or seek separation from Bosnia. Serb "autonomous areas" were set up in the fall, and a plebiscite was held in Serb areas to demonstrate Serbian opposition to Bosnia's secession from Yugoslavia. By early January 1992, Serbian president Milosevic also began transferring Bosnian Serbs in the JNA back to Bosnia in anticipation of hostilities. Meanwhile, Bosnia's president, Alija Izetbegovic, and the SDA grew increasingly committed to Bosnian independence. When the international community recognized both Slovenian and Croatian independence in January 1992, largely as a gambit to end the war in Croatia, it worked. Within two months, however, war had engulfed neighboring Bosnia.

Once Slovenia and Croatia had successfully seceded, Bosnia was left with a Hobson's choice: remain in a much smaller Yugoslavia that would be overwhelmingly dominated by Serbia and, by implication, its own large Serb minority, or leave the Yugoslav federation, a prospect that Bosnian Serbs worried would leave them analogously dominated by Bosnia's Muslim plurality.[9] In the event, Bosnia was recognized as an independent state by the European Community on April 6, 1992, one month after barricades were first raised in Sarajevo city streets, two days after President Izetbegovic ordered a general mobilization of Bosnia's territorial defense forces, and one day after Serb paramilitary forces besieged Sarajevo's police academy and the JNA seized its airport. In short, recognition occurred just as the country was being plunged into war.

During the next three and a half years, Bosnian government forces fought to preserve an independent, unitary state that would enjoy the same borders as the former Bosnian republic and ostensibly offer the same rights to its Serb and Croat citizens that they had enjoyed when Bosnia was a constituent republic of Yugoslavia.[10] The government found itself at war on at least two fronts. From the beginning, and principally, it battled radical Bosnian Serbs, closely tied to and actively supplied by Serbia, who fought to "cleanse" large portions of Bosnian territory of non-Serbs and declare an independent Serbian Republic (Republika Srpska) that might eventually join Serbia proper. Second, it faced Bosnian Croats, closely tied to and actively supplied by their own patron Croatia, who launched their own ethnically driven land grab in central and southern Bosnia in April 1993. The conflict between the Bosnian government and Bosnian Croats was resolved, at least tactically, in 1994, after intensive diplomatic efforts by the United States. Finally, on November 20, 1995, a comprehensive settlement was reached among all three warring parties after twenty-one days of proximity talks in Dayton, Ohio. By the time the Dayton Agreement was initialed, over half of Bosnia's prewar population of 4.4 million had fled their original homes, either to live as refugees outside the country or as internally displaced persons elsewhere in Bosnia; dead or missing were estimated at 279,000, close to 7 percent of the prewar population; nearly half of the country's housing stock was damaged or destroyed; and most of its economic infrastructure was devastated.[11]

International Intervention

Throughout the wars in the former Yugoslavia, the international community found itself deeply divided on multiple levels. Regionally, Europe saw the Yugoslav crisis as a test case of its capacity to make common foreign and security policy; it pitted itself against the United States, which bemoaned European ineffectiveness but was unwilling to step into the breach. Both stood in delicate relationship to Russia, which hinted at grave consequences should the West take sides in the Bosnian conflict. Intergovernmentally, Germany and Austria were seen as the champions of Croatia, France as guided by its historic support of Serbia, Russia as clearly partisan to the Serbs, the new U.S. administration as heavily favoring the Bosnian Muslims—increasingly referred to as "Bosniacs"—and the UK as preternaturally disposed to appeasement. Institutionally, organizations like the UN, the EU, and NATO were each trying to stake their respective claims in the new post–Cold War world. Within governments, interagency divisions between military and political departments closed off a range of policy options that would involve a more robust use of military force. Operationally, as the war progressed, the principal components of international action in Bosnia—peacekeeping, humanitarian assistance, and mediation efforts—became increasingly contradictory.

Effective policymaking was also undercut by competing analyses of what the war was about to begin with and by subsidiary arguments about the nature and behavior of the warring parties. Was the Bosnian war a case of external aggression against an independent state, and an otherwise placid multinational polity at that, or had Bosnia never been a state of any viability to begin with? Was this a civil war in which "ancient hatreds" between neighbors burst to the surface with the end of communist suppression? Was the story instead one of state failure spurred by a hefty dose of mismanagement by outside governments and international financial institutions? What was the balance between such internal factors as weakening state institutions, predatory political elites, and the legacy of previous civil war, and such external factors as Yugoslavia's rapidly declining strategic importance once the Cold War ended, the loss of its historic markets for the same reason, and international recognition of Slovenia and Croatia? As for the parties: Were the Bosnian Serbs fierce and well-trained fighters who would drag any intervening force into a bloody quagmire, or drunken bumpkins who would run scared at the first show of force by the international community? Was this a case of genocide against a completely innocent people, or was there blame for atrocities on all sides? Was there not also in the Balkans a predisposition to blood feuds and grotesqueries of collective violence? Complicating all of such arguments were rival philosophical commitments to different principles of international right and order: national self-determination versus the protection of minorities, the rights of groups versus rights of individuals, and the long-term viability of nation-states versus multinational polities.

Getting to Dayton

Prior to the Dayton Agreement, a series of peace plans had been developed by different international mediating bodies, none of which had been sufficiently acceptable to the parties, or sufficiently backed by major international actors, to become the basis for a comprehensive settlement.[12] Broadly, the Dayton Agreement was possible where settlement had earlier been elusive because of an increasing coherence in international engagement in the conflict that helped create as well as reinforce a changing balance of military power among the parties on the ground.

A first element of this emerging coherence was the changing role of the United States, which began to recognize that it actually did "have a dog in this fight."[13] Under the leadership of National Security Adviser Anthony Lake, the U.S. administration developed for the first time in mid-1995 a serious strategy to bring about an end to the war. Until this point, the U.S. response had been weak and vacillating at best. Under President George Bush, the United States had been all too willing to allow Europeans to take the lead on a crisis they claimed as their own but were demonstrably incapable of handling. Under President Bill Clinton, the United States was far too inclined to issue outraged statements that something be done and to blame its European allies for tying U.S. hands, when his administration was unwilling to take any real risks on Bosnia's behalf—indeed, far fewer than those same European allies, who maintained thousands of their own troops on Balkan ground.

The seeds of a U.S. strategy to bring cease-fire to Bosnia began when the United States brokered the tactical realliance between Bosniacs and Bosnian Croats.[14] Both initially at the receiving end of the Bosnian Serb campaign, Bosniacs and Bosnian Croats became open adversaries by the spring of 1993, their antagonism heavily shadowed by allegations that Croatian president Tudjman and Serbian president Milosevic were playing an endgame to divide Bosnia between themselves.[15] When this second front emerged between the government and Bosnian Croats, actively backed by Croatia, it became even more remote that a territorial formula could be found that would simultaneously provide the basis for a viable, unitary Bosnian state and satisfy the separatist objectives of Serbs and Croats both. In March 1994, this Bosniac-Croat split was provisionally resolved with heavy U.S. backing through the "Washington Agreement," which committed Bosnian Croats and Muslims to unite in a postwar "federation." More critical at the time, it bound the two in a de facto military alliance to roll back Serb territorial gains. While the United States discreetly worked with the Croatian army, Croatia allowed arms and equipment to slip via Croatia to Bosniac forces.[16]

To the Croatian card, Washington added the Serbian, recognizing President Milosevic as the key broker on the Serbian side of the equation. The Americans now worked from the assumption that Bosnia would contain both the Bosniac-Croat Federation and a quasi-independent Republika Srpska and that both entities would be allowed to establish "special" relationships with neighboring Croatia and Serbia, respectively.

A second, arguably more critical element was a lurch into operational coherence among the various components of international Bosnia policy. Since the war began, international mediation, military, and humanitarian efforts had worked at cross-purposes. By mid-1995, they began to function more productively to support a common strategy to end the war. In large part, this coherence was forced upon the international community by the Bosnian Serb army.

Previous calls for more muscular diplomacy in the Balkans had been persistently undermined by the vulnerability of UN peacekeepers and other international personnel on the ground—primarily those deployed in six UN-designated "Safe Areas"—should the use of force by NATO invite reprisals.[17] That a way out of this bind had to be found became shamefully evident when Serb forces took hundreds of UN peacekeepers hostage following NATO air strikes in May 1995.[18] It began to seem increasingly likely that U.S. troops would have to intervene in Bosnia simply for the unexalted task of safely withdrawing the troops of its allies. In the brutal event, this dilemma between the vulnerability of UN peacekeepers and the need for forceful diplomacy was eased when the enclaves of Srebrenica and Zepa fell to the Bosnian Serbs in July, removing along with the thousands of civilians expelled or killed, two of the least tenable deployments of UN peacekeepers in the country.[19]

Involved governments now were ready to align their respective military, humanitarian, and political efforts behind a common objective. In partial preparation for the possibility that the remaining UN peacekeepers would have to be withdrawn, the UN Security Council authorized a military rapid reaction force (RRF) in mid-June, which deployed around Sarajevo by the end of July (and which would become instrumental in NATO's subsequent air campaign). Meeting in London in July, foreign ministers of the UN's troop-contributing countries ended the onerous "dual key" arrangement that required civilian UN approval of NATO action and agreed to use airpower to deter an assault on Gorazde, the next safe area likely to be attacked (at the same time, pulling UN peacekeepers discreetly out of the enclave).[20] The Clinton administration also indicated that U.S. troops might now be involved in enforcing whatever peace settlement was reached. Taken together, these decisions signaled a new unity in international diplomacy and a willingness to back it by force to an unprecedented degree.

A vital third element smoothing the path to Dayton was this new willingness to use force by the international community, especially airpower, as a partner to diplomacy. Various explanations account for the underuse of armed force to respond to the Yugoslav wars, from the nationally parochial through the bureaucratically predisposed and militarily arcane to the ontologically confused. Legal authorizations to use force certainly existed, not least the provision for individual and collective self-defense in the UN Charter, though this was arguably contravened by the existence of a UN arms embargo on the region beginning in September 1991.[21] The UN Security Council resolutions establishing the six Safe Areas in Bosnia had authorized the use of all necessary measures to protect them, and NATO had declared that violators of the military exclusion zone surrounding each Safe Area would be subject to air attack.[22] Later authorization for close air support of UN peacekeepers also enabled the robust use of force. Finally, even baseline rules of engagement permitted UN peacekeepers to resort to force in self-defense, though rarely has this been interpreted to go beyond physical defense of the peacekeeper to permit defense of the peacekeeper's mandate.

Not until the end of the summer 1995, however, did the international community turn seriously to the use of military force to end the Bosnian war. Obstacles to the use of NATO airpower had been removed with the repositioning of UN troops, both forced, in the case of Srebrenica and Zepa, and voluntary, in the case of Gorazde.[23] Bosnian Serb forces also provided NATO with a rationale for air strikes, with a mortar attack on August 28 that killed thirty-seven in Sarajevo's marketplace.

Finally, powerful pressure to reach settlement came from the dramatically changing military balance on the ground between the spring and fall of 1995, itself in no small way a product of U.S. efforts, which brought the territorial holdings of the warring parties into remarkably close alignment with the proposed basis for negotiation.[24] Starting in May, Serb forces suffered a series of defeats at the hands of the Croatian and Bosnian armies that significantly changed their calculus at the bargaining table and that also represented a new level of U.S. commitment to the Croatian military, which at this stage was being openly trained by unofficial U.S. advisers. On May 1, the Croatian army retook Serb-occupied territory in Western Slavonia, defying resident UN forces in this "UN Protected Area."[25] On August 4, it launched Operation Storm, an offensive that toppled the self-proclaimed "Krajina Serb Republic" in just two days, sending close to 150,000 Serb civilians fleeing into Serb-held Bosnia and Serbia.[26] Through the early fall, the Bosnian army in turn advanced dramatically on Serb positions. As EU negotiator David Owen described the situation from September on: "Thereafter, day by day, the map altered."[27] Until this point, Serb forces had held a commanding position territorially, having seized nearly two-thirds of Bosnian territory within the first month of the Bosnian war—which made it exceedingly difficult to extract concessions on the basis of anything less—and controlling almost one-third of Croatia, in Western Slavonia, Krajina, and Eastern Slavonia.

The narrative of the last days of the war demonstrates how effective NATO's subsequent air campaign was alongside these Bosnian and Croatian military gains. NATO and the recently deployed RRF began heavy air bombardment of Serb positions around Sarajevo on August 29–30, just after the Sarajevo marketplace attack, which they resumed between September 5 and 12. On September 8, talks in Geneva produced a "Statement of Agreed Basic Principles" that accepted as a basis for settlement a territorial split of 51 percent under Bosnian-Croat control to 49 percent under Bosnian Serb control and a political subdivision of Bosnia into two coequal "entities." As the Bosnian army and Croat forces advanced on Serb positions in western Bosnia, a cease-fire agreement for Sarajevo was reached on September 14, and "Further Agreed Basic Principles" were established on September 26. Renewed Serb offensives in October were met by resumed NATO air strikes between October 4 and 10, until a cease-fire came into effect midmonth. On November 1, proximity talks began at Wright-Patterson Air Force Base in Dayton, Ohio, and on November 20, Croatian president Tudjman, Serbian president Milosevic, Bosnian president Izetbegovic, and President Kresimir Zubak for the Bosniac-Croat federation initialed the Dayton Agreement. On December 14, the "General Framework Agreement for Peace" was formally signed in Paris.

The Dayton Bargain

The Dayton Agreement effected a compromise between two contending visions of Bosnia: the first, a single state with room and rights for a mix of nationalities; the second, an effective division into three, nationally homogenous ministates. Whether Dayton's mediators sought to have the first vision trump the second, the choices made by its implementers have helped tip the balance toward the latter.[28] It is worth reviewing the settlement's key provisions to assess the quality of the framework for effective peacebuilding that it provides its implementers.

The basic settlement. The Dayton Agreement consists of a short "General Framework Agreement" in which the parties pledged to "welcome and endorse" all provisions outlined in twelve attached annexes, as well as to generally abide by international norms respecting one another's sovereign equality, territorial integrity, and political independence. The meat of the accord is in the annexes, which cover issues ranging from the precise demarcation of the cease-fire line and regional arms control to the protection of human rights and preservation of national monuments.[29]

The political formula for resolving Bosnia's conflict was to create a single Bosnian state that is divided between two "entities," the Republika Srpska and the Federation of Bosnia and Herzegovina, the latter being an uneasy truce between Bosniacs and Croats since its formation in 1994. Bosnia's new constitution is inscribed in the agreement (as Annex 4) and establishes an intricate set of power-sharing institutions at national and entity levels, ironically very similar to those that failed to manage the rivalries that tore apart both Bosnia and Yugoslavia. Under the agreement, these joint institutions are the primary mechanisms to manage tension between the pull toward unity and the push toward partition. These were to begin functioning with the first postwar national elections. The strategy appears to have been twofold: first, to establish an institutional framework that would channel into political contestation any continuing conflict between those who favored an independent unitary state and those who sought significant degrees of autonomy from it; and second, to begin a process of democratization that had been sidelined when Yugoslavia dissolved in a series of wars.

Militarily, the agreement secured the cease-fire line and provided for regional stabilization and confidence-building measures. The military planks called for separation of armed forces along either side of an Inter-Entity Boundary Line (IEBL) that divided Serb areas from the Bosniac-Croat Federation. The provisions further laid out a detailed calendar of obligations governing when the parties had to cease hostilities, withdraw foreign forces, redeploy both forces and heavy weapons, exchange prisoners, and establish mechanisms for military cooperation. They also authorize deployment of a multinational "Implementation Force" (IFOR) under Chapter VII of the UN Charter to implement the territorial and military provisions, most of which were scheduled to be in place within six months.[30] Left for future resolution among the territorial provisions was authority over Brcko, the town that sits astride the narrow Posavina corridor connecting western and eastern Republika Srpska, and to which both Serbs and Bosniacs lay primary claim.[31]

Of no less consequence politically *or* militarily is the agreement's provision for the return of displaced persons, which had powerful implications if taken seriously. According to the agreement, "all refugees and displaced persons have the right freely to return to their homes of origin. They shall have the right to have restored to them property of which they were deprived in the course of hostilities since 1991 and to be compensated for any property that cannot be restored to them." Fulfilling these two sentences alone would dramatically affect all other elements of the Dayton package, especially those related to power sharing and elections. To realize this right of voluntary return for Bosnia's 2.5 million refugees and displaced, the parties at least nominally committed themselves to an extraordinarily progressive course of action. They would refrain from harassment, intimidation, persecution, and discrimination; prevent others from doing the same; repeal legislation and end administrative practices that discriminate against minorities, either in intent or effect; prevent or suppress hate speech whether committed by public officials or private citizens; protect minority populations; and prosecute and punish anyone with public responsibilities (specifically police and other security forces) who violates the rights of minorities.[32] The parties also agreed to establish a commission to deal with property claims and their just compensation.[33] Particularly given the ambitions of two of the warring parties—national homogeneity on territory under their control—and their chosen techniques for accomplishing these—ethnic cleansing—the provisions for refugees and internally displaced persons are possibly the most radical feature of the entire Dayton accord. Indeed, if most Bosnians sought to return, full implementation of these provisions could amount to a flat-out reversal of the entire course of the war.

Bolstering these commitments were the parties' obligations to guarantee human rights, which are detailed both in Bosnia's new constitution and in a separate annex.[34] Although more ink was expended on the institutional balance of power among Bosniacs, Croats, and Serbs, the postwar constitution outlines a full array of rights and freedoms, and an annex to the constitution lists fifteen international human rights agreements to which Bosnia's government must conform. Little is said about implementation in the constitution, though there are provisions for international monitoring, and in the context of the agreement as a whole there has been ample room for external efforts to strenuously encourage compliance. Annex 6 then expanded on the constitutional guarantees, pledging the parties to abide by international standards of human rights, respect the series of conventions designed to protect them, and fully cooperate with international human rights efforts, including the work of the International Criminal Tribunal for the Former Yugoslavia. The parties also committed themselves to establishing a joint Commission on Human Rights, comprising an Ombudsman and a Human Rights Chamber, designed to evolve over the course of five years from an office with significant international involvement to a regular, functioning, and fully Bosnian institution.

Finally, the Dayton accord not only pledged Bosnia's warring parties and its most influential neighbors to a settlement, it also committed various members of the international community to an unprecedented level of involvement in helping those parties implement its military and civilian provisions. Dayton offered a model of third-party implementation in which international military and civilian efforts were assigned to "lead agencies" by sector. Military provisions would be supervised by the sixty-thousand-strong IFOR, which was followed in December 1996 by a thirty-one-thousand-troop NATO-led Stabilization Force (SFOR), which continues to keep peace in Bosnia today.[35] Among the wide range of civilian activities, police monitoring and training would be handled by the United Nations Mission in Bosnia and Herzegovina (UNMIBH) and an International Police Task Force (IPTF), whose peak strength reached 2,027 unarmed personnel by the summer of 1997.[36] Elections were to be managed by the OSCE, which also oversees regional arms control and confidence-building measures. Dayton assigned the return of refugees and displaced persons to the UNHCR, with invited assistance from the International Committee of the Red Cross (ICRC), the United Nations Development Programme (UNDP), and other humanitarian organizations. An independent international arbitrator would preside over the Brcko process. Finally, human rights issues involved several implementing organizations, including the OSCE, the Council of Europe, the UN Commission on Human Rights, and the European Court of Human Rights. Additional major responsibilities, not detailed in the Dayton Agreement proper, included EU administration of the city of Mostar, which was heavily damaged by Croat-Bosniac fighting in 1993 and which remains divided between its Croatian west and Bosnian east,[37] and the management of reconstruction, absent from the Dayton Agreement but to be undertaken by a combination of multilateral and bilateral financial institutions, prominently led by the World Bank.

All told, at least seven major international organizations—NATO, UN, OSCE, EU, UNHCR, ICRC, and the World Bank—possessed principal responsibilities for peace implementation in Bosnia, not counting the active involvement of interested national governments, various special envoys, bilateral initiatives, and hundreds of nongovernmental organizations operating on the scene.

The panoply of civilian efforts was to be monitored and coordinated by an international High Representative—a position filled by a series of European diplomats since the office began in January 1996.[38] Dayton's text gave the High Representative minimal operational authority with which to exercise his responsibility for coordinating international activities, particularly if coordination is viewed as extending beyond information sharing to developing common strategies and implementing common plans with pooled resources. More problematic, the only government that could at the time exert significant leverage over either the parties or other implementers—namely, the U.S. government—was uninterested in giving the High Representative much-needed political backing. What the High Representative did enjoy was textual authority as the interpreter of last resort of the Dayton Agreement's civilian provisions and a capacity to establish new mechanisms (such as commissions or task forces) to help him execute his mandate.[39] In addition, an intergovernmental Peace Implementation Council (PIC) was created to oversee the whole process and "to mobilize international support behind Dayton implementation."[40] The five-nation Contact Group also provided an ongoing opportunity to harmonize the diplomatic efforts of its members and exert appropriate leverage on the parties.

What is missing from the agreement, or the burden on implementation. Notwithstanding the Dayton Agreement's comprehensiveness, several critical elements were missing from its approximately 130 pages of detailed text. In their collective absence, Dayton offered no strategy for implementing its own numerous provisions, let alone for moving beyond them to address issues that its text left unresolved. First, it provided no effective mechanism for dealing with continued conflict between the Bosniac and Croat communities that make up the federation. Should joint institutions be less than fully functioning and complete cooperation from these parties less than forthcoming, it is left to international implementers to develop strategies and instruments for dealing with any obstruction. The beleaguered experience of the European Union in Mostar and of the United Nations and Office of the High Representative since they took over from the EU in later 1996 demonstrates the weight of this burden.

The lesser attention to intrafederation conflict is also symbolically problematic: when the ostensible goal is to strengthen a unitary state and work to diminish mutual distrust among its three communities, it does not send a helpful message to devote most international attention to only one of Bosnia's dividing lines.

Second, the agreement provided no direction to the parties or to implementers on the relative importance of its various provisions or the need to set priorities among them, and no hint of the consequences should those priorities not be established or wisely set. On the strictly military side, the agreement contained implicit priorities with its highly detailed calendar to which the parties were to adhere. On the political and civilian side, however, the agreement seriously imposed a timetable on only two obligations: reaching an arbitration decision on the status of Brcko and holding national elections.[41] Apart from these, the peace agreement amounts to a laundry list of critical issues—demobilization and police reform, elections, constitutional reform, human rights guarantees, refugee return, and so on—with no light shed on the relationship among them. What effect were elections likely to have, for instance, if held in the absence of basic civilian security or confidence among Bosnia's displaced that they would be able to return? What was the likely impact of pushing the issue of return in an economic and security context that only plausibly allowed the displaced to return to majority areas? Could one seriously embark upon police reform and enforcement of human rights should NATO not accept that part of its mandate that involved armed civilian groups, reservists, or paramilitaries? The Dayton Agreement need not have been expected to make such judgments, but its international implementers could not avoid them.

Third, the agreement gave no guidance on how to manage its chief contradiction: namely, between integration and de facto partition. On the one hand, Dayton tried to reunite the warring parties and peoples through pledges to create joint institutions and, more, through a right of return that promised a demographic reversal of the entire war. On the other, the settlement froze the lines of confrontation between Serb and Federation areas and within the Federation and derived political rights from this division, while the accord's principal backer pledged to "equip and train" the army of only one of the three parties, the Bosniac-dominated central government. Such issues would unavoidably give the international community an opportunity to show whether it had overcome the ambivalence it manifested during the Bosnian war or whether it was still of mixed minds about the nature and level of its commitment to an independent, multinational Bosnia.

For these lacunae, the Dayton Agreement was less to be faulted than frankly assessed and supplemented. Having been arrived at by coerced compromise, it contained tension as well as ambiguity among its provisions that would have to be worked out during implementation. This did not make it fatally flawed, as some critics argued, only predictable.[42] The Dayton Agreement, then, offered neither a clear political outcome nor a strategy for building peace. What it offered was a cease-fire amid a daunting set of challenges: parties whose objectives had not changed and who remained in power, plans for power sharing that threatened to consolidate national exclusion rather than mitigate it, and social wounds from a war fought with extraordinary cruelty. While international implementers could hardly be asked to build peace in such a context on their own, they could legitimately be asked to put their efforts coherently and effectively behind a well-conceived course of action. In short, they could be asked to define a set of objectives that would guide their work with Bosnia's parties and peoples, and to design a strategy to achieve them.

Impact of International Intervention

Generally, there is some merit in the conventional view that military implementation was an early success while civilian implementation has flagged. Certainly, those military provisions to which NATO leadership devoted their resources were efficiently implemented according to the agreed-upon timetable. The IEBL was stabilized (with the important exception of Brcko) and multiple small adjustments to it were made peacefully; troops and heavy weapons were redeployed as required and are regularly inspected by NATO-led troops; foreign forces were basically removed; and there has not been a single military-on-military clash since the war ended. This is no mean accomplishment, and no subsequent criticism should eclipse NATO's tremendous achievement in stabilizing Bosnia's cease-fire.

On the civilian side, progress has been much more uneven. Several rounds of elections have been held, the two national-level elections on schedule, although with serious problems, as will be discussed below.[43] Bosnia's joint power-sharing institutions also began to function by late 1996. Although these have been slow to accomplish much substantively and have been characterized as much by backsliding and recalcitrance as by active cooperation, this was to be expected. After all, they represent an institutional attempt to reconcile parties whose aims never changed but who were convinced by circumstance that the battlefield was not the best place to pursue them.[44] Their slow and frustrated progress does not make them a failure; both the parties and their international interlocutors deserve credit that they work at all.[45] In addition, there have been some positive steps on returning Bosnia's refugees and displaced, particularly to majority areas.[46] A fair amount of reconstruction has occurred as well, though little has translated into widespread job creation because of a greater emphasis on infrastructure.[47]

More troublesome, the conditions that have prevailed throughout Bosnia and Herzegovina for several years after the war formally ended, especially in Serb and Croat-controlled areas, worked actively against the resumption of "normal conditions of life" called for in the Dayton Agreement. Residents still face what UNHCR has characterized as a "climate of fear and intimidation," especially in minority areas.[48] The power of nationalist authorities remains essentially unbroken; and dynamics pushing toward effective partition are still stronger than those pushing toward integration. Perhaps worse, choices made and priorities set by international parties during implementation have contributed powerfully to this bleaker side of the picture.

The First Round of National Elections

National elections occupy a pivotal place in Dayton's inventory of provisions as the chief mechanism for launching Bosnia's new power-sharing institutions and giving them democratic legitimacy. The Dayton Agreement put the first round of postwar national elections on a tight schedule, stipulating that they be held no later than nine months after the treaty's entry into force, or mid-September 1996. Dayton authorized the OSCE to oversee all aspects of the Bosnian elections, from certifying whether basic conditions for free and fair elections prevailed to details of their preparation and execution. A Provisional Electoral Commission comprised of both Bosnian and international representatives was also established; among its assignments, it was given the critical responsibility for determining rules for voter registration. The Dayton Agreement placed far greater emphasis on the timing of elections than on establishing or sustaining their necessary conditions, with national elections being the only strictly civilian provision to carry an explicit deadline and with no specific mechanism provided to ensure that the results of elections will be implemented.[49] Perhaps not surprisingly, other components of democratization beyond national elections—such as strengthening the rule of law, protecting basic rights and liberties, and encouraging independent media—are scattered through less enforceable parts of the agreement.

Furious debate attended the lead-up to national elections in September 1996, concerning the wisdom of holding them on schedule, the readiness of the international community—specifically the OSCE—to preside over them, and the longevity of a multinational military commitment to Bosnia in their aftermath.[50] There were two primary arguments in favor of holding elections that September. First, most European and U.S. diplomats expressed the view that elections were the essential first step in getting Bosnia's new joint institutions off the ground, which themselves were crucial to knitting the country's fractured communities back together. This view was strengthened by the tendency among U.S. policymakers, in particular, to equate democracy with elections and neglect the wider array of social, political, and institutional factors needed for democratic success. Second, and arguably decisive, was stark pressure within and from the U.S. government to reinforce their position that Dayton implementation—and U.S. commitment to it—would essentially be over within one year. The year 1996 was a presidential election year in the United States. With the shadow of Somalia not long in the distance, the Clinton administration had promised that U.S. troops would be out of Bosnia by December 1996. Other NATO members had signaled that they would quit Bosnia themselves without a continuing U.S. involvement. Since no one believed that a nationwide poll in Bosnia could be held in the absence of IFOR's substantial military presence, postponement was inconceivable so long as a public commitment to withdraw U.S. troops was maintained. A related but much less persuasive argument was that the Dayton timetable had to be strictly observed in order to keep pressure on the parties to meet their obligations. The arguments against holding elections pointed to the social and political conditions on the ground and the manifest underpreparation of the OSCE. Critics predicted, accurately as it turned out, that the national elections would restore to power the war-time leaderships least likely to commit themselves to building peace, only this time with democratic legitimacy.[51]

Initial ex post facto debate tended to focus on whether the conduct of the elections had been technically free and fair: how many registrations were botched, what number of ballots might have been miscounted, and so on. The independent International Crisis Group, which has been one of the tougher critics of the 1996 elections, identified the following problems: a higher number of voters than was technically possible, poor handling of refugee registration and out-of-country voting,[52] a shortfall of between 5 percent and 15 percent of registered voters from official lists, the decision to locate several polling stations at sites of major war-time violence, technical decisions made without full disclosure to candidates and voters, ballots that were not in the custody of accountable parties when moved from polling stations to counting centers, and the mystifying OSCE decision to destroy all ballots one week after votes were certified based on a regulation adopted the day before elections were held.[53] Of singular destructive impact was a technical judgment made by the OSCE and the Provisional Electoral Commission to allow voters to register where they intended to live, as opposed to where they currently resided or where they had lived before the war. While undoubtedly motivated by sensitivity to the circumstances of the uprooted, the impact of this now-notorious "P-2" form, in the absence of robust safeguards against fraud, was to create a legitimate mechanism, and an open invitation, for parties to manipulate further the ethnic balance of power within communities.

A much greater problem was the prevailing climate of fear and uncertainty; especially in the absence of any confidence that NATO or the United States would stay a course longer than December 1996, the elections could be counted upon to produce a victory for nationalist parties. Indicted war criminals still dominated political life; opposition political figures had been targets of attack;[54] freedom of media and of movement were minimal; civilians who belonged to minority communities were subject to systematic violence and intimidation by authorities; and brute uncertainty prevailed among Bosnia's residents and its refugees about whether their country could be rebuilt as one or would be split into three. In short, Bosnia's climate was one of such manifest insecurity that the rational vote for people to cast was for the nationalist parties, which most reliably, if narrowly, had always promised to protect their interests.

Over time, observers also began to recognize how constraining were the constitutional stipulations imposed by the Dayton Agreement—essentially, that there is no political office requiring a nationwide vote while there are several offices that restrict both voters and potential candidates by resident status in one entity or the other. Concerns over the divisive implications of these power-sharing arrangements have led to increasing and vocal calls either to revise Dayton itself or to embark on a concerted process of "soft amendment" of the Dayton constitution.[55] Given well-founded concerns about the risks of opening up the basic framework for peace established in 1995 for new rounds of negotiation, however, present efforts to escape Dayton's constraints have emphasized the softer option, largely through the laborious process of drafting a new electoral law for the country.[56]

Interpreting the Military Mandate

In the first critical years after the war ended, minority residents and opposition political figures were targets of systematic intimidation and harassment, which was often attributed to gangs but which demonstrably enjoyed acquiescence or active support from authorities. Many incidents took place at night, when international observers were the most remote. Empty houses were destroyed so that refugees could not return to them, returnees were harassed and driven out shortly after they arrived, or minority residents were forcibly expelled; minorities were detained at roadside checkpoints or threatened with arrest as suspected war criminals and sometimes beaten in police custody; mosques and churches were vandalized; haystacks have been burned and agricultural property damaged; and livestock and pets have been poisoned.[57] Dozens of incidents worthy of public report occurred after Dayton's signing, not counting the burning of Sarajevo's suburbs and the exodus of approximately sixty thousand Serbs in early 1996.[58]

Most incidents involved the prospect of return. The following are sadly representative. Between May and July 1996, hundreds of Bosniacs were expelled from Serb-controlled Teslic after a steady wave of verbal intimidation, bombings, beatings, and threats.[59] Croats who remained in Bosniac-controlled Bugojno were forcibly evicted in July 1996.[60] In October, 150 demonstrators stoned a commercial bus making an inaugural run across Croat-controlled territory to East Mostar while police stood by;[61] also in October, 250 displaced Serbs were prevented from visiting their prewar homes in Croat-controlled Drvar, and thirty-five homes were subsequently set on fire.[62] Ninety-six homes and two mosques were destroyed in Prijedor after UNHCR gave Serb authorities a list of Bosniacs who wished to visit their property.[63] All such incidents were paralleled by a pattern of arbitrary arrests, detentions, and harassment by authorities. Moreover, every episode carried a double punch—the event itself and the fear that similar attacks would follow.

While the parties were responsible for the range and frequency of these incidents, significant responsibility also belonged to NATO's political leadership, which decided at an early stage that this arena of confrontation was outside the bounds of IFOR's and SFOR's mandate, even though there was every reason to include it.[64]

The military annexes of the Dayton Agreement generally focused on interentity security, leaving unaddressed those front lines that still existed within the Federation between Bosniac and Croat forces or within Republika Srpska between Serb authorities and any still-resident non-Serb population.[65] However, under provisions for the "Cessation of Hostilities," the agreement included with its military provisions a broad array of security concerns that went beyond the narrowly military or strictly interentity. Here, the text recognized that nonmilitary actors could have military capability and should therefore be subject to the same obligations as the parties:

> Each Party shall ensure that all personnel and organizations with military capability under its control or within territory under its control, including armed civilian groups, national guards, army reserves, military police, and the Ministry of Internal Affairs Special Police (MUP) comply with this Annex.[66]

Dayton also recognized that even those without military capability could pose a security threat: "The Parties also commit themselves to disarm and disband all armed civilian groups, except for authorized police forces."[67] Most significant, the agreement required that:

> The Parties shall provide a safe and secure environment for all persons in their respective jurisdictions, by maintaining civilian law enforcement agencies operating in accordance with internationally recognized standards and with respect for internationally recognized human rights and fundamental freedoms, and by taking such other measures as appropriate.[68]

In addition, the parties were required to cooperate completely with all international personnel, "including investigators, advisors, monitors, observers, or other personnel in Bosnia pursuant to the General Framework Agreement," which itself referred to the International Criminal Tribunal for former Yugoslavia.[69]

Parallel to these obligations placed upon the parties were responsibilities assigned to IFOR. Military Annex 1-A enumerated several supporting tasks for the force, which included assistance to other international personnel, specifically naming UNHCR.[70] More important, IFOR was explicitly "to observe and prevent interference with the movement of civilian populations, refugees, and displaced persons, and to respond appropriately to deliberate violence to life and person."[71] This item carried enormous significance if realized in practice, particularly if read in conjunction with paragraphs three and four of the same article that, respectively, allowed NATO to use its own judgment to establish any "additional duties and responsibilities for the IFOR in implementing this Annex,"[72] and that granted IFOR's commander, "without interference or permission of any Party, [the authority] to do all that the Commander judges necessary and proper, including the use of military force to protect the IFOR and to carry out the responsibilities listed above in paragraphs 2, 3 and 4." Indeed, the Dayton Agreement reiterated on several counts IFOR's license to use any means necessary to fulfill the full measure of their mandate.

IFOR's, then SFOR's, primary responsibility was to ensure that the parties met their military obligations, which clearly included extramilitary components. The loophole was that the NATO-led force was permitted but not obligated to carry out these responsibilities: "the IFOR shall have the right to fulfill its supporting tasks, within the limits of its assigned principal tasks and available resources."[73] At the time of its deployment, IFOR was heavily shadowed by the UN's experience in Somalia and therefore determined to refrain from anything that looked like "nation-building" or "mission creeping."[74] This specter encouraged not only a strict segregation of IFOR's operation from civilian implementation but also an unjustifiably minimalist reading of its own military responsibilities. In the event, NATO's political leadership chose to restrict its focus to the most narrowly military components of its mandate, with the upshot being that a heavily armed multinational force of close to sixty thousand troops (under SFOR, thirty-one thousand) presided over a protracted "security gap" through which Bosnian civilians fell by the day. With them went opportunities to rebuild a state with room for multiple nationalities.

Moreover, although this pattern of violence was not strictly military, it has not been nonmilitary either. Targeting civilians to move them forcibly from one part of the country to another resembled the coercive instruments used for the same purpose during the war. That it was not soldiers per se who were targeting civilians was also less significant a distinction than it might have appeared. Recall that throughout the wars of the former Yugoslavia, belligerents had at their disposal paramilitary groups as well as regular and special police, which they developed and used with extreme ferocity. Civilians and their property were primary targets of military campaigns, the campaigns themselves waged by a combination of paramilitary, police, and reserve forces along with regular military units.

Nor was there evidence that post-Dayton violence was beyond the control of political authorities. Just the opposite: in almost all incidents, local authorities were shown to have been involved, either directly—as in February 1997, when Croatian police in West Mostar fired into a crowd of unarmed Bosniac civilians attempting to visit a cemetery on a Muslim holiday, killing one and injuring twenty—or indirectly, when local police failed to protect civilians or their property when these have been targeted by armed groups.[75] As expressed in a statement of the PIC steering board in June 1997, "the police not only frequently condone violence on ethnic and political grounds, they are often responsible for the violations themselves."[76]

With time, SFOR steadily invigorated its approach to Bosnian intransigence. As of August 1997, SFOR began inspecting and confiscating weapons from paramilitary special police units, making these units subject for the first time to NATO oversight. NATO also authorized SFOR to take all necessary measures against inflammatory radio and television broadcasters whenever requested by the High Representative, which the force has continued to do episodically since 1997. SFOR has also been working more closely with the IPTF and taken some initiatives to give greater protection to returning refugees. In addition, SFOR troops started moving against "persons indicted for war crimes," a trend that was powerfully encouraged by the International Criminal Tribunal's indictment of Serbian president Milosevic during the war over Kosovo in the spring 1999.

In this chapter I contend that such efforts were too little, too late. SFOR's attention to special police, for instance, seemed designed principally to weaken the forces protecting Karadzic and other hard-line Serb leaders after SFOR had publicly committed troops to protecting Biljana Plavsic, the president of Republika Srpska who broke with Karadzic loyalists and was then openly supported by the international community. Analogously, the timing of SFOR's initial challenge to hard-line Serb media suggested a greater interest in shutting down broadcasts that might incite violence against NATO and other international personnel than in contributing to a comprehensive policy to support independent media in Bosnia as a whole. Most critical, the apprehension of indicted war criminals, although a key objective, has yet to be nested within a broader effort to address ongoing threats to civilian security, particularly in the context of return, and to put the peace process in Bosnia on a firmer political and social foundation. Weakening the hold of extremists is tightly linked to protecting civilians and strengthening a peace process. Standing alone, however, it will not redress the institutionalized problems of security forces who answer only to hard-line and deeply entrenched political authorities, none of whom have yet shown a serious commitment to a common and democratic peace.

Protecting Human Rights, Freedom of Movement, and Right of Return

Since the war began and continuing since it ended, a pitched debate has taken place among international observers about whether stability in Bosnia rests on a partitioned country or a united one. Frequently, this debate revolves around speculation about what the popular traffic will bear: at its simplistic worst, either Bosnians have been implacable enemies for centuries and prefer ethnic separation or they have lived in a multinational idyll for centuries and want now to re-create it. Yet the only way to gain purchase on what people truly want—and are therefore likely to sustain—is to enable them to choose under conditions of genuine openness and security.

Unfortunately, questions of human rights and freedom of movement, which centrally affect the possibility of return, commanded a much lower priority than they should have in the first phase of Dayton implementation. Such issues are inherently difficult to address. Their lesser priority is also attributable in no small measure to NATO's unwillingness to address a broader array of security concerns, to the extraordinary pressure to hold national elections, and to a hoary disinclination among international actors to intrude upon the intimate relations between political authorities and their citizens. This disinclination is unfortunate, particularly in a context of third-party peace implementation that already intrudes upon domestic jurisdiction in multiple ways. In the context of Bosnia, according a lesser priority to human and civil rights represented a persistently missed opportunity by the international community to reinforce its commitment to a unitary Bosnian state and to strengthen popular constituencies for peace.

To the pattern of overt violence previously described must be added further impediments to the resumption of normal living conditions. Bosnians have faced enormous obstacles to their freedom of movement across entity or intra-Federation lines since the Dayton Agreement was signed. Literal impediments were imposed in the form of roadside checkpoints. There was initial progress in early 1996 when illegal checkpoints were banned and the parties generally complied, but over the course of 1996 and early 1997, roadside checks began to proliferate again, occasioning a second crackdown by IPTF and SFOR in the spring.[77] Bureaucratic obstacles are also common. Taxes and "visa" fees have been routinely imposed on people trying to move around what is intended to be one country. Wartime property laws actively discourage return and any mobility dependent on fair compensation for property. Access is often denied to personal and official records, to reconstruction and business loans, and to basic services like education and medical care. As in the former Yugoslavia, jobs, pensions, social services, housing, and education remain largely a state prerogative; administrative authorities therefore enjoy a still-unchecked capacity to deny a range of civil and economic rights to minority populations or opposition figures.

Equally daunting, each national community in Bosnia has effectively created its own symbolic exclusion zone with very practical consequences for freedom of movement and normal living conditions. For several years after the war ended, Bosnia operated with three sets of license plates;[78] three international telephone exchanges;[79] three currencies;[80] two alphabets;[81] increasingly, three languages;[82] and especially disturbing, three school systems.[83]

The persistence of such conditions directly militated against Dayton's specific guarantees that Bosnia's residents could return voluntarily to their prewar homes, that they could have their basic human rights protected, and that they could have confidence in a future increasingly respectful of democratic participation and the rule of law. The figures on return tell the statistical tale. In 1996, roughly 252,000 refugees and internally displaced persons returned to Bosnia.[84] During the same year, approximately ninety thousand left.[85] Of the former, most returned to areas where they belonged to the national majority; most of the latter were leaving areas in which they belonged to the minority.[86] In 1997, under 10,000 of a pool of 178,000 returnees were minority returns, in the High Representative's view, "because of continued political, security and administrative obstacles."[87] In 1998, a higher number were considered minority returns—33,359—but the overall pool remained small (127,800 refugees and internally displaced) and most still returned to majority areas.[88] Pressure from host governments to send Bosnian refugees back, coupled with the inadequacy of local conditions, placed UNHCR and other humanitarian groups working on return in the difficult position that they could responsibly facilitate returns only to majority areas.[89]

Only in mid-1997 did international implementers begin focusing serious attention on these issues that so directly affect the prospects for normal life among Bosnia's citizens. When the PIC met in Sintra, Portugal, in May 1997, it reiterated the international commitment to a united, multiethnic Bosnia and took an especially tough stance on issues that relate practically to Bosnia's current and would-be residents: moving toward a uniform system of car registration, integrating the country's telephone systems, opening regional airports, and amending property laws that "place insurmountable legal barriers in the path of return."[90] The Sintra meeting also called for international aid to be made conditional upon the willingness of local authorities to accept minority return. One of Sintra's more dramatic innovations was to give the High Representative authority to curb or suspend inflammatory media, which he actively put into effect against Serb broadcasts in the following months.[91] Seven months after Sintra, the PIC met again in Bonn and reiterated the expanded authority they expected the High Representative to exercise in the face of recalcitrance by the parties. Since then, the High Representative has resorted to his so-called Bonn powers repeatedly in order to make headway on issues from the common national anthem to privatization.

Sintra and Bonn represented a breakthrough, but an ironic one. The PIC's tough language, asserting a different mix of international priorities and according new operational authority to the High Representative, was desperately welcome and has proved to be instrumental in pushing the parties on particular issues. There was nothing in the PIC's assertiveness in late 1997, however, not one item, that could not have happened a year and a half earlier.

Lessons for Bosnia's Future

By 1999, nearly four years after war formally ended in Bosnia, the international operation in Bosnia had settled in for a protracted presence. Most recognize that Bosnia's respite from war is unlikely to be sustainable in the absence of NATO peacekeepers and that beyond the absence of war, social and political peace remain to be built.[92] For any serious headway to be made, the international community will have to redirect its efforts at strengthening the popular stratum of Bosnian society where peace can best be built.

In significant part, this necessitates greater strategic coordination among international efforts. Political resources were squandered for almost two years by divergent strategies among agencies and involved governments. Senior officials at most major implementing agencies persistently described a chaotic blend of different mandates, incompatible timetables, and divided leadership among their respective executive bodies.[93] Early on, doubts about the effectiveness of the High Representative discouraged investment of material and diplomatic resources in that office, which proved the doubts accurate but for the wrong reason. From the very beginning, the office could have attained the capacity it only acquired later at Bonn. Competing agendas among international actors also created a field day for the Bosnian parties who had skillfully manipulated such divisions during the war. The predictable obstruction from local parties and the clear need for ongoing negotiation made it crucial from the outset that international efforts be internally unified and organizationally coherent. One lesson emerging from the Bosnian experience is that the Dayton model of decentralized peace implementation is singularly counterproductive after a negotiated and significantly open-ended settlement.

Of specific importance is greater integration of military and civilian implementation, the lack of which has created a particularly destructive vacuum.[94] Just as it took a serious partnership between military force and diplomacy to bring the Bosnian war to an end, the success of the civilian components of peace implementation depends upon their having integrally available the military capital of SFOR or any successor mission. The impact of IFOR's and SFOR's early inattention to the extramilitary components of their mandate has been corrosive. Allowing several years to pass during which civilians were regularly and predictably targeted, and throughout which they had diminishing expectations that basic security of their persons and property could be assured, strengthened the hands of nationalist authorities and dampened faith that a nonnationalist Bosnia might be possible. Though laudable, SFOR's later efforts to support elected minority politicians risk being insufficient after so much ground had been effectively lost.

Also important is that the first two years of what was widely perceived as IFOR's and SFOR's relative inaction deprived civilian mediators of the leverage that could come from having NATO resources support their efforts. The negotiating does not end with a settlement, after all, particularly when the parties could be expected to try end runs around it.

Most critical, the question of partition lingers. Even had international efforts been coordinated on the ground and civilian activities bolstered with appropriate military resources, a profound ambivalence has existed among international actors about the shape of postwar Bosnia. The Dayton Agreement left this question open, effecting a compromise between unity and division that was unwieldy at best. Dynamics on the ground have pulled in alternate directions, with mononationalism clearly the dominant trend.

It is not always easy to make the case against partition, since some of the best evidence that many Bosnians do not want it exists at the community level, where resources are scarce and media and intergovernmental attention low. It is also tempting to embrace an argument for partition that could help justify the inadequacy of several years of multibillion-dollar international implementation. Whatever one's initial instincts, the debate needs to be had and to be had well, with empirical accuracy and a sober assessment of the impact of international efforts to date, given the implications for other war-torn countries where international interest may run high but political coherence somewhat less so.

Many international observers are inclined to argue that the decision is best left to Bosnians. A fine position but one that begs the question, "Which Bosnians?" Hard-line leaders are happy to decide themselves, since they still control most instruments for steering the population, and therefore the outcome, their way. More moderate leaders and representatives of many citizens' groups also welcome the opportunity to decide but need a good deal of international support in order to do so. U.S. Senator Kay Bailey Hutchison rightly rejected a political solution for Bosnia that was imposed from outside,[95] but equally, one should reject a political solution that is imposed by authoritarian and corrupt politics from the inside. The objective of international efforts should be to establish and stabilize those conditions in which Bosnians can securely and democratically choose. The sheer fact of uncertainty strengthened the position of Bosnia's partitionists, especially in the first two years of implementation. Under persisting conditions, with mononational parties secure in their respective political, administrative, and economic control, who would expect that Bosnia's citizens would not fulfil the prophecy that the only way for them to live is to live apart?

For many, living side by side would take time, and some may never seek it. Yet others clearly do, if only because living multinationally will allow them to return to the areas from which they were driven during the war. In 1996, three-quarters of the refugees returning did so spontaneously.[96] In the 1997 municipal elections, parties representing displaced persons won a majority of council seats in six municipalities (five in the Federation, one in Republika Srpska).[97] In eighty-nine municipalities, displaced voters cast ballots in their prewar municipalities and elected representatives to those councils: forty-two municipalities now have between 20 percent and 49 percent of their seats occupied by representatives of the displaced, and forty-seven municipalities have up to 20 percent of their seats so occupied.[98] Implementing these results has posed a steep challenge that continues to depend heavily on the seriousness of international commitment to see them realized. Furthermore, those familiar with community-level dynamics in Bosnia view this issue through a different lens. They do not describe a population ideologically committed to multiethnicity, but they do see a serious and widespread interest in resuming normal, safe, and productive lives where questions of nationality are marginal.[99]

The Dayton settlement was reached in large part because the balance of forces on the ground changed. Building peace in Bosnia also demands that the balance on the ground shifts, but instead of rearranging the holdings of Serbs, Croats, and Bosniacs, it requires a transfer of power from existing political and administrative authorities to more democratic institutions and constituencies. Although typical of the work of diplomats and large organizations, one of the more disheartening aspects of international activity in Bosnia has been its generally disproportionate focus on Bosnia's ruling elites.

Even though working with political leaderships is essential to implementing a peace agreement to which they are signatories, and while elites enjoy greater capacity to obstruct that process, the international community has chronically missed opportunities to engage directly with those segments of Bosnia's population that could provide the most powerful opposition to the nationalism that tore the country apart. Today, the challenge is not just to sustain the current level of involvement but to redirect it and to channel international resources strategically to those constituencies in Bosnia most committed to a common peace.

Notes

1. After three years at a troop strength of roughly 30,000, SFOR was restructured and downsized to approximately 20,000 troops, based both on perceived security needs in Bosnia and on the need for troops in Kosovo. See http://www.nato.int/sfor/docu/d981116a.htm.

2. For a discussion of peace implementation after civil wars, see Stephen John Stedman and Donald Rothchild, "Peace Operations: From Short-Term to Long-Term Commitment," in *Beyond the Emergency: Development Within UN Peace Missions,* a special issue, ed. Jeremy Ginifer, of *International Peacekeeping* 3, 2 (Summer 1996).

3. The Yugoslav state comprised six republics (Croatia, Serbia, Bosnia and Herzegovina, Slovenia, Montenegro, and Macedonia); two semiautonomous provinces linked to Serbia (Kosovo and Vojvodina); and six constituent nationalities (Croatian, Serbian, Slovenian, Montenegrin, Macedonian, and Muslim, the last having become an official Yugoslav nationality with constitutional amendments in 1974).

4. Unlike other republics, Bosnia also had a collective presidency comprised of two Muslims, two Serbs, two Croats, and one Yugoslav.

5. Among scholars of Yugoslavia, Susan L. Woodward most systematically treats the country's dissolution as an example of state failure, with particular emphasis on its inability to function economically. See her *Balkan Tragedy: Chaos and Dissolution After the Cold War* (Washington, D.C.: The Brookings Institution, 1995).

6. See Stuart Kaufman, "The Irresistible Force and the Imperceptible Object: The Yugoslav Breakup and Western Policy," *Security Studies* 4, 2 (Winter 1994/95): 281–329; David A. Lake and Donald Rothchild, "Ethnic Fears and Global Engagement: The International Spread and Management of Ethnic Conflict," Policy Paper no. 20 (San Diego: University of California Institute on Global Conflict and Cooperation, January 1996); and Barry R. Posen, "The Security Dilemma and Ethnic Conflict," in *Ethnic Conflict and International Security,* ed. Michael E. Brown (Princeton: Princeton University Press, 1993). Each of these authors emphasizes situations of uncertainty and what Posen labels "emerging anarchy" (103) as critically enabling ethnic conflict. The concept of "plausible futures" is from Lake and Rothchild (8–9).

7. Slovenia had expressed its intention to secede in 1989, and of all the moves toward independence, its made the most sense. It was the westernmost republic, nationally homogeneous (over 90 percent Slovenian), with its own language, and economically best poised to operate independently of the rest of Yugoslavia.

8. In August 1990, Serb radicals declared independence, which they effectively retained until mid-1995 when the Croatian army, then better armed and trained, retook the region, expelling virtually all of its Serb population.

9. According to the last prewar census in 1991, Bosnia's population was 44 percent Muslim, 31 percent Serb, 17 percent Croat, and 8 percent Yugoslav and other. Figures cited by Woodward, *Balkan Tragedy,* 33.

10. Fear that such rights might disappear was not without basis, though it was also extravagantly stoked and manipulated by Serbian and Croatian leaders. Yugoslavia's delicate balance of powers among its republics and constituent nationalities would be called into question, at least constitutionally, once a republic became an independent state. Croat, Serb, and Muslim status as constituent nations of the Federal Republic of Yugoslavia (along with Slovene, Montenegrin, and Macedonian) did not guarantee them equal status as constituent nations of Bosnia. It did not ease concern when Izetbegovic announced that the SDA opposed national power sharing in Bosnia in favor of one man, one vote, a change that favored the larger Muslim population. See Laura Silber and Allan Little, *Yugoslavia: Death of a Nation* (New York: TV Books, Inc., 1995), 209.

11. Dr. Kemal Hrelja, "Review of the Economic and Social Situation in Bosnia and Herzegovina, 1986–1996," paper presented at a workshop on Reconstruction, Reform, and Economic Management in Bosnia and Herzegovina, sponsored by UNDP, UN Department of Development Support and Management Services, and the Vienna Institute for Comparative Economic Studies (Vienna, October 8–9, 1996), 42–57. See also the World Bank reports prepared for the Second Donors' Conference for Bosnia and Herzegovina, "Towards Economic Recovery," Discussion Paper no. 1 (April 2, 1996); and "Bosnia and Herzegovina: The Priority Reconstruction and Recovery Program: The Challenges Ahead," Discussion Paper no. 2 (April 2, 1996).

12. Beginning with the Carrington Plan of 1991, which was designed to prevent the war from ever breaking out, these included the Cuteiliero Plan in March 1992 (both under the auspices of the European Community Conference on the Former Yugoslavia, or ECCY); the Vance-Owen Peace Plan of 1993 (which proposed a division of Bosnia into ten ethnically balanced cantons); the Union of Three Republics Plan, and the Invincible Plan (all three generated by the EC/EU–UN International Conference on the Former Socialist Federal Republic of Yugoslavia, or ICFY); and the five-nation Contact Group's proposals of 1994, which were revived in the form of the Dayton Agreement. One of the more detailed accounts of the negotiating history is that of David Owen, for almost three years cochairman of the ICFY steering group. See his *Balkan Odyssey* (New York: Harcourt Brace & Company, 1995).

13. After U.S. Secretary of State James Baker traveled to Belgrade and Zagreb on June 21, 1991, in an eleventh-hour effort to defuse the crisis over Croatia and Slovenia, he explained the absence of U.S. interests in Yugoslavia with the phrase: "We don't have a dog in this fight." Silber and Little, 201.

14. On U.S. strategy and the role of the Bosniac-Croat alliance within it, see Daniel Serwer, "A Bosnian Federation Memoir," in *Herding Cats: Multiparty Mediation in a Complex World,* ed. Chester A. Crocker, Fen Osler Hampson, and

Pamela Aall (Washington, D.C.: United States Institute of Peace Press, 1999), 547–586.

15. The full-throttle confrontation that began in April 1993 has been partially attributed to the Bosnian government's rejection of the Vance-Owen Peace Plan, whose terms were particularly favorable to Bosnian Croats. See for example, Misha Glenny, "Yugoslavia: The Great Fall," *New York Review of Books* 42, 5 (March 23, 1995): 63. Though a contributing cause, active Bosniac-Croat conflict began months before Vance-Owen was revealed and had in fact been presaged by mutual hostilities from the time Yugoslavia began to disintegrate. Particularly good on this subject is Chapter 22 in Silber and Little, 291–302.

16. This was not just about Bosnia, since Serbs in Croatia still held the territory they had gained in 1991–1992 in Krajina and Western Slavonia, where the autonomist Serb rebellion began in 1990, and in Eastern Slavonia.

17. A United Nations Protection Force was established in February 1992 to facilitate cease-fire in Croatia and as a complement to ongoing international mediation efforts. UNPROFOR's mandate was subsequently extended to Bosnia and came to include responsibility for six designated "Safe Areas." The first Safe Area declared was Srebrenica. See Security Council Resolution 819, UN Doc. S/Res/819 (1993), paras. 1–4. The safe-area concept was extended to Sarajevo, Tuzla, Zepa, Gorazde, and Bihac with SCR 824, UN Doc. S/Res/824 (1993), paras. 3–4.

18. After the first strike against a Serb ammunition depot near Pale on May 25, the response was Serb bombardment of all UN-designated Safe Areas except Zepa; seventy-one people were killed in Tuzla alone. After the second strike against the Serb depot on May 26, the response was to take close to four hundred UN personnel hostage over the following few days. *Report of the Secretary-General Pursuant to Security Council Resolutions 982 and 987*, UN Doc. S/1995/444 (1995). See also Stephen Engelberg and Eric Schmitt, "Air Raids and UN Hostages Mark a Turn in Bosnia's War," *New York Times*, July 16, 1995, A1.

19. Srebrenica fell on July 12, six days after the Serb assault began. Zepa fell on July 25. The assault on Srebrenica stands as one of the most atrocious events of the war. Between 5,000 and 7,000 Muslim men are estimated to have been slaughtered during the week in July in which the town was taken by Serb forces. Beyond the obvious responsibility borne by Serb authorities for this bloodletting, many others have been accused of contributory culpability: the commander of local Bosnian forces who never arrived to help defend the town, the UN authorities who never managed to order the close air support when it was desperately needed, the U.S. authorities who are alleged to have known in advance but did nothing to prevent the assault on the town. On the UN role, see David Rohde, *Endgame: The Betrayal and Fall of Srebrenica, Europe's Worst Massacre Since World War II* (New York: Farrar, Straus and Giroux, 1997). On what U.S. authorities may have known, see Charles Lane and Thom Shanker, "Bosnia: What the CIA Didn't Tell Us," *New York Review of Books* 43, 8 (May 9, 1996), 14.

20. Silber and Little, 360. When defense of Gorazde was discussed in London, there was no mention of Zepa, which was under attack at the time.

21. SC Res. 713, UN Doc. S/Res/713 (September 25, 1991), para. 6, called for the embargo. In 1993, the Council drafted a resolution that was never adopted, which called for lifting the embargo against the Bosnian government on the grounds that it violated Bosnia's inherent right of self-defense. See UN Doc. S/25997 (June 29, 1993). U.S. congressional advocates of lifting the arms embargo also based much of their case on Bosnia's right to defend itself.

22. SC Res. 836 authorized UNPROFOR and regional organizations to use force to defend the safe havens.

23. As David Owen describes the situation at the end of August 1995: "For the first time since the autumn of 1992 UNPROFOR was no longer spread out across the whole of Bosnia-Herzegovina and vulnerable to Bosnian Serb retaliation and hostage-taking. UNPROFOR was out of Zepa, Srebrenica and Gorazde. Bihac was now safe. There were no significant UN forces in Serb controlled areas anywhere in Bosnia-Herzegovina. . . . It was inevitable, therefore, that the UN and NATO would take action against the Bosnian Serbs for the mortar bomb attack, which was a flagrant breach of the heavy weapons exclusion zone in Sarajevo." Owen, *Balkan Odyssey,* 331.

24. U.S. and European mediators were advocating as a basis for settlement that Bosniac and Croat forces would hold 51 percent of Bosnia's territory, and Serb forces the remaining 49 percent. The 51:49 formula had been floated by Contact Group negotiators in July 1994 but was rejected at the time. Owen, *Balkan Odyssey,* 279–286.

25. The UN Protected Areas (UNPAs), all in Croatia, were part of UNPROFOR's original mandate and distinct from the Safe Areas later established in Bosnia.

26. Another 50,000 soldiers fled as well. Søren Jessen-Petersen, UNHCR Special Envoy, remarks at a joint UNHCR-IPA conference, "Healing the Wounds: Refugees, Reconstruction and Reconciliation" (Princeton, NJ: June 30–July 1, 1996).

27. Owen, *Balkan Odyssey,* 335.

28. The tension underlying this compromise meant that the final political outcome for Bosnia remained fundamentally uncertain, as it still does. Susan L. Woodward was an early and outspoken commentator on this issue of Dayton's open-endedness. See her "Implementing Peace in Bosnia and Herzegovina: A Post-Dayton Primer and Memorandum of Warning," Brookings Discussion Papers (Washington, D.C.: Brookings Institution, May 1996), especially 10–13; and "America's Bosnia Policy: The Work Ahead," Brookings Institution policy brief no. 2 (Washington, D.C.: Brookings Institution, July 1996).

In this the Dayton Agreement differed qualitatively from the other peace accord reached that fall between Croatia and Serbia over the final status of Eastern Slavonia. See *Basic Agreement on the Region of Eastern Slavonia, Baranja and Western Sirmium,* UN Doc. S/1995/951 (November 15, 1995).

29. For the full text of the accord, see General Framework Agreement for Peace in Bosnia and Herzegovina, December 14, 1995, 35 I.L.M. 75 (hereafter, Dayton Agreement). Dayton's annexes, which make up approximately 130 pages of text, are numbered and titled as follows: (1-A) Military Aspects, (1-B) Regional Stabilization, (2) Inter-Entity Boundary Line (IEBL) and Related Issues, (3) Elections, (4) Constitution, (5) Arbitration, (6) Human Rights, (7) Refugees and Displaced Persons, (8) Commission to Preserve National Monuments, (9) Bosnia-Herzegovina Public Corporations, (10) Civilian Implementation, and (11) International Police Task Force.

30. IFOR was a NATO-led force, under the authority and command of the North Atlantic Council, though it included troops from non-NATO members.

31. The parties are required to settle its fate by "final and binding" arbitration within one year of the Dayton Agreement's signing, or by December 15, 1996. Dayton Agreement, Annex 2, art. V, para. 5.

32. Ibid., Annex 7, art. I, paras. 1–3, cover the basic obligations described.

33. Ibid., Annex 7, art. VII, establishes the Commission for Displaced Persons and Refugees, to be comprised of international and Bosnian members.

34. Ibid., Annex 4, art. II, covers human rights, as does Annex 6 on "Human Rights and Fundamental Freedoms."

35. During its operation, until early 2000 when it was reduced to 20,000, IFOR troop strength ranged near 50,000; SFOR's troop strength has ranged between 31,000 and 36,500. Figures are cited in the monthly reports submitted by NATO to the Security Council. See, for example, the eleventh IFOR report, UN Doc. S/1996/880, para. 1, and the eighth monthly SFOR report, UN Doc. S/1997/718, para. 1.

36. *Report of the Secretary-General on the United Nations Mission in Bosnia and Herzegovina* (UNMIBH), UN Doc. S/1997/468, para. 3.

37. This job was subsequently transferred to the United Nations and the Office of the High Representative in late 1996.

38. Former Swedish prime minister Carl Bildt held the position from 1996 to April 1997. Bildt was succeeded by Spanish diplomat Carlos Westendorp who was followed in 1999 by Austrian Wolfgang Petritsch.

39. "The High Representative is the final authority in theatre regarding interpretation of this Agreement on the civilian implementation of the peace settlement," Dayton Agreement, Annex 10, art. V; which is analogous to the IFOR commander's being named the "final authority in theatre regarding interpretation of this agreement on the military aspects of the peace settlement" in Annex 1A, art. XII.

40. *Conclusions of the Peace Implementation Conference in London,* UN Doc. S/1995/1029 (December 12, 1995), para. 3. The PIC was created out of the remnants of the International Conference on the Former Yugoslavia that had been in operation since August 1991.

41. Other civilian provisions had deadlines but in practice they were much less consequential, largely because they were more technical or more easily obstructed: for example, the obligation to bring existing constitutions into conformity with the Dayton Constitution. Dayton Agreement, Annex 4, art. XII, para. 2.

42. Hutchison, for instance, calls on Clinton to "reconvene the Dayton parties to reassess the accords." Ivo H. Daalder makes a more substantial case for revising the Dayton Agreement in "Bosnia After SFOR: Options for Continued US Engagement," *Survival* 39, 4 (Winter 1997–98): 5–28.

43. Following the first round of national balloting in September 1996 were a "special" election for the Republika Srpska (RS) National Assembly in November 1997 after a split within the previously elected RS government; a second national ballot in September 1998; and two rounds of municipal balloting, in September 1997 (after three postponements) and April 2000, respectively.

44. Their functioning has been repeatedly obstructed from different sides, particularly Serb and Croat, over everything from timing of meetings to location.

45. The Office of the High Representative deserves special credit, as it has worked particularly hard on this issue of getting joint institutions up and running.

46. The phrases "majority/minority areas" or "majority/minority return" are shorthand to describe the return of individuals to areas where they belong to the majority national group or where they are in the minority.

47. Author interviews, Sarajevo, August 1998. See also Zlatko Hertic, Amela Sapcanin, and Susan L. Woodward, "Bosnia and Herzegovina," in *Good Intentions: Pledges of Aid for Postconflict Recovery,* ed. Shepard Forman and Stewart Patrick (Boulder, CO: Lynne Rienner, 2000), 326.

48. UNHCR, Humanitarian Issues Working Group, *Bosnia and Herzegovina: Repatriation and Return Operation 1997,* UN Doc. HIWG/97/2 (Geneva: April 23, 1997) (hereafter UNHCR Working Group), para. 40.

49. The Dayton text does itemize conditions for free, fair, and democratic elections in Annex 3, art. I, and in an attached OSCE document, "Attachment to Annex 3 on Elections."

50. Representative of this debate: Misha Glenny, "Decision Time in Bosnia," *New York Times,* September 8, 1996; Stephen S. Rosenfeld, "Sticking to the Dayton Accords," *Washington Post,* June 23, 1996; and Morton I. Abramowitz, "Bosnia: The Farce of Premature Elections," *Washington Post,* May 24, 1996.

51. Glenny writes: "Editorial writers have joined forces with such influential commentators as the financier and philanthropist George Soros and former Prime Minister Haris Silajdzic of Bosnia. All say roughly the same thing: that holding the elections will guarantee that Humpty remains dismembered and that the results of ethnic cleansing will be sanctioned by what is a bogus democratic gesture." *New York Times,* September 8, 1996.

52. This is not terribly surprising since registration for over 800,000 refugees living in dozens of host countries began just three months before the elections.

53. The International Crisis Group documents these and other flaws in the elections in "Elections in Bosnia and Herzegovina," ICG Bosnia Report no. 16 (September 22, 1996).

54. U.S. Special Envoy Richard Holbrooke brokered a deal on July 18, 1996, in which Radovan Karadzic agreed to step down as president of the Republika Srpska and refrain from public political activities. He nonetheless remained an active figure behind the scenes, as he does in a more beleaguered form today. The most widely reported incident was the physical attack on Haris Silajdzic, Bosnia's war-time foreign minister (then prime minister). As a candidate for a new multinational party, he was attacked on June 15, 1996, by a gang carrying SDA flags in Cazin. Jovan Kovacic, "Assault on Bosnian Leader Highlights Tension," *Reuters World Service,* June 16, 1996, available in LEXIS, News Library, Reuwld File.

55. Author interviews, Sarajevo, August 1998; New York, February and April 2000.

56. A draft permanent election law for Bosnia and Herzegovina was submitted to the Bosnian Parliamentary Assembly at the end of 1999 but by mid-2000 had yet to be adopted.

57. Interview, UN Civil Affairs Officer, Sarajevo, November 1996.

58. UNHCR, Executive Committee of the High Commissioner's Programme, "Update on Regional Developments in the Former Yugoslavia," UN Doc. EC/47/SC/CRP.18 (April 9, 1997), para. 3. The infamous burning of the suburbs began in early March 1996, in anticipation of their transfer to Federation authority. See also Dan De Luce, "Fires Burn in Lawless Sarajevo Suburb," *Reuters European Community Report,* March 9, 1996; and Chris Hedges, "Sarajevo District Burns," *New York Times,* March 18, 1996, A6.

59. UNHCR, Office of the Special Envoy, "Information Notes" (May 1996), 5. See also "Update: Non-Compliance with the Dayton Accords," *Human Rights Watch/Helsinki Report* 8, 12 (August 1996): 5.

60. Report of the Special Rapporteur on Former Yugoslavia, UN Doc. E/CN.4/1997/56 (January 29, 1997).

61. Office of the High Representative, Bulletin no. 22 (October 24, 1996), para. 9. From Internet: www.ohr.int/bulletins.htm.

62. The Drvar incident was repeated almost identically in May 1997, when twenty-four houses were set ablaze following a visit from an international mediator who called for Serbs to be able to return. Patrick Moore, "Croats Block Serb Refugees from Returning Home," *OMRI Daily Digest,* Part 2, no. 200 (October 15, 1996), archive available online at www.omri.cz/publications/DD/index.htm/; International Crisis Group, "House Burnings: Obstruction of the Right to Return to Drvar," ICG Bosnia Report no. 24, June 16, 1997, 1.

63. International Crisis Group, "Going Nowhere Fast: Refugees and Internally Displaced Persons in Bosnia and Herzegovina," ICG Bosnia Report no. 23, May 1, 1997, 43.

64. It should be made plain that all criticism of the NATO-led forces in Bosnia is directed at NATO's political leadership, not at the force commanders or troops on the ground who have operated within a particularly tight chain of command that gives them little interpretive leeway in fulfilling their mandate.

65. Parties are obliged not to "threaten or use force against the other Entity" or engage in "offensive operations," which is defined as "projecting forces or fire forward of a Party's own lines." Dayton Agreement, Annex 1-A, art. I, para. 2(a) and art. II, para. 1.

66. Ibid., Annex 1-A, art. II, para. 1.

67. Ibid., para. 3. This reference to Bosnian police stands in awkward relationship to the military provisions. On the one hand, the military annexes include the parties' obligation to ensure civilian security and to guarantee the professionalism of any security personnel operating within their jurisdiction. On the other hand, the only explicit mechanism provided for ensuring that police respect basic human rights and professional standards is the presence of a UN International Police Task Force, authorized under Annex 11.

68. Ibid. This phrase repeats identically the language in the new Bosnia Constitution, Annex 4, art. III, para. 2(c).

69. Ibid., Annex 1-A, art. II, paras. 1–4. See Article IX of the GFA for reference to the International Criminal Tribunal.

70. Ibid., art. VI, para. 3(c).

71. Ibid., para. 3(d).

72. Ibid., para. 4.

73. Ibid., para. 3.

74. Among other things, this led NATO governments to make the awkward distinction between "mission creep" and "mission evolution," in order to explain the extension of their mandate under SFOR.

75. Remarkably, this incident was caught on film. For official reports on this incident, see IPTF report, UN Doc. S/1997/204 (March 7, 1997); High Representative report, UN Doc. S/1997/201 (March 7, 1997); Bosnian government report, UN Doc. S/1997/183 (March 3, 1997); and follow-up IPTF report, UN Doc. S/1997/351 (May 5, 1997).

76. *Conclusions Reached at Sintra,* UN Doc. S/1997/434 (June 5, 1997), para. 55. The recognition that police were the primary abusers of human rights led

to a new authorization in December 1996 for IPTF to conduct independent investigations.

See also *Report of the Secretary-General:* "It has become apparent that most of the violations of human rights which occur in Bosnia and Herzegovina (by some estimates as many as 70 per cent) are the work of the police forces of the Entities themselves. This creates the need for independent investigation of such cases. It was therefore proposed by the United Nations at the second Peace Implementation Conference that this responsibility should be entrusted to IPTF, a proposal which attracted widespread support and was incorporated in the Conclusions of the London Conference." UN Doc. S/1996/1017 (December 9, 1996), para. 15.

77. "Vehicles bearing the license plates of the other entity, or the other party in the Federation, are regularly stopped and harassed by the local police, thereby preventing the population from exercising its right to move freely around the country." *Report of the Secretary-General on the UNMIBH,* UN Doc. S/1997/468 (June 16, 1997), paras. 5–6.

78. License plates display the red-checkered Croatian shield in Croat areas, the blue-and-gold fleur-de-lis in Bosniac areas, and Cyrillic letters and the orthodox cross in Serb territory.

79. Until late September 1997, one could not call across entity lines. Even from outside the country, one had to dial Republika Srpska via Serbia, and Croat parts of the Federation via Croatia.

80. The Croatian kuna, the Yugoslav dinar, and the Bosnian dinar, although deutschmarks are welcome almost everywhere.

81. Latin and Cyrillic.

82. Serbo-Croatian always had a Serbian and a Croatian variant and two alphabets. Croatia's early reassertion of national enthusiasm (preindependence) involved resurrecting old Croatian vocabulary to distinguish its language from its more Balkan sibling. Serbs have similarly reinforced historical differences that distinguish the variants. Bosniacs, in turn, who could hardly be expected to speak Serbian or Croatian, have begun to incorporate Turkic and Arabic vocabulary.

83. Interviews with Svjetlana Derajic, International Council of Voluntary Agencies, Sarajevo, November 1996; Peggy L. Hicks, Human Rights Officer, Office of the High Representative, Sarajevo, November 1996; and Julia Demichelis, Washington, D.C., October 31, 1997. See also Lee Hockstader, "In Bosnia, Classes Open on School Segregation," *Washington Post,* October 19, 1997, A20.

84. Of this number, 88,039 were refugees and 164,217 were internally displaced persons. See UNHCR Working Group, Annex I and Table 6, respectively.

85. Office of the High Representative, Bulletin no. 36 (February 11, 1997). From the Internet: www.ohr.int/bulletins.htm.

86. Among internally displaced, for example, 94 percent returned to majority areas. See UNHCR Working Group, Table 6.

87. Report of the High Representative to the Security Council (October 16, 1997), para. 61. From Internet. Statistics from UNHCR, Sarajevo Office, Statistical Summary, November 1998.

88. Ibid.

89. The numbers of Bosnians still without a durable resolution are daunting: 815,000 refugees outside the country and roughly 866,000 displaced internally within it. Among the refugees, UNHCR estimates that over half originate

from areas where they would now be a minority, underscoring the importance "for rapid progress in minority returns." UNHCR Working Group, paras. 17, 22.

90. Conclusions of the ministerial meeting of the PIC Steering Board, S/1997/434 (June 5, 1997), passim. The deadline for car registration was set at January 1998. The deadline for telephones, set at mid-July 1997, passed without progress; however, by September, some telephone communication across entity lines became possible for the first time since the war ended. It is extremely limited, however, allowing only for Sarajevo to place calls to Banja Luka, not reliably vice versa and not broadened beyond these major cities.

91. "The High Representative has the right to curtail or suspend any media network or programme whose output is in persistent and blatant contravention of either the spirit or letter of the Peace Agreement." Conclusions of the ministerial meeting of the PIC Steering Board, S/1997/434 (June 5, 1997), para. 70.

92. In the words of SFOR's new Force Commander, General Montgomery Meigs, "It's starting to come together . . . but it's been awfully slow—too slow." Craig R. Whitney, "And Still, Serbs Bar Muslims in Bosnia," *New York Times,* October 8, 1999.

93. Interviews with representatives of UNHCR, UN Civil Affairs, IPTF, Office of the High Representative, and OSCE in Zagreb, Sarajevo, Mostar, Banja Luka, and Brcko, November 1996; in Sarajevo, August 1998; and in New York, September 1999.

94. The counterexample is the UN Transitional Administration for Eastern Slavonia (UNTAES), which fully integrated its military and civilian components under a single command and which used this leverage repeatedly to positive effect. Interview with Jacques Paul Klein, former Transitional Administrator, November 25, 1997, Vukovar, Croatia.

95. "The United States is trying to re-create Bosnia in the American multiethnic, multicultural image—an Americanization of the Balkans, if you will," *New York Times,* September 11, 1997.

96. Annex 1, HIWG/97/2. Another indicator of such sentiment, even before the first municipal elections, was the success of the "Coalition for Return," the network of Bosnian and international organizations representing returnees and the right to return independent of nationality. The coalition was formed in 1996 at the initiative of then Deputy High Representative Michael Steiner, who believed that displaced persons and refugees had common interests that could unite them as a political movement.

97. The Republika Srpska municipality is Srebrenica, where representatives of the displaced won 52 percent of the seats.

98. International Crisis Group, ICG Analysis of 1997 Municipal Election Results (October 14, 1997). Press release taken from Internet. The total number of municipalities electing councils was 135, with a total of 4,789 seats. Total voter turnout was estimated at 87 percent.

99. Interviews with UN volunteers, UN Civil Affairs Officers, and staff of international and local NGOs in Sarajevo, Banja Luka, Pale, and Tuzla, November 1996.

Few analysts have written systematically about community-level peacebuilding in Bosnia, although anecdotes are abundant. A recent exception is work by Julia Demichelis and Iain Guest for the United States Institute of Peace. See Iain Guest, "Moving Beyond Ethnic Conflict: Community Peace Building in Bosnia and Eastern Slavonia (Croatia)," paper presented at the USAID conference, Promoting Democracy, Human Rights, and Reintegration in Postconflict Societies (Washington, D.C., October 30–31, 1997).

6

Building Peace in El Salvador: From Exception to Rule

Robert C. Orr

In less than a decade, El Salvador has transformed itself from a country whose name was once synonymous with death, torture, and destruction into what many now consider to be a "model" of reconciliation. Prominent international figures have hailed El Salvador as a "negotiated revolution," a "jewel in a crown of thorns," and "almost a miracle," and more important, Salvadorans on both sides of the conflict have acknowledged that the process has been successful, with many thinking it could be a model in helping other countries bring their own wars to an end.[1]

El Salvador was not always a source of optimism; in fact, quite the contrary. During the twelve-year civil war that began in 1979, approximately eighty thousand Salvadorans were killed, over half a million people were internally displaced, and over one million sought refuge in other countries, principally the United States.[2] This exodus from the country represented more than one-fifth of the prewar population of 4.8 million. The Salvadoran economy, once the envy of Central America, was devastated, with up to $2 billion in physical infrastructure destroyed.[3] Political and social institutions throughout the country suffered great reverses due to underfunding, corruption, and disuse, while in conflict zones (sixty-eight municipalities out of 262), no recognized government functions were being performed at all. The social fabric of Salvadoran society was severely damaged, as ideological polarization predominated and middle ground virtually disappeared.

Finally in 1990, after more than a decade of conflict and many failed efforts to secure peace, the United Nations became a central actor in the search for peace in El Salvador. The UN entered at a time when the Salvadoran conflict was increasingly "ripe" for a negotiated solution. A military stalemate had developed, and both sides were looking for a way out. This was reinforced by the fact that outside support for both sides was beginning to dry up with the end of the Cold War. After a two-year negotiation, in what the UN's principal mediator later called "almost laboratory conditions," the parties came to final agreement at the stroke of midnight on December 31, 1991.[4] On January 16, 1992, representatives of the Salvadoran government and the Farabundo Marti National Liberation Front (FMLN) signed a comprehensive peace agreement in Mexico City's Chapultepec Castle, officially bringing to an end twelve years of war. The UN's instrumental role in bringing about this peace and nurturing it through its delicate first years led many to hail El Salvador as a victory for UN peacemaking and peacekeeping efforts.

Indeed, in the broader international context of peace efforts, El Salvador stands out for its successes. In 1999, seven years since signing peace accords, El Salvador has avoided a return to war, the human rights situation has dramatically improved, a variety of new institutions have been built, the economy has grown, and democracy is increasingly taking hold. In addition, the United Nations peace mission has pulled out and the United States has dramatically reduced its presence in the country, proving the country's internal capacity to sustain the peace process beyond an extensive, intrusive international presence.

Despite these very real gains, however, the fundamental bases of peace in El Salvador are not yet consolidated. Many of the root causes of the war have yet to be meaningfully addressed, and vast elements of Salvadoran society have yet to enjoy the full benefits of peace. Although international peacemaking and peacekeeping efforts proved successful, the longer-term peacebuilding effort to solidify self-sustaining peace in El Salvador is much less assured.

This chapter will explore the root causes of the war in El Salvador, international attempts to address them and the ensuing results, and some general conclusions that can be drawn from El Salvador for other countries attempting to make the lasting transition to peace.

Roots of the Conflict

The road to armed conflict in El Salvador was a long, tortuous path that can be traced back at least as far as 1932, when between ten thousand and thirty thousand peasants and labor organizers were slaughtered in what became known as "La Matanza." Following decades of social tensions rooted in El Salvador's agrarian structure, volatile labor relations, and authoritarian government, El Salvador entered a particularly tumultuous period in the 1970s. An acute land shortage boiled over when hundreds of thousands of landless peasants were forced back into El Salvador from Honduras following the 1969 "Soccer War."[5] During the 1970s, a rapidly accelerating downward spiral of widespread repression and social mobilization culminated in a series of high-profile killings and massacres that gave rise to a military opposition to the government. While identifying the immediate catalysts of El Salvador's civil war is difficult, it can safely be said that increasing assassinations of popular leaders, including those of Father Rutilio Grande in 1977 and Archbishop Oscar Romero in 1980, as well as repeated massacres of demonstrators and civilians, such as at Plaza Libertad in 1977, Archbishop Romero's funeral in 1980, and the Sumpul River in 1981, helped to radicalize existing opposition organizations and convince them that armed force was the only possible way to protect themselves and achieve their social, economic, and political goals.[6] On October 10, 1980, five revolutionary organizations joined together to form the FMLN. On January 10, 1981, the FMLN launched a general offensive in various departments around the country, marking the start of a countrywide civil war.[7]

If the immediate catalysts of armed conflict in El Salvador were multiple, so too were its root causes. At least four major root causes can be identified, as well as two additional sustaining factors. The first of these causes was El Salvador's dramatic *social and economic inequality and poverty*, a factor cited by virtually all analysts of the war. In 1976, according to ministry of planning statistics, 50 percent of the urban population of El Salvador lived in poverty (unable to buy two basic food baskets) and 20 percent in extreme poverty (unable to buy one basic food basket), while the remaining 60 percent of the population living in rural areas was even worse off; GDP per capita was $200, less than one-fourth that of urban areas.[8] Even more than the grinding poverty, however, the pervasive inequality—economic and social—set the backdrop for the social explosion that would escalate into armed conflict. According to the World Bank: "An underlying cause of the civil war in El Salvador stems from the inequitable social and economic structures developed during colonial rule which led to the creation of a coffee oligarchy that controlled most of the country's land area and exploited the cheap wage labor of the rural population."[9] And according to the UN: "There is wide agreement that the root causes of the conflict were twofold: the power of the armed forces and the depth of social injustice, particularly in terms of land ownership."[10] Even the U.S. National Bipartisan Commission on Central America ("Kissinger Commission"), which emphasized the role of communist infiltration in the region, acknowledged the crucial role of social and economic inequality in causing and furthering the war.[11] Within El Salvador itself, representatives of both the left and the center also emphasized the role of social and economic inequality in causing the war.

A second root cause of the conflict in El Salvador, and again one identified by virtually all analysts and most participants in the war, was the *lack of political space* for dissent and opposition in the country. While elections were held throughout the war, there was never any possibility of participation for those parties left of center. Indeed, the left had learned the hard way what participation in the political system meant for them—in 1980, all six of the leftist leaders of the Revolutionary Democratic Front (FDR) had been killed, and as Constituent Assembly elections approached in 1982, all FMLN leaders' names were on published death squad lists. Even the U.S. ambassador and the Central Election Commission acknowledged that if the left chose to participate in the political system, it would have to "campaign from outside the country."[12] For years many who suffered exile, repression, and exclusion from the political system pointed out that few means of opposition remained, short of supporting armed resistance to the government, but this point of view was belatedly acknowledged by sectors of the governing regime. In fact, the reformist, right-wing National Republican Alliance (ARENA) government headed by Alfredo Cristiani that negotiated the peace became the most insistent in identifying lack of political space as the principal cause of the war. President Cristiani himself argued that "since the lack of political space lay at the root of the conflict," efforts to end the war needed "to focus on opening political space and ensuring a democratic system."[13]

A third root cause of the war, in some ways a specific subset of the general poverty and inequality concerns, was the *highly skewed land tenure* and a correspondingly desperate situation for many in the agrarian sector. Before the war, El Salvador had one of the five most extreme concentrations of land in the world.[14] Indeed, the largest 5 percent of farms controlled 70 percent of the land, while the smallest 20 percent of farms had only 1 percent of total land.[15] This led to a volatile situation in which over one-third of the total Salvadoran population was comprised of landless peasants with few ways to maintain themselves and extremely limited opportunities to improve their situation.[16] With over 55 percent of the prewar Salvadoran population depending on agriculture for its subsistence, this situation was totally unsustainable.[17]

A fourth root cause was the endemic politically directed violence, in particular *massive human rights abuses, and an absence of justice.* In the late 1970s and early 1980s, El Salvador was responsible for introducing the term *death squad* into the lexicon of people around the world. By 1983, death squads were responsible for as many as forty thousand deaths (far outstripping battle deaths), principally among labor organizers, bureaucrats, office workers, professionals, politicians, priests, and progressive military officers.[18] The trade union movement, in particular, was decimated. As one former high-ranking U.S. State Department official complained, the Salvadoran armed forces have "always found it easier to kill labor leaders than guerrillas," making El Salvador the third most dangerous country in the world for trade union activity.[19] Killings represented only one dimension of the human rights abuses in El Salvador, as people were routinely tortured and freedoms of press, speech, and association were severely curtailed. In the face of monumental violations of human rights, the justice system proved itself totally inadequate. As the State Department reported in 1983, "the legal system is in a state of virtual collapse," and "convictions in serious criminal cases, in particular those with political overtones of any kind, are virtually unobtainable because of intimidation and corruption of judges, lawyers, witnesses, and jurors."[20] Having no recourse to the legal system to obtain justice, people turned increasingly to the logic of armed conflict.

A fifth major cause of the war was external. While not a root cause of the initial conflict, *active international support* for the war quickly became a dominant factor in expanding and sustaining the conflict. The Reagan administration, spurred by the belief that conflict was the result of "a global Communist campaign coordinated by Havana and Moscow to support the Marxist guerrillas in El

Salvador," began to pour military and economic assistance into the country.[21] By the end of the war, the United States had contributed over $4.5 billion in military ($1.2 billion) and economic ($3.3 billion) assistance.[22] On the other side, Nicaragua and Cuba played an active, if much smaller role in supporting the FMLN with arms, logistics, and political backing.[23] While the roots of the war were internal, there is little doubt that significant international support, especially from the United States, was key to expanding the scope of the war and to ensuring its longevity. Not surprisingly, since Cold War tensions helped feed the war, the end of the Cold War concomitantly had a significant impact on ending it.

Like international involvement, a sixth causal factor developed over the course of the war and helped prolong the conflict for twelve years, namely a profound *militarization of Salvadoran society*. Initially an effect of the war, militarization became a crucial cause in sustaining it. Not only did the military and its influence expand rapidly and affect the government and political institutions, the economy became a war economy and the society became militarized. The army ballooned from less than ten thousand in 1979 to sixty-three thousand in the mid- to late 1980s, dramatically increasing the military presence throughout the country, especially in conflict zones. Formal governmental institutions ceased to exist in sixty-eight of 262 municipalities. Government social expenditures dropped dramatically in order to channel resources to the war effort, and many of the remaining social expenditures became just another form of counterinsurgency policy. The economy became dependent on massive inflows of U.S. assistance tied to the war, and a distorted, statist economic model designed to help win the war failed to provide economic returns, as evidenced by the –3.2 percent GDP growth experienced between 1977 and 1987.[24] Finally, a war culture developed throughout Salvadoran society, both inside and outside the official conflict zones. Resolution of disputes through violence became the norm—labor disputes and protests of all kinds were often put down by force, and proliferation of firearms led to increasing violence in resolving personal quarrels. Cynicism, fatalism, hatred, and distrust prevailed in many parts of public and private life.

Most analysts and participants in the peace process, both within the country and outside, would agree that militarization, like the other five major causes of the protracted Salvadoran civil war previously mentioned, would need to be addressed to bring peace to El Salvador. The challenge would be how to do so.

International Involvement

As noted above, significant international involvement in El Salvador served to expand the scope of the civil war and to help sustain it throughout the 1980s. Not surprisingly, therefore, the end of the Cold War facilitated the search for peace. By 1989, the FMLN's outside support from Cuba and Nicaragua had begun to dry up, and its sense of isolation had increased. On the other side, under the Bush administration the United States lost interest in the military effort in El Salvador, thereby forcing the government to consider alternatives to the military victory it had long pursued and opening up a real possibility of a negotiated solution.

Indeed, negotiated solutions had been sought by outside actors since an early stage of the conflict. The Contadora Group (Colombia, Mexico, Panama, Venezuela) initiated regional peace efforts in Central America in 1983. Central American countries themselves became involved in the peace efforts for the first time approximately a year later. By 1987, the Central American governments had become principal actors in peace efforts, drafting and signing the Esquipulas I (1986) and Esquipulas II agreements (1987), marking the "official" birth of the Central American peace process.[25] When regional efforts failed to move the process forward, however, Central American leaders called on the UN to facilitate the process. Up to this point, the UN had been involved only peripherally, providing encouragement through resolutions and other forms of moral support but doing little in the way of concrete involvement. After receiving the go-ahead from both parties, UN Secretary-General Perez de Cuellar became personally involved in the talks in 1990, and UN leadership of the process was established.

Over the course of the next two years, the UN facilitated a comprehensive series of agreements designed to end armed conflict by political means, promote democratization, guarantee human rights, and reunite Salvadoran society.[26] In exchange for a phased demobilization of the FMLN's forces, the government of El Salvador signed specific agreements to ensure unrestricted human rights; pass constitutional reforms to stipulate subordination of the armed forces to civilian authority, improve the judicial system, and ensure neutrality of the electoral oversight body; establish a "Truth Commission" to investigate violence in hopes of fomenting reconciliation; create a representative National Commission for the Consolidation of Peace (COPAZ) to monitor agreements and draft secondary legislation;

downsize and reform the armed forces; abolish three military police forces and replace them with a new civilian police force; promote reintegration of belligerents through land transfers to former FMLN and government soldiers as well as squatters in conflict zones; ensure political participation by the FMLN; and address a limited number of economic and social questions by forming a National Reconstruction Plan, adopting measures to alleviate the social cost of structural adjustment programs, and establishing the multisectoral Forum for Economic and Social Consultation.[27]

Not only were the peace accords broad-ranging but so too was the UN's role. The UN-sponsored peace process in El Salvador was in fact one of the most ambitious peacebuilding efforts in the history of the organization. It was responsible not only for verifying the accords but also for mediating between the parties, providing good offices over a long period of time, providing logistical assistance, and coordinating the inputs of various national, international, and multilateral bodies. The UN, in some instances, even became a "conscience" and quasienforcer of the accords when the parties themselves sought to cut deals in contravention of the signed accords.

Despite the peace process's comprehensive attention to immediate peacemaking and peacekeeping concerns, neither the peace accords nor the UN structure designed to help implement them provided much of a framework for long-term peacebuilding. Peacebuilding issues were addressed, but for the most part not in the same concrete, structured manner as the more immediate concerns. In part this is because of the inherently more profound, long-term nature of peacebuilding issues. There are other reasons for slighting peacebuilding, however. In some areas, the government asserted its prerogative to remove key issues from the agenda, as it did in the case of a thoroughgoing review of economic concerns. In other areas such as justice issues, the parties simply failed to understand the extent and importance of the problem. International actors also contributed to the problem by being turf-conscious and opting for loosely coordinated spheres of influence in certain substantive and geographic areas, rather than working actively to form an integrated, well-coordinated international presence in the country. Significant weaknesses resulted from this "every agency for itself" approach, and serious efforts have been made to form a much more cohesive international agency presence in neighboring Guatemala.[28] In El Salvador, however, the individualistic tendencies of international actors combined with the preferences of the warring parties and the idiosyncrasies of the negotiating process to produce an uneven patchwork of programs and strategies for solving Salvador's huge peacebuilding challenges.

Peacebuilding Progress

Demilitarization

Of all the main causes of prolonged conflict in El Salvador, the one that the accords most directly and aggressively addressed was that of the country's profound militarization. Within twelve months of the signing of the Chapultepec accords, the FMLN's eight thousand–strong fighting forces were concentrated, disarmed, and fully demobilized.[29] Simultaneously, the Salvadoran armed forces began the substantial transformation laid out in the peace accords. Not only had the size of the military been dramatically reduced from its wartime strength of sixty-three thousand to approximately seventeen thousand by 1998,[30] the military had undergone an intensive reorienting and professionalization process as well. As mandated by the accords, the mission of the armed forces was fundamentally redefined to include only the defense of "the sovereignty of the state and the integrity of its territory." Accordingly, the armed forces were restructured, and previously held responsibilities for public security were civilianized. An "Ad Hoc Commission" was also set up under the accords to purge the armed forces of serious human rights violators, a process that was ultimately accomplished through UN intervention despite government attempts to avoid fully complying.[31] Further, the accords provided for reforming the educational system of the armed forces in order to emphasize new doctrine, increase technical competence, and expand humanistic studies. In recent years, "Plan Arce 2000," an expanded program developed by the El Salvador military for education and training, has increased professionalization in the ranks, improved overall civil-military relations, and has gone a long way toward ending the old system of promotions obtained through cronyism.

Perhaps as important for demilitarizing El Salvador as the demobilization of the guerrillas and structural transformation of the armed forces was the civilianizing of police functions. One of the most important concrete achievements of the peace process was the disbanding of the National Police and the Treasury Police, and the transfer of public security functions to a newly created National Civilian Police

(PNC) force. In addition to civilianizing police functions, this new body was designed to facilitate the process of demobilization, reintegration, and reconciliation of excombatants. The force was to be comprised of 20 percent former guerrillas, 20 percent former military, and 60 percent new recruits. With strong support from the United States, the United Nations, and the European Union, the new National Police Academy was able to train and field 250 officers and seventy-two hundred agents in a remarkable twenty-six months.

The achievements of the PNC have been many: reconciliation among former combatants within the ranks has been notable; the force gained popular confidence in a short period of time and used this to good effect during the most fragile early days of the peace; and the new force drastically reduced corruption and the use of police as a political tool. At the same time, however, the PNC seems to have been overwhelmed by a postpeace crime wave. Undermanned and outgunned in the country with the highest per capita murder rate in the Western Hemisphere, the PNC has lost over 1 percent of its members (an average of one police officer is killed every nine days), and over 10 percent of the force have been injured. Initial projections for necessary force strength at 10,000 had to be revised to 16,000 and again to 20,000 (current force levels are 18,000). Still, the force has been unable to handle the crime wave, and public confidence has dropped dramatically. Some "old" elements have been discovered in the new force, and over five hundred police officers have been dismissed due to abuses of their responsibilities.

Demilitarization of the economy has had a more unambiguous development. The defense budget that consumed 21 percent of overall government expenditures in 1988 consumed only 6 percent a decade later in 1997. At the same time, expenditures for the new civilian police climbed from 5 percent in 1988 (for the previous police forces) to 10 percent in 1997. Government spending on health and education has also climbed, albeit more slowly, from 2.3 percent of GDP in 1991 to 3.7 percent of GDP (or 25 percent of the budget) in 1997.

Political Space/Democratization

The accords also directly took on the issue of creating political space for individuals and parties of all political affiliations to participate in the democratic process. Of all the root causes of the war, the lack of political space produced some of the most dramatic results. The peace accords offered significant constitutional reforms aimed at establishing a balance of executive, legislative, and judicial powers, putting structures in place to thwart human rights abuses, and pressing electoral reforms designed to depoliticize the electoral process and put parties on equal footing, including that of the former guerrillas. They opened the possibility of real change in a tightly closed oligarchic system that, through organized violence, government restrictions, and overt manipulation of the political process, had kept large segments of the population from participating in it.

The 1994 elections, the first following the accords, were the most inclusive and cleanest elections in the history of the country, and they established the former FMLN guerrillas and their supporters as the second largest political party in the country by capturing 287,811 votes and fourteen seats in the Legislative Assembly. In 1997, with fears of a resumption of war receding, the FMLN increased its votes by 25 percent and picked up twenty-seven seats in the Legislative Assembly, falling just one seat short of the governing ARENA party's plurality in that eighty-four-seat body. The FMLN also won fifty-three municipal elections, including seven of the ten largest and the coveted capital, San Salvador, giving them responsibility for local governance over nearly half the Salvadoran population. In 1999, the ARENA party retained its hold on the presidential palace with a decisive electoral victory, but the FMLN and opposition parties again won the second largest bloc of seats in the Legislative Assembly (twenty-seven of eighty-four) and retained power in key municipalities.

The three postwar elections have revealed important advances for democracy in El Salvador. The political system has opened significantly, with former rebels and their supporters allowed to compete in elections and to occupy seats they have won in the Legislative Assembly and at the municipal level. Not only has the governing ARENA party accepted the results of elections that have dramatically reduced its proportional influence in the Legislative Assembly, it has also acquiesced as the Legislative Assembly has been progressively strengthened vis-à-vis the executive branch of government, introducing a previously unheard-of level of competition into the process of governing. In some instances, opposition forces have even been able to rally support to block major policy initiatives such as former president Calderón Sol's attempts to increase the value added tax, deregulate the energy sector, and dramatically downsize the public sector.

This said, there remain important impediments to a truly open and competitive electoral system. The new Supreme Electoral Tribunal created by the accords remains politicized, with unfair advantages being meted out to the governing party. A truly neutral oversight and regulatory electoral institution is necessary if further progress is to be made in the democratization process. Key electoral reforms agreed to by the president and the opposition in 1994 to increase participation, representation, and transparency (proportional representation on municipal councils, a single national identification card used for voting, local precinct voting, and a new, comprehensive national registry of citizens) remain unrealized. Thus, while significant progress has been made, a fully open electoral system has not yet been instituted. The apathy threatening the democratic system, demonstrated by the systematic decrease in voter participation in 1994, 1997, and 1999, is less than encouraging. Indeed, the ultimate gauge of openness—ceding power to an opposition victory in the presidential contest—has yet to be put to the test. Only at that point will El Salvador's new political system have proved itself totally.

Despite these challenges, progress is indisputable. While the peace accords opened the door for this change, sustaining the progress has depended on significant financial support from the United States for key aspects of the electoral process, including voter registration, education, and the institutional needs of the Supreme Electoral Tribunal.[32] In addition to direct support for elections and electoral machinery, the United States has also been a major supporter of strengthening the Legislative Assembly and of building up the governing capacity of municipalities.[33] This financial support has been complemented by increasing work by the Inter-American Development Bank in these areas. The high level of U.S. support in the years immediately following the peace accords depended to a great extent on the U.S. historical involvement in El Salvador. As time has passed, overall U.S. financial support has dropped to a mere $34 million in 1999, compared to $292 million in 1992 and more than $500 million annually at the peak of the conflict.[34] Nonetheless, the United States has timed its financial support, even though much reduced, to strengthen El Salvador's democratic process at key junctures (for example, during 1992, when the accords were signed, and in 1994, when the first postwar elections were held) and at times has exerted significant political pressure to improve and expand the country's electoral process.

Human Rights and the Administration of Justice

The above-mentioned progress in democratization would have been impossible without dramatic improvements in the human rights situation in El Salvador. This, in fact, is exactly what has happened. According to the Secretary-General of the United Nations:

> Massive human rights violations no longer occur. The systematic practice of forced disappearances, torture, the holding of prisoners incommunicado, acts of terrorism and summary and arbitrary executions on political grounds is a thing of the past. In an atmosphere of greater tolerance and pluralism conditions exist in which nongovernmental human rights organizations can freely go about their work. The democratic freedoms of expression, of association and of public organization, as well as the exercise of political rights, have been substantively strengthened.[35]

This progress has been facilitated by extensive international involvement in the area of human rights. Indeed, one of the key innovations of the UN in El Salvador was to address human rights at the earliest possible stage of the peace process and then use progress in this area as an important confidence-building measure to advance the peace process in other areas as well. The San Jose Agreement struck by the parties in July 1990 and subsequent UN Observer Mission in El Salvador (ONUSAL) deployment of 100 human rights monitors in July 1991, even before the peace accords were completed, were essential in providing momentum for the peace process, a presence to dissuade parties from violence that could endanger that process, and an incipient international presence upon which an expanded international mission could be built.

ONUSAL broke new ground for the UN, pioneering an "active verification" methodology that consciously sought structural remedies to systematic human rights violations.[36] In addition, the peace accords explicitly called for the establishment of an Ad Hoc Commission to "purify" the armed forces of human rights abusers, a Truth Commission to investigate serious acts of violence, and through the Truth Commission, a Joint Group for the Investigation of Politically Motivated Illegal Armed Groups. In the end, while many recommendations of the Truth Commission and Joint Group were ignored by the government, the Ad Hoc Commission helped to cleanse the armed forces, the Truth Commission created a more public accounting for violence than many deemed possible, and all three bodies helped keep pressure on the government to improve the human rights situation in the country.

The peace accords also called for important constitutional and legal reforms, established new institutions such as the National Counsel for the Defense of Human Rights (Ombudsman), and called for El Salvador to ratify various human rights treaties. In compliance with the accords, the Salvadoran government has ratified some of these, and the National Counsel for the Defense of Human Rights has developed into a crucial institution that has given victims of abuse an avenue of recourse and has proved its ability to help defuse volatile situations such as land invasions and large protest marches.

Improvements in the administration of justice have become possible with the creation of a new Supreme Court in 1994 and the National Council of the Judiciary, designed to evaluate and remove incompetent and corrupt judges. Development of the new justice system, however, has been characterized alternately by advances and reverses. While the Salvadoran government has agreed to assign a percentage of the national budget to the judicial system in order to ensure its financial independence, the vetting of judges has proceeded at a frustratingly slow pace.[37] Even though the constitution was democratically reformed for the first time in the history of El Salvador, a host of crucial legal reforms was not ratified by two successive Legislative Assemblies, as required by the new constitution. New criminal legislation has been passed and has come into force, but the entire system is overwhelmed by a tidal wave of violence.

Even as systematic human rights abuses have been dramatically reduced, violence remains a pervasive problem. With the country awash in surplus arms following the conflict, and the demobilization of the organized coercive forces (large parts of the army and guerrillas), an explosion of "privatized violence" has ensued. Homicide rates have soared to the second highest in the world, and the justice system is not up to the challenge.[38] Indeed, even on the high-profile human rights cases, no justice has been rendered, despite over $30 million spent by the United States in this area.

In short, although the Ad Hoc and Truth Commissions, active verification by ONUSAL, constitutional reforms, the new Supreme

Court, and new institutions like the National Counsel for the Defense of Human Rights have all helped the country move away from total impunity, the justice sector continues to require significant attention and resources if it is to have any chance of meeting the immense challenges of personal security and justice in postwar El Salvador.

Economic Inequality

The FMLN made many attempts to place economic and social issues on the agenda of the peace negotiations. The Salvadoran government, however, was very leery of letting the peace process undermine the outward-oriented, free-market model it had worked so hard to create.[39] As a result, economic and social issues were addressed very late in the negotiating process and received little concerted attention. As Alvaro de Soto, the UN's lead negotiator, later acknowledged about the accords, "The chapter on economic and social issues . . . was a jerry-built, last minute compromise that left many loose ends."[40] Unlike the parts of the accords that changed the fundamental organizing principles of political and military life in El Salvador, the accords' social and economic components only affected those sectors overall around the margins. The Social and Economic Forum, a mechanism designed to bring business and labor together to work on pressing economic and social problems, was disbanded soon after its inception. Other mechanisms created under the accords survived, such as the Social Investment Fund designed to temporarily cushion the impact of structural adjustment, but none fundamentally reordered economic or social priorities or left any permanent institutions behind.

As Alvaro de Soto and Graciana del Castillo noted in 1994, the peace process and the economic strategy of the government, backed by the International Monetary Fund (IMF) and the World Bank, operated on separate tracks. De Soto and del Castillo likened the situation to that of doctors operating on a patient with a curtain drawn across the middle of his body, with the doctors on one side not necessarily knowing or accounting for what the doctors on the other side of the curtain were doing.[41] As chief architects of the accords and the land transfer program respectively, de Soto and del Castillo were concerned that the stringent fiscal policies of the government demanded by the multilateral lending agencies were hampering the development of the new National Civilian Police and the land transfer program—central elements of the UN's peacebuilding strategy. This is not entirely surprising, however, since the government's economic program predated its peace negotiations, and the international financial institutions tended to give precedence to the economic goals when these conflicted with the peace process.

To be sure, the economic half of the patient worked on by the economic doctors sought to address poverty concerns as part of the program. In his inaugural speech and subsequent major policy addresses, President Cristiani promised that "the only ones privileged by this government will be the poorest of the poor" and that his government would adopt measures to address the needs of the poor, "the likes of which have never been seen before [in El Salvador]."[42] Despite this rhetoric, however, efforts to address the needs of the poor in El Salvador since 1989 have been relatively limited and certainly more routine than they have been pathbreaking.

The strategy to reduce poverty put forward by three successive ARENA governments (Cristiani, Calderón Sol, and Flores), backed by international financial institutions and bilateral donors, consisted of three basic pillars: economic growth, temporary compensatory programs, and over the longer term, investment in human resources (principally through restructuring the delivery of health and education services).[43] The first of these pillars, the underlying premise of the strategy, was that growth and distribution were not compatible and that growth must be pursued first, the idea being that benefits would eventually trickle down, albeit with some help in the short run. As one key government think-tank publication put it: "Experience shows that the sequence which eventually makes it possible for a country to eliminate extreme poverty . . . consists of *sustained growth first in order to distribute the fruits of growth later.*"[44]

The second part of the poverty-alleviation strategy—the concrete backbone of the government's social policy—was the implementation of two different compensatory programs. The first, the Social Rescue Plan (SRP) announced by President Cristiani only two months after taking office, included a $120 million compensatory component designed to cushion the effects of initial stabilization efforts over an eighteen-month period. The program consisted principally of subsidies and job creation programs, virtually all of which were either ongoing, repackaged, already funded and about to be implemented, or extensions of existing programs.[45] The second, the Social Investment Fund (SIF), was a truly new mechanism created in 1990 for a fixed four-year term (later extended multiple times) that was designed to address the "most pressing needs of the poor, especially the extremely poor," and in so doing to "help facilitate national reconciliation, promote productive activities, and human development."[46] Through July 1994, the SIF had channeled over $119 million, 93 percent of which had come from the Inter-American Development Bank, to demand-driven projects with local groups, principally in the areas of education (41 percent), and sewage, water, and health (40 percent).[47]

Despite a certain level of success in delivering needed services quite efficiently in virtually all parts of the country, these compensatory, safety-net programs suffer from some important deficiencies. The first is a mismatch between the temporary, compensatory nature of the programs and their assigned mission of bearing virtually the entire burden of poverty alleviation in a country where over half the population is poor or extremely poor.[48] Second, these programs have had a very difficult time reaching the target population, not only because of technical and administrative hurdles and a lack of institutional capacity to target but also due to the politicization of the programs.[49] Third, the compensatory mechanisms have depended almost exclusively on foreign funding, calling into question the Salvadoran government's commitment to poverty-alleviation efforts.[50] Fourth and most important, a safety-net approach alone does little if anything to address the deep-rooted causes of poverty in social and economic structures. Despite government claims to the contrary, poverty in El Salvador was not caused primarily by the war, and most certainly it is not a temporary phenomenon. Patterns of poverty have persisted before, during, and after the war, leading to the conclusion that poverty is primarily associated with land tenure, poor soils, population pressure, and low technical levels of peasant farming.[51] These are precisely the types of structural problems that the temporary compensatory mechanisms have not even sought to touch.

The third part of the Salvadoran government's poverty-alleviation strategy—building human resources through improvements in health and educational services—was clearly necessary. While attention was given to these issues and dollars spent in health and education increased, expenditure as a percentage of GDP remains at an extremely low 1.0 percent and 1.7 percent, respectively, and spending on these areas as a percentage of current government expenditure actually decreased between 1989 and 1993, from 6.5 percent to 4.4 percent and 16.8 percent to 14.5 percent, respectively.[52] By 1997, education and health expenditures had reached 3.7 percent of GDP, or 25 percent of the government budget, compared to 2.3 percent of GDP in 1991. In addition, El Salvador's primary-school enrollment ratio remains the lowest in Latin America and is growing only slowly.[53] Increased attention and funding to health and education on the part of the United States (since 1992) and the World Bank, in particular to the quality of education through the World Bank–supported EDUCO program, is a move in the right direction.[54] After very dramatic declines in the 1980s, however, both health and education need much more attention, especially through institutionalized, Salvadoran mechanisms.

In terms of concrete results, the government's three-pronged strategy for addressing poverty and equity concerns has yielded modest returns. According to the World Bank, poverty rates in El Salvador have declined from about 60 percent in 1990 to 48 percent in 1995, and extreme poverty rates from 28 percent to 18 percent over the same period.[55] These numbers would be much worse if it weren't for the offsetting, cushioning effects of the large remittance flows pouring into the country over this same period. As various studies have demonstrated, these remittance flows have had a strong redistributive and poverty-ameliorating effect as they represent direct transfers to the poor sectors of society.[56]

Clearly, more needs to be done in this area if a stable Salvadoran polity is to be built over the medium term. According to the Secretary-General of the United Nations, "To say that there is a need to implement social policies that gradually reduce poverty and exclusion is to state the obvious."[57]

Land and the Agrarian Situation

One of the central elements of the peace process was the Land Transfer Program (Programa de Transferencia de Tierra, or PTT) designed to facilitate the reinsertion of forty thousand former combatants and squatters in previous conflict zones into peacetime productive life. Though the PTT was beset by delays—and was completed only when the United States stepped in to press the Salvadoran government and provide additional financing (85 percent of the total)—it was ultimately successful in transferring about 10 percent of El Salvador's agricultural land to over thirty-five thousand recipients by the end of 1998.[58]

While land has been successfully transferred, however, the viability of the new landholders is anything but assured. Problems with agricultural pricing, debt, credit, and a lack of technical assistance are endangering the land transfers made as part of the peace process. On one hand, skyrocketing prices and the PTT's attempt to use market mechanisms to value the land left the program short of funds and the new landowners with over $100 million in debts.[59] At the same time, they have suffered from insufficient credit and woefully inadequate technical assistance to increase their productivity.[60] Finally, the economic liberalization program of the government has put intense pressure on commodity prices, leaving many in the countryside worse off than before. Imports have flowed in, but smallholders have had insufficient experience, infrastructure, and credit to engage in the lucrative export markets. Many have been left behind.

While PTT land recipients have struggled, it is important to place their struggles in the overall context of Salvadoran agriculture. The vast majority of the three million Salvadorans living in rural areas were unaffected by the PTT. Despite previous attempts at agrarian reform in the 1970s and 1980s, and the land transfer program following the war, 1 percent of property owners continue to hold 50 percent of the land, while 95 percent own only 30 percent, with over 50 percent of the active rural population being landless or land-poor and 87 percent of farmers cultivating basic subsistence crops on three hectares or less.[61]

What has all this meant for political stability and the prospects for avoiding a return to war? Despite all the above-mentioned problems in the agricultural sector, El Salvador is unlikely to face a broad-based rural insurgency any time soon. Since the beginning of the war in 1979, two major developments have helped to ameliorate the "agrarian question" in El Salvador: land reform efforts from 1980–1983 and through the PTT following the war, and dramatic migration from the countryside to the cities and abroad.[62] Not only has the PTT program addressed some of the needs of those most likely to return to war, it combined with the more dramatic land reform of 1980–1983 to redistribute a full 30 percent of El Salvador's agricultural land. In the words of one analyst, "The peace and stability that El Salvador has achieved today rest in part on the fact that political tension in the countryside has been reduced because the short-term demands of organized campesino groups for land redistribution have been at least partially addressed."[63] No less important, however, has been the massive shift of population from the Salvadoran countryside, due both to increasing opportunities in the cities (and decreasing opportunities in the countryside) and to the war itself. The net result has been a dramatic reduction of the economically active population engaged in agriculture, from 60 percent in 1961 to 47 percent in 1971, 43 percent in 1980, and only 33 percent in 1991.[64]

This is not to say, however, that the problems of structural poverty have improved or that the potential for discontent in this area has been eliminated. This is borne out by the problems that El Salvador has had with numerous land invasions since the signing of the peace accords. These invasions have been resolved peacefully for the most part, in no small part because of the critical roles played by the new National Civilian Police and the National Counsel for Human Rights—key creations of the peace accords. In a broader sense, the peace process has also been instrumental in ameliorating potential conflict by channeling problems in the countryside into the newly representative political process created by the accords. The "crisis of agriculture" has been a major campaign issue in the last two elections in 1997 and 1999, leading to serious attempts on the part of the government to address the problems of debt and on the part of the World Bank and other donors to address the credit, technical assistance, and pricing problems.

Lessons Learned

Mahatma Gandhi said that there are two kinds of peace—the peace that silences the guns and the peace that makes guns irrelevant.[65] El Salvador has clearly achieved the first, a self-enforcing cease-fire, and is working diligently on pursuing the second, broader goal of self-enforcing peace. The peacebuilding process in El Salvador has faced many bumps along the way and has a long way to go. At the same time, the hard-won record of success that El Salvador has managed over the last seven years is sufficient to provide some important lessons not only for ongoing efforts in El Salvador but also elsewhere. Before reviewing them, however, it is important to point out the propitious conditions for peace in El Salvador that are not likely to be replicated elsewhere. First, the end of the Cold War and external support for both sides during the war was a unique historical window. Second, El Salvador is a very small country that received immense financial support from the international community. From 1990 to 1995, El Salvador received a whopping $2.4 billion in overseas development assistance (including $1.2 billion from the United States and $654 million from multilateral donors).[66] Finally, El Salvador was decisively affected by its relationship to the United States, the preponderant economic, political, and military power in the region. Not only did the U.S. shift in approach toward El Salvador dramatically enhance the prospects for securing peace accords, the extensive economic ties (remittances, trade, investment) helped open new economic opportunities, even as old military ties helped facilitate the transition of the Salvadoran military to play a new role in Salvadoran society.

While El Salvador's success to date derives from unique circumstances and thus cannot be "replicated," there are a number of general lessons that can be learned and applied elsewhere.

Political processes. The development of a truly democratic political process is one of the seminal successes of the Salvadoran peace process. Because political space was opened and increasingly democratic institutions advanced through the peace process, the Salvadoran system has begun to manage the dramatic socioeconomic challenges in rural areas without resorting to the use of arms. While there is much left to do in this area, the level of political attention now devoted to this question bodes well for ultimately finding acceptable ways to address the problems.

Early action. The international community's experience in El Salvador suggests that action must embed processes and institutions to address root causes at the earliest possible stage of the peace process. Institutional change is much more difficult as time passes. This has been proven in various social and economic arenas in El Salvador, especially in terms of agreeing upon a comprehensive rural strategy early on and in terms of building poverty-alleviation concerns into the broader economic model being pursued.

Attention to conflict zones. A careful balance must be struck between giving priority to peacebuilding in conflict zones and addressing countrywide needs. In the immediate aftermath of the war, El Salvador's principal conflict zones were in great need of rebuilding economic, social, and governmental infrastructure. El Salvador's National Reconstruction Plan helped to catalyze resources for these purposes and was ultimately quite successful in fostering progress both in physical reconstruction and democratic strengthening.[67] At the same time, peacebuilding activities tailored to conflict zones are no substitute for effective national action in establishing genuine political dialogue and effective economic and social policies. In El Salvador, this is nowhere more evident than in the search for a long-term solution to the immense needs in rural areas.

Integrated peacebuilding strategy. While establishing a functioning, representative political dialogue is essential, as noted above, this is by no means a substitute for an integrated peacebuilding strategy that weaves together political, economic, and social programs. Operating on a patient with a curtain drawn down the middle is both dangerous and unnecessary. Economic and political causality flows both ways. The international community should not support exclusively privileging one set of goals—in the case of El Salvador, structural adjustment—over needs in other areas. This was dangerous and could have been fatal to the Salvadoran process in key areas such as the land transfer program and the National Civilian Police, if the United States had not been willing and able to step in with significant resources and political pressure to address the failings at various points. As evidenced by vast improvements in neighboring Guatemala, the international community has begun to learn the importance of coordinating external actors.

Coordination of external actors. As evidenced by the greatly improved results in the justice sector when the UN and the United States began to work together, this is of primary importance. Because the United States had been working on improving the administration of justice in El Salvador for years before the accords, the U.S. and the UN agendas did not always mesh. Rather than resolving these differences, however, these two major players tended to pursue their own agendas in the sector for quite some time. Finally after some real failures, the two actors began to work together in earnest. Only once their work was coordinated was the international community able to bring appropriate pressure to bear on the government with respect to purging the new National Civilian Police forces of old elements and fully supporting this crucial new institution.

Remittances. Over one million people fled El Salvador during the war. Although the product of immense human suffering, this massive movement of people produced a crucial income stream for El Salvador in subsequent years in the form of remittances from abroad. According to the World Bank, remittances from abroad exceeded $1.3 billion in 1996.[68] These monies have cushioned the living standard of large segments of the Salvadoran population and have enabled development of certain sectors of the Salvadoran economy. At the same time, massive remittances from expatriates have distorted the economy and made management of the macroeconomic framework more difficult. Though other countries may not have remittances to the extent of El Salvador, all countries in conflict will have some because of the displacing of population. Both local governments and international actors should thus explicitly seek to understand and be prepared to address both the opportunities and challenges presented by remittance flows. They should also be prepared to address the impact of the ultimate demise of remittances once peace has been established, refugee flows stop, and links between expatriates and their families back home gradually loosen with time.

Balancing multiple UN roles. In El Salvador, the UN artfully combined its mediation, verification, and institution-building roles. While there is clearly tension between these different roles at certain points of any peace process, El Salvador proves that these tensions can be managed. If strategically combined, the UN's leverage over domestic actors and their decisions that fundamentally affect the prospects for peace can be enhanced.[69] In El Salvador, for example, the UN effectively combined those roles to support the creation and development of the office of the National Counsel for the Defense of Human Rights. Despite its very slow start, this office has become one of the lasting accomplishments of the peace process.

Balancing pragmatism and principled action. While a UN peace mission should always be pragmatic, long-term peacebuilding efforts are best served if the UN and other external actors stick to their principles in key situations. As William Stanley and David Holiday point out, in El Salvador, "while the UN consistently supported pragmatic agreements between the two parties to adjust the timetable for implementation of the accords, it refused to sanction agreements by the two parties that undercut elements of the peace accords that the UN considered vital to the integrity of the peace."[70] ONUSAL refused, for example, to participate in government-FMLN negotiations to delay purging the military and to transfer existing investigation units into the new police force. This latter decision made it possible two years later for the mission to insist that the old units be fully retrained at the civilian police academy, a stance that eventually led to their resignation, thus ending their threat to the integrity of the new police force.

Peacebuilding as a local process. Peacebuilding is ultimately a local process, and thus for long-term sustainability, much of the responsibility for the peace process and peacebuilding activities should remain with or be transferred to local people and institutions as soon as realistically possible. In El Salvador, the UN effectively accomplished keeping the onus on the parties, even when it temporarily substituted for them when they defaulted on their responsibilities at key moments of the peace process. At the same time, the UN slowly but steadily reduced and reconfigured its presence in El Salvador in order to keep the greatest share of the burden on Salvadorans themselves.[71] In this regard, the UN presence in El Salvador does provide a template for successful missions in the future.

Notes

1. For quotes of senior UN representatives, see Mark Levine, "Peacemaking in El Salvador," in *Keeping the Peace: Multidimensional UN Operations in Cambodia and El Salvador,* ed. Michael W. Doyle, Ian Johnstone, and Robert C. Orr (New York: Cambridge University Press, 1997), 227. In 1999, U.S. Ambassador Anne Patterson stated, "It's almost a miracle what's happened here," *New York Times,* March 7, 1999, A-8. Former President Alfredo Cristiani has stated, "Clearly, El Salvador is a model from which many lessons can be learned" (author interview, Washington, D.C., February 23, 1995); his successor, Armando Calderón Sol, argued that "El Salvador has become a model for how to proceed" (*North-South,* Miami, Sept.–Oct. 1994, 18). FMLN Commandante Joaquin Villalobos has stated that while "the path to peace and democracy in El Salvador cannot be replicated by others, it can serve as a general model" (author interview, Carlisle, PA, September 9, 1994).

2. The Stockholm International Peace Research Institute (SIPRI) estimates the death toll of the twelve-year war at 77,000–82,000, rather than the commonly cited 75,000. Estimates of those displaced within the country and those going abroad are inexact, but most sources place the numbers in the range of 500,000 to one million, respectively. See, for example, UN staff member Blanca Antonini's "Mision de Observadores de las Naciones Unidas en El Salvador (ONUSAL): Memoria," unpublished manuscript, 11; and Edilberto Torres-Rivas, "Insurrection and Civil War in El Salvador," in *Keeping the Peace,* ed. Doyle, Johnstone, and Orr, 226.

3. Antonini ("Mision de Observadores," 11) estimates the value at $1.6 billion, while other UN sources place it between $1.8 and $2 billion (as cited in *Keeping the Peace,* 224).

4. UN Assistant Secretary-General for Political Affairs Alvaro de Soto clarified what he meant by "laboratory conditions": "The Salvadoran conflict was ripe for a negotiated solution, and the parties were willing to reach a politically negotiated solution. They realized that the military solution was no longer an option, and there was a tacit understanding between them that many changes—societal and institutional changes—had to come about to ensure that peace truly would be reestablished." Alvaro de Soto, "The Politics of Post-Conflict Reconstruction," in *Making Peace Work: The Role of the International Development Community,* ed. Nicole Ball (Washington, D.C.: Overseas Development Council, 1996), 12.

5. The loss of the Honduran "escape valve" for landless peasants was a significant factor in increasing tension in El Salvador's agrarian sector during this period. See World Bank, *The World Bank's Experience with Post-Conflict Reconstruction,* Vol. 3: *El Salvador Case Study,* Report no. 17769 (Washington, D.C.: World Bank Operations Evaluation Department, 1998), 6. For a historical analysis of the origins of El Salvador's armed conflict, see Torres-Rivas, "Insurrection and Civil War," 209–226.

6. According to the legal office of the Archdiocese of San Salvador, over 800 community leaders and leaders of opposition organizations were killed in the first nine months of 1979 alone. See Torres-Rivas, "Insurrection and Civil War," 217.

7. Armed encounters had been taking place for at least two years by that time, but the offensive marked the first time that a military balance of forces could be said to exist.

8. Ministry of Planning statistics based on multipurpose household surveys, as cited in World Bank, *El Salvador: The Challenge of Poverty Alleviation,* Report no. 12315-ES (Washington, D.C.: World Bank Operations Evaluation Department, 1994), Annex A, 3. For information on rural poverty, see World Bank, *Economic Memorandum on El Salvador,* Report no. 1313a-ES (Washington, D.C.: World Bank Operations Evaluation Department, 1977).

9. World Bank, *El Salvador Case Study,* 5.

10. United Nations, *United Nations and El Salvador, 1990–1995* (New York: UN Department of Public Information, 1995), 7.

11. Henry A. Kissinger et al., *Report of the National Bipartisan Commission on Central America* (Washington, D.C.: Government Printing Office, 1984).

12. For the statement of the Central Election Commission, see Americas Watch Committee and American Civil Liberties Union, *Supplement to the Report on Human Rights in El Salvador* (Washington, D.C.: Center for National Security Studies, 1982), 154. For the statement of U.S. Ambassador Deane Hinton, see Walden Bello and Edward S. Herman, "U.S. Supported Elections in El Salvador and the Philippines," *World Policy Journal* 1, 4 (Summer 1984): 851–869.

13. Author interview, Alfredo Cristiani, Washington, D.C., February 23, 1995.

14. According to Charles Lewis Taylor and David A. Jodice, *World Handbook of Political and Social Indicators* (New Haven: Yale University Press, 1983), El Salvador's Gini coefficient for the 1970s was a stunning 83. Cited in Mitchell Seligson, "Thirty Years of Transformation in the Agrarian Structure of El Salvador, 1961–1991," *Latin American Research Review* 30, 3 (1995): 44.

15. World Bank, *Economic Memorandum on El Salvador.*

16. According to the 1971 census, 34 percent of the Salvadoran population was comprised of rural landless. Cited in Lisa North, *Bitter Grounds: Roots of Revolt in El Salvador* (Westport, CT: Lawrence-Hill, 1985), 48.

17. World Bank, *Economic Memorandum on El Salvador.*

18. Christopher Dickey, "Behind the Death Squads: Who They Are, Why They Work, and Why No One Can Stop Them," *New Republic*, December 26, 1983, 17.

19. William Bollinger, "El Salvador," in *Latin American Labor Organizations*, ed. Gerald Michael Greenfield and Sheldon L. Maram (New York: Greenwood Press, 1987), 360. Benjamin C. Schwarz, *American Counterinsurgency Doctrine and El Salvador: The Frustrations of Reform and the Illusions of Nation Building*, prepared for the Undersecretary of Defense Policy (Santa Monica, CA: Rand Corporation, 1991), 25. The ranking as the third most dangerous country was by the International Labor Organization, as cited in "The Economic Intelligence Unit: Guatemala, El Salvador, Honduras," 4 (Geneva: ILO, 1990): 22.

20. Department of State, *Report on the Situation in El Salvador with Respect to the Subjects Covered in Sections 728(d) and (e) of the International Security and Development Cooperation Act of 1981 as Amended P.L. 97–113* (Washington, D.C.: GPO, 1983), 11.

21. Secretary of State Alexander Haig to NATO representatives, *New York Times*, February 21, 1981, 6.

22. Figures are for FY 1980–1992, based on Congressional Research Service, *El Salvador, 1979–1989, A Briefing Book on U.S. Aid and the Situation in El Salvador* (Washington, D.C.: April 1989); Department of State, *U.S. Economic and Military Assistance, FY 1991, FY 1992, FY 1993* (Washington, D.C.: GPO, 1992), and other U.S. government documents as compiled by Herman Rosa, *AID y las Transformaciones Globales en El Salvador: El Papel del la Politica de Asistencia Economica de los Estados Unidos desde 1980* (Managua: CRIES, 1993), 114.

23. See Jorge G. Castaneda, *Utopia Unarmed: The Latin American Left After the Cold War* (New York: Knopf, 1993); and William LeoGrande, *Our Own Backyard: The United States in Central America, 1977–1992* (Chapel Hill: University of North Carolina Press, 1988).

24. World Bank, "El Salvador at a Glance," September 21, 1999 (www.worldbank.org).

25. For a more complete description of the negotiations that ultimately led to the Salvadoran peace accords, see Jack Child, *The Central American Peace Process, 1983–1991: Sheathing Swords, Building Confidence* (Boulder, CO: Lynne Rienner, 1992); and Mark Levine, "Peacemaking in El Salvador," in *Keeping the Peace*, 227–254.

26. The Geneva Agreement, April 4, 1990, UN Doc. A/45/706–S231931, Annex I, in *El Salvador Agreements: The Path to Peace* (New York: United Nations, 1992), 1.

27. For details and an analysis of the accords, see Timothy A. Wilkins, "The El Salvador Peace Accords: Using International and Domestic Law Norms to Build Peace," in *Keeping the Peace*, 255–281.

28. In Guatemala, the UN has led the way on coordination by developing a common "UN Development Assistance Framework" and establishing an active country team—composed of all UN agencies, the World Bank, the Inter-

American Development Bank, and other bilateral and intergovernmental assistance agencies—that meets regularly.

29. The peace process was seriously threatened in the early days by discovery of FMLN arms caches that had not been disclosed as mandated under the accords. With UN intervention, however, the disarmament process was put back on track and completed. Demobilization was to be completed originally by October 15, 1992, but was delayed until December 15, 1992, in exchange for a "recalendarization" of the implementation of the Ad Hoc Commission's recommendations for purging the armed forces of human rights violators.

30. As of March 1998; see U.S. State Department, "Background Notes on El Salvador" (http://www.state.gov/www/background_notes_/el_salvador_0398_bgn.html).

31. See Ian Johnstone, *Rights and Reconciliation: UN Strategies in El Salvador* (Boulder, CO: Lynne Rienner Publishers, 1995), 31–33.

32. Author interview, Salvador Novellino, USAID's staff person in charge of electoral promotion activities, San Salvador, August 17, 1994.

33. The United States has spent over $50 million in direct electoral assistance over the last decade, as well as $2 million for Legislative Assembly strengthening between 1990 and 1995, and tens of millions of dollars in strengthening municipal governance. The estimated USAID budget for 1999 for the promotion of more inclusive and effective democratic governance is over $6 million, within the "Democracy" budget estimated total of over $33 million.

34. U.S. Embassy in San Salvador figures, as quoted in *New York Times,* March 7, 1999.

35. Report of the Secretary-General, "Assessment of the Peace Process in El Salvador," A/51/917, July 1, 1997, 5.

36. Johnstone, *Rights and Reconciliation,* 24–29.

37. Report of the UN Secretary-General, *The Situation in Central America: Procedures for the Establishment of a Firm and Lasting Peace and Progress in Fashioning a Region of Peace, Freedom, Democracy, and Development: Assessment of the Peace Process in El Salvador,* Report A/51/917, July 1, 1997, 6.

38. Serge F. Kovaleski, "Murders Soar in El Salvador Since Devastating War's End: Some Jobless Ex-Combatants Turn to Life of Crime," *Washington Post,* October 1, 1997, A22. In 1995, El Salvador suffered a rate of 139 homicides per 100,000 people, second only to South Africa's 140, while the United States experienced 9.5 per 100,000.

39. See Robert C. Orr, "Paradigm Lost?: U.S. Democracy Promotion Efforts in Developing Countries" (Ph.D. diss., Princeton University, 1996), 276–333.

40. Alvaro de Soto and Graciana del Castillo, "Post-conflict Peace-building in El Salvador: Strains on the United Nations System," May 1993, manuscript cited in *Keeping the Peace,* 275.

41. Alvaro de Soto and Graciana del Castillo, "Obstacles to Peacebuilding," *Foreign Policy* 94 (Spring 1994): 69–83.

42. See Cristiani's inaugural speech, reprinted in *Estudios Centroamericanos* 488 (June 1989): 521–527, and his 1991 presidential New Year address, *La Prensa Grafica,* January 15, 1991.

43. See Juan Belt and A. Lardé de Palomo, "El Salvador: Politica social y combate a la pobreza," manuscript, 1994. Belt was the senior economist at USAID/San Salvador.

44. FUSADES, Martes Economico, *La Prensa Grafica,* February 9, 1993 (emphasis in the original).

45. Peter Sollis, "El Salvador Issue Brief #2—Poverty Alleviation in El Salvador: Fighting Poverty Under the Cristiani Government" (Washington, D.C.: Washington Office on Latin America, 1993), 6.

46. FIS, *Fondo de Inversion Social de El Salvador: Información Básica* (San Salvador: FIS, Julio 1994), 3.

47. FIS, *Reporte de Avance No. 37* (San Salvador: FIS, Julio 1994).

48. According to one former head of the SIF, the government "gave the SIF a mission way too big for its capacities . . . this is not a long-term solution for all our problems" (author interview, Mirna Lievano de Marques, San Salvador, August 30, 1994).

49. On the lack of institutional capacity, see World Bank, *Challenge of Poverty Alleviation,* Annex A, 32. On politicization: the National Reconstruction Program in particular had a hard time overcoming the counterinsurgency roots of the implementing agency CONARA, but the SIF also has problems with patronage politics, as evidenced by the correspondence of projects to political distribution rather than poverty distribution throughout the country. See Fondo de Inversion, *Social, Reporte de Avance No. 37,* 17.

50. According to FIS, *Reporte de Avance No. 37,* 93 percent of FIS funding comes from the Inter-American Development Bank.

51. See Sollis, "Poverty Alleviation in El Salvador," 4.

52. Ministry of Finance, 1994, as cited in World Bank, *Challenge of Poverty Alleviation,* Annex A, 8.

53. See James Boyce, ed., *Economic Policy for Building Peace: The Lessons of El Salvador* (Boulder, CO: Lynne Rienner Publishers, 1996), 5; and World Bank, *Project Completion Report* (Loan 3293-ES).

54. The Educatión con Participación de la Comunidad (EDUCO) program was developed in an effort to modernize the education system in El Salvador and enable it to respond to the current economic and social demands. It was premised on the delivery of educational services through community participation in the provision of preschool and primary education in rural areas, especially the most impoverished ones.

55. According to the 1997 World Bank Country Assistance Strategy for El Salvador, as cited in World Bank, *El Salvador Case Study,* 10.

56. See, for example: CEPAL, *El impacto económico y social de las migraciones en Centroamérica* (Santiago, 1993); USAID/San Salvador, FY 1993 ESF Economic and Democratic Reform Program, Program Assistance Approval Document, San Salvador, 1993; S. Montes, *El Salvador 1987: Salvadoreños refugiados en Estados Unidos* (San Salvador: Instituto de Investigaciones, Universidad Centroamericana, 1987).

57. UN Secretary-General, *The Situation in Central America: Assessment of the Peace Process in El Salvador,* A/51/917: 17.

58. See UN Secretary-General, *The Situation in Central America,* A/52/1008, September 24, 1998; and Michael W. Foley, *Land, Peace, and Participation: The Development of Post-War Agricultural Policy in El Salvador and the Role of the World Bank* (Washington, D.C.: Washington Office on Latin America, 1997). On the U.S. role in funding $65 million for the process, see the statement of Nicholas Burns, State Department spokesman, February 26, 1996, in San Salvador.

59. Recognizing the problem, the Salvadoran government passed a debt-restructuring law in May 1996, writing off 70 percent of the debt. Cancellation

of the remaining 30 percent was subsequently agreed upon in 1997. UN Secretary-General, *The Situation in Central America,* A/51/917: 10.

60. Between 1992 and 1997, the international community did provide a number of diverse agricultural training programs to excombatants, but a study by UNDP in 1997 concluded that the technical assistance programs did not achieve their goals and reached only 25 percent of total PTT beneficiaries. See UN Secretary-General, *The Situation in Central America,* A/51/917: 11–12.

61. World Bank, *Challenge of Poverty Alleviation,* Annex A, 4, 19. For statistics and analysis of land-poor population, see Seligson, "Thirty Years of Transformation," 30.

62. Seligson identifies three reasons for the relative "decline" of the "agrarian question": urbanization, international outmigration, and land reform efforts. See Seligson, "Thirty Years of Transformation," 43–73.

63. Foley, *Land, Peace, and Participation,* 3.

64. Seligson, "Thirty Years of Transformation," 61.

65. As quoted in David Rieff, "Almost Justice," *New Republic,* July 6, 1998: 38.

66. World Bank, *El Salvador Case Study,* 17.

67. See Orr, "Paradigm Lost?" Chap. 9. See also Secretary-General, *The Situation in Central America,* A/51/917: 9–10.

68. World Bank, *El Salvador Case Study,* 11.

69. William Stanley and David Holiday, "Peace Mission Strategy and Domestic Actors: UN Mediation, Verification and Institution-building in El Salvador," *International Peacekeeping* 4, 2 (Summer 1997): 22–49.

70. Ibid., 45–46.

71. The mission passed through four distinct phases: 1) The United Nations Observer Mission in El Salvador (ONUSAL) under Security Council mandates between July 26, 1991, and April 30, 1995; 2) the Mission of the United Nations in El Salvador (MINUSAL) under a General Assembly mandate from May 1, 1995, to April 30, 1996; 3) the United Nations Office of Verification in El Salvador (ONUV) from May 1, 1996, to December 31, 1996; and finally, 4) a tiny support unit for UN headquarters of four, then two individuals who have been housed within the UNDP structure in the country from January 1, 1997, to the present.

7

Conclusion

Chetan Kumar

The arguments made in this volume suggest that the key to lasting peace within a society is an ability on the part of its members to manage tensions and disputes before the eruption of violent conflict. Though this ability might emerge outside of formal political arenas, it will eventually need to take the form of political processes that are resilient when faced with multiple crises, that have both authority and increasing legitimacy, and that are capable of being institutionalized. The five cases examined in this volume show that such processes cannot flourish—even if their design appears promising—if they do not emerge from the appropriate kind of relations between the different groups, actors, and sectors within a society. These healthy relations, in turn, will be both facilitated by as well as manifest in such conditions as a capacity for dialogue and compromise among the relevant groups, a secure public space in which voices that seek moderation and engagement can be heard and in which moderate constituencies can be mobilized, and participation by major groups at different levels in key areas of decisionmaking. Other case-specific factors will also affect the capacity for conciliatory intergroup relations.

The central argument of this volume is that international peacebuilding efforts should focus on those factors that allow stable political processes to emerge and flourish. An exclusive emphasis on the form of political institutions may not be enough or may even be counterproductive, if the right factors that will allow these institutions to work and be consolidated over time are not present. Without stable political processes, even useful efforts to rebuild the economy, the environment, or infrastructure will come to little long-term effect.

It is important to distinguish between the conception of politics as discussed in this volume and specific political mechanisms or structures devised to help manage various social or political tensions. The latter range widely, from various federal and consociational arrangements to territorial and institutional power-sharing mechanisms. Included in this range have been instruments for formal political participation by groups and individuals, from Western-style democracy to local adaptations thereof.[1]

A political focus for peacebuilding, as suggested in this volume, encompasses and transcends these different structural forms. Hence, international peacebuilders should not focus primarily on prescribing or operating specific political structures but on facilitating or enforcing[2] the conditions that constitute an appropriate context for these structures to emerge.[3]

A political focus for peacebuilding does not necessarily imply the primacy of those international actors that deal expressly with political issues, such as the UN's Department of Political Affairs. Rather, we suggest that all programming that involves societies in conflict should be conceived with political impact in mind. Across the range of actors, from foreign ministries through relief and development agencies, programs and policies should be alert to their effect on prospects for the emergence of sustainable conflict management structures, eventually in the political arena. If desperately needed short-term economic and humanitarian assistance has the potential for generating long-term distortions in the relations between actors and sectors in a country, then steps for future correction should be built into the program itself. Similarly, development and reconstruction programs should emphasize not just the final programmatic objectives but also the processes through which these programs are accepted and sustained by the local actors concerned. If these processes are sound and rooted in tolerance and compromise, then the long-term basis for not just successful economic management but also a sustainable polity can be laid.

The cases examined here indicate that international policymakers must take a series of simple but important and often neglected steps in order to identify and promote those factors that will allow the emergence of viable political processes.[4] These steps include:

- *Substantive, nuanced knowledge of the political landscape of a society,* including an understanding of the goals and interests that underlie the stated ideologies of major actors within the affected society;
- *Carefully considered strategy,* based on this knowledge, for promoting those factors that will allow the establishment of authoritative and legitimate political processes and institutions;
- *Coordination of international efforts,* civilian and military, and among segments of civilian assistance (humanitarian, developmental, and political);
- *Implementation characterized by learning and feedback,*[5] so that the means used by international actors to achieve their goals can be adjusted as the situation demands and so that temporary setbacks do not prevent or derail longer-term accomplishments.[6]

Treating Peace as Process

While longer-term, structural contributors to political violence must be understood and fully appreciated, international peacebuilding efforts will be most effective if they focus principally on a society's political capacity to manage tensions arising from these causes, rather than on redressing specific long-term factors as such.[7] Keeping the focus of peacebuilding on politics, as we propose, is distinct from, though meant to inform choices about specific institutional forms or their operation in particular situations. Whatever the precise institutional forms, the creation or revival of these structures is often contingent on several sets of relations:[8] between political actors; between political and civic actors; between the relevant sectors in that society; and between all of these and various external actors, governmental and nongovernmental, active in that country. The important link between political relations and sustainable peace[9] has been examined by John Paul Lederach, who has drawn an important distinction between horizontal and vertical relations:

> Most peacebuilding work, particularly in the sub-field of conflict resolution, has been aimed at improving aspects of relationships through negotiation, dialogue, and mediation by getting counterparts to meet with each other. However, if we ask the question "who meets each

> other to develop relationships?" we find this answer: people who are at a relatively equal status within the context of the conflict. Community people meet community people, mid-range leaders encounter each other, and of course, top level political leaders in the limelight sit across negotiation tables. . . . The most significant gap in interdependence we face is rooted in the lack of responsive and coordinated relationships *up and down the levels of leadership in a society affected by protracted violent conflict* [emphasis added]. This is what I have referred to as *vertical capacity.*[10]

Lederach's concept of *vertical capacity* suggests that if these relations are to foster legitimate political capacities, then they have to encompass not just healthy relations between different actors but also between different actors at various levels of society. If healthy and appropriately managed, these relations provide the right context for the establishment of authoritative and viable political processes.[11]

While the specific factors behind healthy intergroup relations may vary from one society to another, the chapters in this volume suggest some common ones:

- *Capacity for dialogue and compromise* among concerned actors.[12]
- *Public security* that guarantees heterogeneity of expression and debate among multiple groups and actors.[13]
- *Participation* by all key actors and sectors in the formulation and operation of the political structures that manage conflict.[14]

For international actors, the key peacebuilding role is, therefore, to facilitate the emergence of appropriate structures by actively promoting these enabling factors.[15] Structures that are not firmly rooted in the right kind of intergroup relations will soon collapse or require massive international assistance to stay viable, no matter how well conceived they may be in theory. These factors are being increasingly recognized by major players in the formulation of approaches to peacebuilding, such as the OECD's Development Assistance Committee.[16]

Developing the Peacebuilder's Role

Intergroup relations evolve over time and are especially fluid in the context of violent conflict. They are also shaped unavoidably by both internal and external actors, the positions each take, and the material and normative resources each brings to bear. As long as international actors are involved in peacebuilding at all, they will affect indigenous developments in multiple, not always salutary ways. In order to anticipate their likely effect and direct it as best as possible to the support of an ongoing peace process, the peacebuilder's first task must be to map the evolving patterns of relations between key actors and sectors within the affected society, both domestic and international. Several specific questions quickly concentrate this analysis:

- Who are the key players? What are their interests and whom do they represent?
- What are the different contexts in which the conflict is occurring?
- What are the possible impacts of international intervention on relations among various parties and sectors?
- What are the consequences of implementing a peace agreement *as signed* for longer-term relations between groups and sectors?

Only after having provisionally mapped the political landscape—and continuing to improve their understanding of the terrain—can policymakers move on to the second task of reliably identifying factors likely to help transform intergroup relations into viable political processes that are both lasting and legitimate. The third step then becomes determining an appropriate international role in creating or strengthening these factors. This determination, as well as the fulfilling of the role, will ideally be coordinated between different international actors. The final step will be to ensure that this role is carried out flexibly after an adequate assessment of the extent of time and commitment that may be required in fulfilling it.

Before considering these steps in greater detail, it is important to recognize the difficulties that policymakers face in collecting and using information while developing policy, and particularly in creating coordinated strategies on the basis of this information. In practical terms, both these goals are very difficult to realize.[17]

For instance, given the constraints of time under which they operate, policymakers may simply not have the time to sample and make decisions on the basis of available expert knowledge on a particular issue or country.[18] In addition, the number of situations that strained bureaucracies have to deal with necessitates the expenditure of smaller amounts of time and effort on those cases that are not politically urgent or visible (the much-debated, so-called CNN effect). Even for those cases that do receive attention, it requires considerable effort for policymakers to push for certain courses of action within their own systems of government, let alone within the bureaucracies and institutions of other actors and governments.[19] These constraints imply that while some thought might be given to the nature of conflict and the best means for addressing it, rarely is a systematic and coordinated strategy based on independent input and analysis developed and applied to particular internal conflicts. In some cases, given a willingness of political leaders in intervening states, high-level conversation between top leaders might establish very broad political parameters for intervention. However, this does not imply that these parameters were correctly established or that top-level political agreement translated into coordinated implementation on the ground. The restoration of ousted President Jean-Bertrand Aristide in Haiti, the creation of a "multiethnic" Bosnia, and the revival of the Somali state are examples of agreement on broad parameters by the intervening parties without a concomitant coordinated strategy to follow.

Given these problems of development and implementation, policymakers should perhaps prioritize—in the limited time they may have—developing an understanding of the determinants of the political relationships between the key actors and sectors (and not just the primary protagonists) in a society. This understanding will help identify critical factors that will sustain viable political processes within the affected countries. Similarly, to the extent that some political exchange for achieving a minimal level of coordination takes place between top leadership of intervening actors, peacebuilding should be targeted toward reinforcing and providing support for those factors that will allow resilient and authoritative political processes to emerge in conflicted societies. A political focus for peacebuilding efforts, therefore, may not only be substantively justified but may also represent the most productive use—given the numerous limitations faced by multiple actors in generating common options and political will for action—of international resources and time in the short run.

Mapping the Political Cartography of Conflict

Players

The players in the conflict are critical.[20] Frequently, the primary protagonists in a conflict, by dint of their weight in materials and resources, draw the most attention. International organizations and actors, who are often used to dealing with governments and political hierarchies, also tend to focus primarily on prominent actors with the biggest international outreach. Firm settlements are seen as being most easily reached between a few of these big players rather than a host of smaller ones. However, merely identifying the top players may not be sufficient.[21] In some cases, these players may actually benefit from the further continuation of conflict (either directly or through the possibility of a future all-out victory over others) and may view cease-fires and accords as tactical maneuvers rather than as moves toward peace. In these situations, where the players are primarily interested in the power or resources that accrue from the conflict, any of a host of ideologies ranging from nationalism to democracy may be articulated in order to justify continuing the conflict.[22] Hence, it is important to attempt to segregate the stated rationales of the primary protagonists from their real interests. Furthermore, even where the primary protagonists claim ideological motivation, in actuality they may not be legitimately representing the ideologies in question outside of their immediate constituencies.

In Haiti, for instance, although Aristide was considered the most legitimate representative of Haiti's democracy movement during the years of his first presidency, many in this movement no longer consider him to be their best or most capable interlocutor. However, the tendency of many external analysts to divide the Haitian political spectrum between Aristide's partisans and the elements who have traditionally opposed him tends to further polarize an already conflicted political system; this division diminishes the role of many actors who might in fact be more willing to build consensus and compromise. Similarly, Ameen Jan's analysis makes it clear that many Somalis did not consider the warlords' military campaigns as the best means for obtaining security for their land and pastures. Hence, both Haiti and Somalia demonstrate the importance of tapping into constituencies and actors other than primary protagonists.[23] Should the primary protagonists prove unwilling to make peace, other actors and constituencies could, under certain circumstances, provide an alternative route to peace.[24]

The first step in correctly mapping intergroup relations, therefore, is to identify the primary protagonists, in addition to developing a nuanced understanding of their actual and stated interests and the degree to which they represent the constituencies on whose behalfs they state their claims. In this context, it is also important to have knowledge of those elements in a society that may not provide direct allegiance to one or other of the primary protagonists.

Context

In most cases of internal conflict that have prompted international intervention, the obvious context is not only the immediate cause of the intervention but also the primary determinant of the course of that intervention. However, it is often in the more subtle, underlying context that the key to peacebuilding efforts can be found.

In the case of Somalia, the visible context was that of a humanitarian disaster. The ensuing international response was first to provide humanitarian relief and subsequently, to try and revive the Somali state so that it could assume the burden of providing for its own citizens. However, before its collapse the Somali state had become a bone of contention among a number of actors none of whom had the wherewithal to transcend traditional precolonial and colonial cleavages.[25] There was no guarantee that a state apparatus restored through international munificence would have been any less contested. The Somali crisis was, therefore, perhaps less an issue of humanitarian crisis resulting from a violent dispute over power sharing and more an issue of the fundamental reordering of the concept of Somali statehood within Somalia itself.

In the light of this subtler context, the option of using force and persuasion to push the warlords toward re-creating the centralized Somali state was perhaps not optimal. A less obvious but perhaps more successful approach might have been to work with those groups already inclined toward peace at the local level (local clan and religious leaderships and leaders of the breakaway fragments of the former Somali state, such as Northern Somaliland) to create conditions in which trade and agricultural activity could resume locally. The long-run aggregate outcome of these efforts might have been the reemergence of a centralized Somali state; but such a state, particularly one dominated by the primary protagonists, did not appear essential for the immediate well-being of most Somalis.

In Bosnia, the humanitarian disaster appeared to have been the result of a conflict based upon ancient ethnic antagonisms. Grim-faced international officials spoke about the intractability of "centuries-old" conflict. Hence, the Dayton accords and their implementation sought to use sticks and carrots to persuade the primary protagonists to live in a "multiethnic" Bosnia. However, the primary goal of the leaders of the conflict was arguably not ethnic vindication but the pragmatic pursuit of power by all means. This provided a subtler context for the Bosnian conflict, which was created by regimes that resolved the issue of ethnic differences by *forcing* people not to live next to each other. The primary peacebuilding task was therefore not "multiethnicity" but the creation of more democratic regimes.[26] In this regard, Dayton's electoral provisions should not have been viewed as the only route—and arguably not the most auspicious—to a more tolerant Bosnia. In fact, the decision of international implementers to hold early elections on schedule consolidated the power of nationalist parties.[27] Under a different strategy, these arrangements would have been treated as temporary, while a highly intrusive international administration in Bosnia moved to empower locally (if only on a transitional basis) those elements that did not stand to benefit directly from prolonging ethnic conflict.[28] Some of the measures that were taken after elections to undermine the authority of ethnonationalists and to enforce free movement and residence across interethnic boundaries should in fact have been taken before elections. Elections held in a more democratic environment might have, among other outcomes, led to a political process more capable of dealing with issues arising from the different identities of Bosnia's citizens.

In Haiti, the obvious context involved the overthrow of a democratic regime through illegal means and the resulting refugee overflow to Haiti's neighbors. The international response was to restore that regime and then to take steps to consolidate the democratic institutions that had been overthrown. However, the crisis was more than the overthrow of a democratic regime by a few miscreants. When Aristide became the first democratically elected president of Haiti in 1991, his recently politicized supporters did not see him merely as the head of an elected government. They saw him as the harbinger of a revolution that would transform the country's social and economic relations. Nor did the dominant oligarchy view him as the head of an elected government. They saw his vision of a corruption- and monopoly-free economy as a mortal threat to their lives and fortunes. Aristide's elected government was thus subjected to pressures from both the impatient masses and the reluctant elite. It faced the contradictory challenge of trying to deliver a quick and revolutionary transformation through gradual means that satisfied all. When the elected government was restored in 1994, this contradiction was also restored, and it has stymied all subsequent efforts to make Haiti's nascent democratic institutions work. Intergroup relations in Haiti are hence primarily characterized not by machinations directed at elected government but by deeper concerns regarding the longer-term fortunes of individuals and groups in a rapidly changing environment. Given this more subtle context, the international response to Haiti's crisis should have featured not just the restoration of democratic processes but also the creation of wider processes of building consensus and compromise (akin to the process in Guatemala) between different social sectors that had previously interacted only spasmodically and violently.[29]

In Cambodia, the obvious context for peacebuilding efforts was the negotiated end to civil war and the implementation of a peace agreement. As Michael Doyle correctly points out, however, the subtler context for the conflict was a struggle to dominate a parasitic state apparatus that was urban-based and, in a manner similar to Haiti, that treated the country's rural expanse as a periphery to be exploited. In the absence of a differentiated economy and polity, this apparatus was also a primary source of political rewards and patronage, and hence highly contested. This contest defined intergroup relations in Cambodia. Of the groups involved in the contest, the Khmer Rouge, in losing its Cold War relevance, also lost its temporary legitimacy. An alternate strategy for Cambodia might have involved the facilitation of a power-sharing arrangement between the other parties to the conflict that focused explicitly on the state apparatus. The government resulting from this arrangement could have pursued the delegitimized Khmer Rouge (which is in fact what happened, as a joint CPP–FUNCINPEC government created through the UN-sponsored elections waged war on the Khmer Rouge). Simultaneously, a program for refocusing the state apparatus toward delivery of public service, involving dialogues, seminars, and training sessions among the partisans of all parties constituting this apparatus could have been an important first step in ensuring that the state was more than an expression of factional interest. Another important and simultaneous step might have been to encourage the emergence of autonomous political and economic activity in rural areas, so that the Cambodian polity could have greater depth beyond the interests of urban-based factions. Elections held in this rejuvenated context might have led to results seen as more than a tactical maneuver on the part of the factions.

While the UN-sponsored elections under UNTAC were an important expression of the Cambodian people's need for democratic participation, both those elections as well as subsequent ones after the Hun Sen coup in 1997 have done little to address the fundamental context of the Cambodian conflict.

In El Salvador, contrary to the other four cases, a subtler context to the conflict did not exist. The country's civil war, both obviously and fundamentally, was a result of the political inability of the ruling oligarchy to deal with the majority's demands for more land and equality. This in turn, in a manner similar to Haiti's, was a result of a historic absence of appropriate relations and linkages between the different social sectors and classes. The absence of equality was further vitiated, as Robert Orr points out, by the militarization of society that had taken place during the civil war. Demilitarization was therefore crucial to the creation of healthy intergroup relations, as were a series of confidence-building and participation-generating exercises that would allow all actors to participate in political decisionmaking on the basis of agreed-upon procedures. The UN-mediated peace settlement identified and helped to create many of the institutions and political practices that have successfully obtained both demilitarization as well as commonly accepted participation by the key actors in the political process. However, also as in Haiti, many of the key sectors have not yet acquired the ability to negotiate or compromise their way around or build a consensus on some of the fundamental differences on social and economic policy between them. This inability is manifest at the local level in areas such as land disputes and at the national level on issues such as privatization. Hence, while the peacebuilding effort in El Salvador has correctly recognized the explicit and underlying issues, steps remain to be taken to address and redress these.

In most cases, prompts—such as refugee crises, humanitarian disasters, or threats to international/regional security—are merely the symptoms of the conflict's primary dynamics and not the dynamics themselves. The constraints of sovereignty may require that the UN and other external actors intervene only when these prompts become manifest and overwhelming. However, it is the peacebuilders' capacity to address the underlying context of the conflict, in order to discern and act upon the more fundamental of these prompts, that must be developed at this second step in the peacebuilding process.

Immediate Impact of External Involvement

The potential impact of international intervention in conflicted societies is often assessed in terms of its ability to achieve goals that have been set by the intervening parties themselves, or in terms of the relations between the intervening parties and the local actors. Rarely ever is intervention assessed in terms of its impact on the longer-term relations between various sectors and actors—civil and political—within the affected society itself. Yet the resources and ideas of the intervening parties are a key variable in determining whether intergroup relations within a society can take the form of viable conflict management processes or not. This understanding of the consequences of intervention behooves external parties to spend more time on determining and anticipating the *political* impacts of their resources and strategies. These impacts can be both intended as well as inadvertent, positive as well as negative.

The inadvertent negative consequences could include the intensification of fault lines between various groups and sectors in a society as a result of increased struggle over international resources. In societies with manifest rifts between a minority elite and an underprivileged majority, the elite are often better able to organize and interact comprehensively with external actors and to receive external assistance. Hence, in societies emerging from prolonged conflict over issues relating to political and economic domination by a minority elite, loosely targeted international assistance can further widen differences and perhaps reignite violent conflict.

Should external intervention occur during a conflict, international resources can become the target of competition among the combatants, as happened in Somalia. There, combatants violently contested the right to be awarded transport and logistics contracts by international officials and fought over materiel captured from or left behind by international troops. In this situation, depending upon the volume and geographical distribution of international resources, international intervention can even affect the balance of conflict. Uneven access to contracts awarded by the international community might strengthen one party not only at the expense of its primary opponents but also at the expense of alternate voices that challenge the existing constructions of conflict.

A history of prior relationships between the intervening parties and the primary protagonists can also affect the evolution of the political process in a particular society. For instance, a perception that some Haitian organizations specializing in international policy in Haiti tilted in the past toward the elite has tarnished current international efforts to build lasting peace in that country. Well-intentioned international support for efforts to strengthen Haiti's frail institutions is seen by some as evidence of elite domination of the institutions, thus making it difficult for these institutions to play intermediary roles between the different sectors. Although these are not insurmountable difficulties, they require international parties to be more conscious of the political implications of their roles and activities and to make decisions and policies based on awareness of these implications.

In Bosnia, Elizabeth Cousens describes NATO's interpretation of its military mandate as "minimalist." Along with the unwillingness of international actors to consider postponing the first round of postwar elections, this reticence allowed a sufficient deterioration in the political and security environment for which international actors have arguably overcompensated by adopting increasingly interventionist policies at a later stage. As a consequence, instead of international actors supporting the appropriate evolution of intergroup relations, they have become a dominant player as one among other groups in Bosnia's intergroup relations. The IFOR example is a powerful illustration of the argument that any mapping of the political terrain, and of any subsequent design of international approaches to it, should involve key international actors.

Cambodia provides another strong illustration for this argument. Doyle points to the impact of UNTAC's rather heavy economic footprint in skewing Cambodia's economy even farther away from the rural areas and toward an urban bias. Clearly, the consequences of UNTAC's presence in Cambodia were not neutral, and all dimensions of the operation should have initially been conceived while keeping in mind that UNTAC was a critical determinant not just of the transition from civil war to a stable polity but of the key parameters of that stable polity itself.

Long-term Consequences of Peace Accords

Experts have argued that the most significant question with regard to civil wars is why certain civil wars do not resume after a cease-fire or an agreement. They point out correctly that most external peacemaking attempts focus on altering the warlike relations between the primary protagonists through various incentives and disincentives designed to induce compromise. These compromises could be formalized by signing accords or agreements between the protagonists. Should these arrangements not evolve into resilient political processes, however, they may collapse in the future. A significant factor in this collapse has been the transformation of former wartime allies into enemies. According to Pierre Atlas and Roy Licklider, "Outsiders should not assume either that wartime cooperation will continue in peace or that 'normal' peacetime behavior will appear naturally of its own accord. Indeed, they should probably anticipate that ad hoc wartime alliances are likely to dissolve with the risk of renewed civil violence."[30] This conclusion suggests that accords and agreements, even when implemented, may of themselves be insufficient to guarantee sustained peace. Ideally, these accords should be seen as starting points for activities transforming compromises and negotiated arrangements into the types of lasting intergroup relations that constitute sustainable political processes.

The nature of the compromise reached by protagonists directly affects the prospects of longer-term relations between them. Compromises reached for reasons of expediency or immediate material gain last only as long as these continue. Compromises made for material gain can also be expensive for their international promulgators, who must maintain the supply side in order to ensure that the primary protagonists do not return to conflict. Elsewhere, shotgun compromises enforced by external actors might require the continued use of the shotgun in order to stay enforced, as is evident in Bosnia. Sometimes, compromises that are important to the external parties but do not address the primary issues among the domestic parties may collapse quickly, as happened with the short-lived Governors Island Agreement between Haiti's military junta and President Aristide in 1993.

An easier way to obtain peace might be through decisive victory by one side. This tends to be far easier to consolidate than peace that arrives via a compromise, especially when there are significant economic resources available for reconstruction. Unfortunately, peace by victory is also likely to bring with it repression by new authorities and violent reprisals against former adversaries.[31] By contrast, a negotiated peace may be less likely to be followed by massive abuses of human rights, but it can also be highly resistant to taking root.[32] Negotiated settlements have better odds over the long term, according to conventional wisdom, when the parties have reached a "hurting stalemate" on the battlefield.[33] People, armies, and leaders weary of war begin to realize that they may be able to accomplish their aims via political battle instead of military confrontation. El Salvador and Guatemala stand as the exemplars of this logic. In these instances, even if the original compromise no longer stands, the broader situation still prevents a relapse into wider conflict.

Negotiated settlements based on short-term compromises may also have better longer-term odds if they contain provisions for strategies and actions that gradually alter some of the factors such as misperceptions, insecurity, exclusion, or personal animosities that have poisoned intergroup relations. The primary protagonists, on their own, are unlikely to systematically create such provisions. The urgency that characterizes the negotiation of most settlements may also prevent a systematic consideration by international mediators of such provisions. Overall, the cases in this volume demonstrate that negotiated compromises require a systematic follow-through in which factors affecting longer-term intergroup relations, and hence the prospects for creating resilient political processes, are addressed. It is unlikely that this systematic follow-through can be concretely or adequately incorporated into an initial agreement, given the obstacles to reaching any negotiated settlement at all. Peace agreements, therefore, need to be seen less as comprehensive blueprints for postwar polities to be implemented exactly as conceived on paper, than as launching points—and possibly flawed ones—for processes that must adapt over time and are only likely to evolve in the long term into successful polities and economies.[34]

The Cambodian experience validates this point. Doyle points out that in response to the criticism that UNTAC did not do enough to reform the Cambodian state apparatus, UNTAC's defenders assert that it was difficult enough to get any type of reform-oriented role for UNTAC into the Paris accords to begin with. However, once the accords were signed, it might have been possible to creatively interpret UNTAC's considerable mandate and to jointly explore initiatives for reform with different levels of the state of Cambodia.

Hence, the fourth step in mapping intergroup relations should be to develop an understanding of the kinds of relations that produced the initial compromises, the expectations that various groups have of these compromises, and the manner in which these compromises affect the subsequent evolution of intergroup relations. Knowledge of these elements will assist international actors in determining the factors that will transform these relations into sustainable conflict management processes.

Identifying Factors Enabling the Emergence of Resilient Political Processes

Provided that the relations among the various groups and sectors have been mapped reliably, the factors that lead to resilient and adaptive political processes can then be identified in each country's case.

Haiti

In Haiti, the biggest determinant of intergroup relations has been the various chasms of inequality, misperception, and exclusion that have traditionally separated different sectors of Haitian society from one another. The primary factor in building a viable political process in the country will therefore have to be the consolidation of engagement, consensus, and compromise among all these sectors. A public process of engagement between the government and various sectors of Haitian society on key national issues is needed. In effect, greater participation in government by all sectors of society is essential for legitimizing the Haitian state. This participation will be ensured not just by democratic elections where the winner takes all but by a political process where even the losers of the elections are able to agree that they have a stake in maintaining an impartial political system. Indeed, this lesson also applies to the other cases in this volume, where international priorities have focused on finding a political solution that will end the violence but where deepening whatever peace may have been achieved requires giving a stake to broader segments of the society in the political system. To the extent that this has not yet happened in Haiti, a tremendous sense of alienation, directed both at the government and the international community, has developed among the population. Specific methods such as the decentralization of economic decisionmaking as well as participatory project implementation, along both geographical and social lines, may not only help to reduce this sense of alienation but provide a way around the current political paralysis.[35]

With adequate encouragement and protection, Haiti's population could provide a sense of forward momentum to the country's deadlocked political class. Certainly, this kind of engagement by the population will constitute an important domestic conflict management asset.[36] While Haiti's ruling elite in the cities have had a long tradition of violent conflict over scarce state resources, the peasantry has an equally long tradition of cooperative activity in times of distress, which are frequent in a rugged rural environment. Indeed, contrary to what many believe, the largest peasant movements were not created by Aristide but in fact helped to launch him and the Lavalas bandwagon. These movements suggest that there are dynamic alternatives in Haitian politics that have yet to be seriously tapped.

Problems of misperception also vitiate intergroup relations in Haiti. Many among the elite continue to see grassroots organizations as tools of populist vendetta; conversely, many ordinary Haitians continue to see most members of the elite as cold-blooded killers. The implementation of many worthy projects and plans has suffered as a result of the disruption of political processes caused by these schisms. Actual participation in projects by actors drawn from diverse social sectors and geographic areas of a country may perhaps help to heal these schisms. In Haiti, most development projects have not provided this kind of inclusion. In fact, many of these projects, depending on who were seen as the ultimate beneficiaries, have heightened animosities along class or sectoral lines. Notable exceptions include the USAID project at Fond Jean-Noel, described earlier. In rural areas where participatory projects are being implemented, members of the rural elite and the peasantry have all laid down arms to rebuild rural communities as a result.

The key factors, therefore, in creating a resilient political process in Haiti are extensive engagement and compromise between all sectors, as well as genuine participation by all sectors in the political process.

Somalia

In Somalia, the key factor undermining intergroup relations was the exacerbation of clan and subclan cleavages. Peace in Somalia, therefore, fundamentally required the absence of political violence between and within clans and the reconstruction of civilian political authority that could provide effective governance at local and zonal levels. However, the assumption that undergirded international efforts in Somalia, as evident in the Addis Ababa agreement and UNOSOM II's mandate, was that a central government would end the conditions of anarchy and violence producing the famine. The various efforts of UNOSOM II from 1993 to 1995 at political accommodation among the factions, grassroots political development, and institution building all arose from the concept of a functioning central government in Somalia as the desired end-state of the intervention. John Hirsch and Robert Oakley point to the limitations of externally derived understandings of desirable political development in Somalia:

> Policy and operational decisions initially made by the Bush administration for UNITAF were expanded for UNOSOM II . . . The changes, however, were not clearly thought through in terms of their potential difficulties and pre-requisites for success. The UN Security Council and the Secretary-General, with US support, began to impose their judgments about what would constitute acceptable political evolution and to set up an intrusive administrative structure supported by military force. When challenged by Aideed and the SNA, the United Nations responded by designating them the enemy, politically and militarily. The outcome was devastating, for Somalis and the peacekeepers, for US foreign policy, and for peacekeeping itself.[37]

Both the historical patterns of Somalia as a stateless, pastoral, nomadic society and the manner in which Siad Barre exploited clan divisions pointed to the difficulty of re-creating a unitary state in Somalia in the short run.[38] Hence, instead of viewing the declaration of secession by "Somaliland" as the result of a renegade clan leadership, Jan argues that the international community should have recognized from that case the difficulty of putting Somalia back together again.

In the years preceding Barre's fall and during the subsequent civil war, the country was de facto divided, as in "Somaliland," into various autonomous, clan-based zones. In some of these zones, clan leaders had in fact embarked on a process to reconstitute political authority and re-energize local mechanisms for conflict management. International assistance supporting these clan-based efforts to reconstitute political authority in Somalia should have entailed, first of all, a reduction in the structural impact of the international presence that froze many indigenous political processes. With a leaner, civilian-oriented political operation, the UN could have identified past and emergent clan leaders in addition to the faction representatives, supported local efforts to provide security, offered appropriate technical support to local administrations, and funded efforts at demobilization. Once peace had returned to the bulk of Somalia through the strengthening of clan-based political authorities, a united federal state with a clearly delineated institutional mechanism that defined the respective functions of the center and the clan-based zones may have been possible.[39]

One of the key obstacles to clan-level reconciliation in Somalia was the perhaps unwarranted international focus on the leaders of the conflict. The conditions created by the intervention—both intentionally and inadvertently—catapulted these leaders to the political apex of Somali society and further narrowed whatever limited space there was for alternate clan-based civilian political leaderships to emerge. Jan argues that a reconfigured international role in Somalia could have been supportive of these broader clan-based leaderships. This role would have included facilitating inclusive political dialogue at the clan level, which would have comprised civilian elements in addition to faction leaders. Such dialogue should have been conducted within Somalia, rather than at high-level international conferences, and should have allowed sufficient time for agreements to be reached so that they were durable. International efforts to assist in building local, civilian institutions of governance would have helped to bolster the process of consensus building within and between the various clans. International intervention to support these delicate political dynamics should have been sufficiently light and nonintrusive so as not to inhibit their development.[40]

It is clear from Jan's arguments that to the extent that the primary determinant of intergroup relations in Somalia is clan cleavages rather than the struggle to re-create a unitary state, the single most important factor in creating lasting political processes, and hence lasting peace, in Somalia is to provide for peaceful and secure relations among the clans themselves.

Cambodia

Doyle has established that the emergence of a polity that can viably manage disputes in Cambodia remains highly contingent on creating a less factionalized and corrupt state apparatus, particularly the military, and the state's ability to serve not just a small urban population but the entire country. While yet another power-sharing arrangement was worked out in 1998 between Prince Norodom Ranariddh and Hun Sen under pressure from Cambodia's international donors, the state remains fundamentally unable to deal with issues affecting the majority of Cambodia's population and hence does not have the capacity for long-term conflict management. While the current power-sharing arrangement may be more stable given the greater comfort level of CPP and the final extinction of the Khmer Rouge, the fact that most of the state apparatus owes allegiance to CPP does not augur well for a sustainable polity. In addition, while elections may be contrived and even fairly conducted in the near future, a continued lack of performance by the state may generate an upsurge of social discontent that could reignite the conflict in the midterm.

Recent experience shows that the CPP-dominated state is amenable to a certain degree of persuasion by donor governments. The latter should encourage the state to build bridges with the rural population, both in terms of political relations as well as resource distribution. UNDP's SEILA project, highlighted by Doyle, could form the model for a national project. In fact, such an exercise would be beneficial for the CPP-led state as it would allow it to trade its narrow urban base for a more substantial national foundation. A broader base may also make it easier for the CPP-led state to decentralize and dismantle parts of the bureaucracy, thus precipitating a more open political and economic environment.

A key element of this project would include, as suggested by Doyle, educating state officials in techniques of consultation, outreach, dialogue, and dispute resolution, but more broadly, in seeing themselves as national civil servants and not as CPP functionaries. Given the dimensions of this effort, those functionaries tasked with managing critical resources could perhaps be targeted first.

Simultaneously with this effort, a systematic nationwide discussion could be launched through a number of forums on the parameters of a polity that is both open and stable. This discussion could engage civic organizations as well as local levels of government in providing specific inputs. Assured of another term in power, the current CPP leadership might be amenable to an enterprise of this nature, particularly since it may soon wish to turn to the question of leaving behind a legacy that is viewed favorably in domestic and international circles. Included in this discussion should be a number of concrete proposals, including several highlighted by Doyle, for making Cambodia's institutions more transparent and accountable.

While the options suggested above do not entail an investment of resources from the international community, they involve a sustained commitment to political facilitation when needed, including a well-coordinated approach to Cambodia's political development, so that the message for political reform is heard loudly and clearly by the concerned Cambodian parties.

Bosnia

In Bosnia, as suggested earlier, the various short-term strategies adopted by international actors have greatly complicated the task of building sustainable political processes. Attempts to create a multiethnic Bosnia by delineating ethnic territories may in fact have strengthened authoritarian tendencies and complicated intergroup relations. For instance, the international community supported in 1994 a military alliance between Muslims and Croats in Bosnia to counter and roll back the Serb military advances. The success of this approach led to the Dayton Agreement that redefined the territorial boundary of the two entities. The United States also trained and equipped Bosnian military forces in order to help create an internal military balance after the withdrawal of international military forces, while NATO secured the cease-fire line agreed to at Dayton. Essentially, the international community enforced a peace agreement in Bosnia while it militarily strengthened the previously weak side. However, it is difficult to predict whether this strategy of creating a military balance will be able to maintain peace once the international community withdraws from Bosnia. Problems are already apparent with the approach. First, the Bosnians have been strengthened to the extent that a possible future military confrontation between Bosnians and Serbs may result in a Bosnian victory. Given the recent history of Serb atrocities against Muslims, a military campaign against the Bosnian Serbs by the Bosnian leadership in the aftermath of a NATO drawdown is not an entirely unlikely scenario. Second, the "Equip and Train" program has strengthened the militaristic leaders within the Bosnian-Croat entity, weakening the more moderate constituencies. While these measures taken by the international community may have been necessary to stop the civil war, they may equally but inadvertently cause a return to war if they are not replaced or supplemented by steps to create more lasting intergroup relations.

The constitution created for Bosnia under the Dayton Agreement includes new power-sharing institutions that would hopefully channel management of conflicts within the rubric of a unitary state. However, several deep-seated problems remain that cast a shadow over the workability of these complex arrangements. First, not enough attention has been given to ensuring the longevity of the Bosniac-Croat Federation. Second, while elections have been the preferred international vehicle for composing the new national power-sharing institutions, the 1996 Bosnian elections legitimized and empowered the nationalist political forces by having them elected. The time and political space for moderate leaderships to emerge was very limited.

The most critical factor in building viable political processes in Bosnia will therefore be the creation of conditions under which political moderates can emerge, build a constituency, and be able to challenge the nationalist leaderships.[41] The rise of more moderate voices will also lead to healthier intergroup relations, which lie at the heart of viable political processes.

El Salvador

Of the cases examined in this volume, El Salvador presents the most striking example of the factors leading to resilient political processes being correctly identified and significantly addressed. Of course, much more remains to be done. Orr points out that the UN's political role in El Salvador, as well as that of key external actors such as the United States, was central to establishing a participatory Salvadoran polity able to manage issues between different groups and sectors more capably than ever before. In addition, the gradual manner of the UN's political pullout, with increasing ownership of previously UN-led processes by local actors, has created a high degree of sustainability and certainly provides a model for peacebuilding in the future. An important area in which these processes were initially deficient but subsequently corrected was the lack of international coordination on key issues. For a brief period, this posed the risk that local processes generated in tandem with internationally led processes could be skewed and uncoordinated, particularly in the area of the rebuilding of judicial system.

As Orr indicates, the new Salvadoran polity is adequately able to give cognizance to and deal with the largely socioeconomic questions of land and poverty that are important to the majority of the population. However, much more may still need to be done before reliable capacity to manage disputes in these areas resides both within the formal political processes as well as in civil society at large.

The issue here is not that of finding consensus between what may be fundamentally irreconcilable divisions between the left and right on economic strategy, but of building pragmatic compromises on policies that attract and keep foreign investment in El Salvador, maintain a degree of fiscal stability, and invest any modest short-term surpluses in health and education. In this framework, land disputes could be resolved not on the basis of a national ideology but practically and at the local level, with the interests of the conflicted parties in mind. However, the framework in which policies are pragmatic and oriented toward dispute resolution should be developed nationally. This development involves the further acquisition of skills in dispute management and dialogue by all concerned sectors.

Apart from these case-specific factors, a number of factors are critical for all the cases here. The role of moderate political forces grounded in stable and conciliatory relations is paramount and depends on the provision of adequate security.[42] Where war-time leaders dominate political exchange, it takes enormous courage for those who would change the political dynamics from hostility toward accommodation to speak out, not least because their presence is threatening to the leaders who wield military power. In Bosnia, for instance, those who seek to return to their prewar homes are quickly targeted by leaders whose political base is threatened by multiethnicity provisions of the Dayton accord. The constituencies most vital for sustaining peace are often the most vulnerable to security threats.

Mindful of the critical need for internal security, the international community has focused its attention on establishing independent and effective police forces in postconflict societies.[43] Emphasis has also been placed on demobilizing and reintegrating former combatants. The international community's record in both areas in several different cases is commendable. However, and often in spite of good intentions, it is difficult to establish credible and capable police forces hastily. Moreover, even the best police forces may not be sufficient to ensure protection against those who insist on using force to achieve their political ends. In such cases, resolute external action might be the only way to remove primary obstacles to sustainable conflict management within societies.[44]

In Haiti, for instance, political change was unlikely to have emerged without the internal backing of President Aristide's decision to abolish the army. Haiti's new, neutral police force has played an important role in providing the security umbrella under which broad political debate can occur. When political disputes between President René Preval and the opposition reached a head in Haiti in January 1999, both sides called for strikes and demonstrations. For the first time in the country's history, the only armed force in the country, the Haitian National Police, did not take sides in the political dispute but stayed neutral and helped maintain public order. A political dispute of this magnitude a few years previously might have prompted a coup d'état, possibly accompanied by rioting and civilian killings. The international community's role in creating a neutral police force in Haiti was instrumental in preventing such violence.

In contrast to Haiti, which has had some success in creating neutral state institutions to provide internal security, Bosnia suffers from problems attendant with the lack of local security institutions. These problems are exemplified by the difficulties of those who have attempted—utilizing the right accorded by the Dayton Agreement—to return to areas they fled during the war. In most cases, these returnees form part of the minority community, and they have frequently become targets of violence by those who want to maintain a strict ethnic division of the country. The fact that neutral police forces have not been able to protect them from targeted violence makes it highly unlikely that significant returns will take place. Nor has the international military presence in Bosnia provided security for these returnees. In addition, the fact that the Bosnian political stage is still occupied by semiauthoritarian parties makes it difficult to imagine the emergence of moderate political voices that want to change the polarized political choices facing Bosnia's population.

Somalia indicates the possibility of security institutions emerging indigenously without the assistance of the international community. Following the UN's withdrawal from Somalia in 1995, various local initiatives to enhance security at grassroots and clan levels emerged across the country. At the local level, these took the form of Islamic courts that were headed by the community's religious leaders. These communities organized their own police forces that reported to the Islamic courts, and law and order was maintained effectively by dispensing justice in accordance with *shari'a*.[45] The functioning of this system of internal security was in marked contrast to the Somali police that the international community had attempted to reconstruct from the remnants of the previous national police force, which functioned independently in the absence of any local political authority. Shortly after the UN's withdrawal, this new police force quickly folded in most locations where it had been established.[46] At the clan level, too, Somalia has been reconstructing institutions of governance and security. Conditions within many of these areas permit broad-based political dialogue that includes many sectors of Somali society in addition to the faction leaders. This development has allowed alternate voices, often of elders and traditional leaders, to emerge as important determinants of political change within their society.

While El Salvador has done significantly better than many others in developing the abilities of its political institutions to manage tensions before they lead to violence, the growing problem of criminal violence in the country may erode public confidence in the new institutions. Perhaps the best way to address this problem in a rounded fashion might be to use some of the new mechanisms for participation to generate public debate on strategies and options for curbing criminality. Options implemented after public consultation will allay fears of the revival of an authoritarian state, reduce support that criminal elements might have among the population, and actually help to further political development by democratizing the discourse on law enforcement. This will be particularly significant given the country's history of state repression.

In Cambodia, the particular problem of insecurity continues to be that of fear of physical harm among the political factions should they stop attempting to control a significant chunk of the state apparatus. Physical insecurity, therefore, is one of the key factors making the state a contested ground. The reported extrajudicial execution of FUNCINPEC partisans by Hun Sen's supporters during the 1997 coup has certainly worsened matters. The numerous attacks on political opponents, the hounding of civil society groups by the government's allies, attacks on the independent media, and human rights violations have all fostered an atmosphere of fear and suspicion that is nonconducive for generating sustainable political processes. In the ruling party particularly, the moderates are highly unlikely to hold sway.

As Doyle points out, even though UN and other types of human rights monitoring have an important role to play in this situation, the long-term solution lies with Cambodia's small but emerging civil society. Particularly important will be the ability of these activists to monitor the domestic situation, articulate their demands and concerns on the basis of international and domestic laws and norms, reach out to actors within the region and beyond for support, and present viable options for both domestic and international actors. While abuses have been frequent in Cambodia in recent years, the state has not indulged in widespread and systematic repression. This leaves windows of opportunity open for civic organizations, particularly if they receive training in developing and promoting their agendas.

Determining and Implementing the Appropriate International Role

After mapping the parameters of intergroup relations in a conflicted society, and deriving therefrom the factors that will sustain a viable political process in that society, the next step should be to build an appropriate international role in light of these parameters and factors. This step can only be undertaken simultaneously with the coordination of the different actors' roles and a collective determination by these actors of the boundaries of success and the external resources needed to achieve that success.

It is critical that the process determining the international role should be well coordinated among the key actors. First, long-term objectives and organizational imperatives of the various actors may be contradictory or even in conflict with each other, in addition to being unaligned with the broader imperatives of sustaining peace in the target country. Second, cooperation between actors *across* issue areas is still infrequent. For instance, strategies pursued to revive agriculture may not be congruent with initiatives in the areas of fiscal policy, revival of industries, job creation, and so on. This is a serious problem because it often leads to the dissociation of a country's polity or economy, whereby different sectors develop vertical linkages of dependency with external donors rather than developing horizontal linkages of interdependence with one another. Finally, there is often a lack of congruence between the short-term imperatives of the international community for providing emergency humanitarian relief in situations of dire emergency and the long-term imperatives of peacebuilding. This situation was clearly manifest in the Great Lakes region of Africa from 1994 to 1997, where steps taken to provide emergency humanitarian relief became an obstacle to building lasting peace.

Despite the need for coordination, several practical concerns identified earlier in this chapter can severely limit the extent of coordination. However, certain noteworthy attempts have been made to ensure prior political coordination, particularly within the UN. The revamping of the UN's Department of Humanitarian Affairs into the Office for Coordination of Humanitarian Affairs and the creation of executive committees for different issues at UN headquarters addressed some of the lacunae in coordination within the United Nations system. The "Friends of the Secretary-General" mechanism also allows states that are particularly interested in a UN operation or initiative to coordinate their strategies. No commensurate mechanisms exist outside the UN, however, to ensure coordination of the efforts of multiple international organizations and actors.

Where international peacebuilding is part of a multilateral effort, as in the cases here, the most obvious locus of coordination is the office of the Special Representative or the Special Envoy of the Secretary-General, as in the case of a UN-led operation (or a regional representative in case of a regional initiative), or where necessary, an Office of a High Representative of the international community, as in Bosnia.[47] Once authorized, this office, in the earliest stages of planning for intervention, should ideally work toward ensuring coordination among the key actors on issues ranging from objectives to the appropriate strategies for intervention. Much depends, however, on the personality and leadership qualities of the individual appointed to head this office and on the relations of this individual with policymakers in the key countries contributing to that intervention. The selection criteria, therefore, ought to be especially rigorous. Recently, suggestions have been made to enhance in creative ways the information and resources available to the position. These include linking, via the Internet, of this individual's office with groups of experts, strategists, and policymakers within member governments who could brainstorm electronically in support of an international role.

Once a certain degree of coordinated planning and strategic thinking is ensured and before the parameters of the international role are pinned down, careful thought should be given to whether a high-level political international role (as opposed to the activities of private and humanitarian groups) is actually needed and justified, within the context of a particular conflict.

As the cases discussed in this volume show, intervention raises an important strategic question as to whether it will help or hinder a society's achieving a stable and just political system. One could even argue that a period of violence is in some cases necessary to overturn a social order that is structurally unjust and undemocratic—the French and Russian revolutions and the English and American civil wars are notable examples.

There is no easy answer to the philosophical question of whether military intervention that freezes a conflict may also apprehend the overhaul of a fundamentally unjust political system. Indeed, it is difficult to imagine—and even more difficult to justify morally—the international community silently witnessing widescale atrocities for the sole reason that such violence is necessary in order for a new and more just society to emerge. What is clear, however, is that when international intervention in conflicted societies does occur—for reasons of national interest, humanitarianism, or a combination of the two—a political consensus among the intervenors as to the objectives of the intervention is paramount. Is the intervention a short-term fix to bring to a temporary halt a humanitarian emergency or a genocidal campaign? Is it intended to freeze the lines of confrontation between warring parties for an indeterminate period of time? Or is it an effort to transform the fundamental political processes that led to the conflict in the first place, which if unaddressed will likely plunge the society into future rounds of violence?

Once the concerned external parties have given due consideration to these factors and general consensus exists on the need and legitimacy for intervention, further discussion should take place on certain commonly held criteria under which the intervention could be deemed a success, the manner in which these criteria will be translated into specific goals for the intervening actors, and the resources and time required to achieve these goals. Given the constraints described earlier on inter-actor coordination, one can hope for only a modest consideration of common criteria and specific goals. The cases here clearly demonstrate that the most significant criterion for success ought to be the extent to which relations among various domestic actors and sectors have evolved into a viable political process. The hallmark of this process would be the extent to which it permits the different actors and sectors to decide, by consensus, not just the manner in which the country is to be rebuilt but also the nature of the problems that need to be addressed through international assistance. Quite often, depending on where they stand in the political and economic landscape of a country, different actors and sectors have very different understandings of the causes of political violence in a society. Should external actors proceed to address the causes of conflict only on the basis of an externally derived understanding of these causes, they run the risk of inadvertently empowering those internal actors who might be sympathetic to that understanding and disempowering those who are not. Hence, a viable political process should bring together both domestic and external actors into a comprehensive process for considering existing problems, identifying their causes, and seeking support for remedies both from abroad as well as from within the affected society. In this manner, the process addresses factors causing tensions among various groups before these tensions lead to violence.

It is important to emphasize again that in its initial stages, a viable process may not reach the pinnacle of institutional definition. Better-defined institutions and relationships might emerge over time as the process evolves. In fact, the cases here suggest that an excessive early emphasis on institutional forms and boundaries derived from exogenous contexts might even prevent the development of sustainable indigenous processes. The most important early characteristic of a viable political process is therefore not its degree of institutional definition or complexity but the extent to which it receives trust and participation from its constituents—in other words, the degree of its popular legitimacy. On this parameter, existing political processes in Haiti, Bosnia, and Cambodia, as well as the aborted unitary state that the international community sought to revive in Somalia, have proved highly inadequate, despite being institutionally complex and multifaceted. The political process in El Salvador has done much better and is certainly farther along than the rest in terms of sustainability.

If the criterion for the success of international intervention to sustain peace is the successful launch of a viable political process, then international actions and strategies should seek to achieve this goal in the most expeditious manner possible. Certainly, where possible, short-term humanitarian assistance or reconstruction efforts that may hinder the longer-term evolution of such a process should be avoided or implemented with the greatest care. Most significant, international efforts should focus with great urgency and care on those factors that will enable the emergence of a viable process. This will prevent a scenario where, as happened briefly in Somalia and appears to be a growing trend in Bosnia, the international presence dominates politics in the affected society.

What will be the length of time and the amount of resources required for creating viable political processes? Most existing conceptions of efforts to build lasting peace envisage everlasting commitments and infinite resources, a prospect that justifiably causes acute anxiety among officials in donor governments. The bulk of expenditures involved tend to go toward deploying veritable armies of international officials who take over all aspects of a country's life and attempt to rebuild them from scratch. Even in places such as Haiti or El Salvador that do not become de facto international protectorates, international commitment is perceived as having to be long lasting in order to ensure sustainable outcomes. To the extent that international officials are seen as running entire countries in the aftermath of civil conflict, one apparent school of thought emphasizes the restoration of legitimate local authority at all costs as a means of providing the international community with an exit strategy from an eternal commitment. Once local authority has been revived, international officials could ideally hand over decisionmaking to them and limit their own role to supporting peacebuilding projects conceived by the local authority.

However theoretically sound, this approach may fall apart in practice. The rush to revive local authority without ensuring that the conditions that can sustain a viable political process are in place can lead to circumstances in which the leaders of conflict acquire authority once again. The very first conceptualization of international time and resources needed to sustain peace should, therefore, involve moving very rapidly to create the conditions in which the right kinds of political processes can be revived. The issue here is not putting an arbitrary cap on the time and resources needed but ensuring that the latter are available in appropriate amounts.

When the international community disengaged from Somalia in 1994, critics touted nation building as the primary cause of international failure in that country. Subsequently, several American critics, most prominently former secretary of state Henry Kissinger, have argued for a move away from a foreign policy centered on humanitarian intervention and the reshaping of domestic politics toward one focused on more traditional cornerstones of U.S. policy abroad, such as great-power relations.[48] Most such arguments suggest that costly military interventions abroad have placed a tremendous strain both on U.S. defense capacity and on its relations with other key states. Ironically, however, it is the Somali example that demonstrates that peacebuilding centered on political processes in conflicted societies can be done effectively and efficiently with only a light military footprint. The alternate strategies for international intervention identified by Jan at the end of his chapter on Somalia clearly establish that the revival of sustainable political processes can be facilitated without heavy military or economic investment but with a lot of political foreknowledge and savvy.

The recommendations made in this volume for developing coherent and appropriate international strategies, while appearing to be idealistic under certain conditions, nonetheless need to be accommodated where possible. Arguably, given the nature of international politics (and domestic politics within the political systems of key actors), it may be difficult to have any kind of strategy at all. In that case, the best that one could insist on and hope for would be a clear focus on political processes as being central to the success of the broader peacebuilding enterprise and an attempt, however tenuous, to understand relations between the key groups and sectors in a society, and hence the factors that will sustain viable political processes based on these relations.

Lightly Treading in the Quagmire

Attempts to build lasting peace in war-torn societies continue to be dogged by perceptions that peacebuilding is a quagmire in which external forces should not get bogged down any longer than can be avoided. This problem is best addressed by changing the proverbial baby's bathwater, in other words through a shift in one's understanding of the peacebuilding enterprise rather than through terminating peacebuilding efforts themselves. The chapters in this volume provide several suggestions for bringing about this conceptual and policy change:

- International involvement is not an open-ended commitment but is specifically targeted to achieve a limited objective—that of establishing conditions (dialogue, public security, and participation) under which viable political processes can flourish.
- It is not the burden of any external actor—the United States, UN, or other major donors or agencies—to cure all that ails a country. These are tasks that should be carried out internally by the revived political system, with external actors providing

assistance for specific initiatives where such assistance has been sought.

- While the international community can certainly facilitate the emergence of viable political processes and institutions, it may also need to aggressively create the conditions in which such politics can emerge and grow. Otherwise, external actors could end up babysitting the nascent political systems for a very long time.

In the end, it should be recognized by all concerned that there is no way to guarantee that any political system will always be adept at managing tensions before they lead to violence or be resilient enough to endure without periods of external assistance. Indeed, success or failure cannot be easily anticipated in advance, no matter how diligent or accurate the intelligence and analytical input. Issues of short-term success or failure, and hence of right or wrong exit strategies, should perhaps have less piquancy in major-power capitals than they currently do. Perhaps the optimal approach is to make the best possible determination of the most appropriate intervention, recognize that perfect solutions will always be elusive, and design and implement peacebuilding policies with consequent sensitivity and accountability.

Notes

1. Connie Peck offers a comprehensive survey of various structural forms designed to manage conflict in "Finding Structural Solutions to Conflict," *Sustainable Peace: The Role of the UN and Regional Organizations in Preventing Conflict* (Washington, D.C.: Carnegie Commission on Preventing Deadly Conflict; Lanham, MD: Rowman and Littlefield, 1998), Chapter 4. The Harris and Reilly volume produced by International IDEA also documents an extensive array of institutional options as well as indicates conditions in which various mechanisms may be most helpful in managing existing or prospective tensions. See Peter Harris and Ben Reilly, eds., *Democracy and Deep-Rooted Conflict: Options for Negotiators* (Stockholm: International Institute for Democracy and Electoral Assistance, 1998).

2. A valuable example of an international role of this nature was the pressure exerted by international financial institutions on Malawi in the early 1990s. According to Nicole Ball, Jordana D. Friedmann, and Caleb S. Rossiter, "The Role of International Financial Institutions," in *The Price of Peace: Incentives and International Conflict Prevention*, ed. David Cortright (Washington, D.C.: Carnegie Commission on Preventing Deadly Conflict; Lanham, MD: Rowman and Littlefield, 1997): "From 1992 to 1994 World Bank pressure—in coordination

with aid suspensions by major bilateral donors—helped a remarkable citizens' protest movement in Malawi topple one of Africa's toughest and oldest dictatorships and establish a democratic form of government" (252–254).

3. This distinction between political structures and the context by which they are enabled and in which they are embedded is broadly analogous to (but not the same as) the distinction between "state" and "regime" that Pierre du Toit makes while offering his revised formulation (state–regime–civil society) of Joel Migdal's classic state–civil society framework. According to du Toit, "A regime comprises the values, norms, rules, procedures, and structures of authority that shape the ordering of power within and among the various organizational sites of the state." See Pierre du Toit, "State Building and Conflict in Divided Societies," an appendix to Pierre du Toit, *State Building and Democracy in Southern Africa: Botswana, Zimbabwe, and South Africa* (Washington, D.C.: United States Institute for Peace Press, 1995), 254.

4. Richard Haass develops an analogous template for determining the appropriate modus operandi for intervention in *Intervention: The Use of American Military Force in the Post–Cold War World* (Washington, D.C.: Carnegie Endowment for International Peace, 1994): "One must begin with an assessment of whether intervention is desirable, then address its feasibility, and then return to the question of desirability" (156).

5. Gerald E. Dirks of Ontario's Brock University, citing D. Gallagher, points out that "political and social systems are dynamic. Especially in post-conflict circumstances, they must be constantly monitored to ensure that the prescribed solutions needed for the realization of stability and security are appropriate for the changing conditions. A one time fix cannot be expected to constitute a durable solution." See Gerald E. Dirks, *Population Movements and Refugee Repatriation: The Impact of Returnees on the Stability of States in Post-Conflict Situations* (Halifax, N.S.: Centre for Foreign Policy Studies, Dalhousie University, 1995), 2–3.

6. According to Michael W. Doyle, Ian Johnstone, and Robert C. Orr, "Conclusions and Lessons," in *Keeping the Peace: Multidimensional UN Operations in Cambodia and El Salvador,* ed. Doyle, Johnstone, and Orr (Cambridge: Cambridge University Press, 1997): "UN peace operations, it appears, need to be ready to improvise their functions dynamically" (388).

7. Barnett R. Rubin (with Susanna P. Campbell) argues in the Introduction to *Cases and Strategies for Preventive Action,* ed. Barnett R. Rubin (New York: The Century Foundation Press, 1998), that "all prevention is political" (18).

8. A similar argument, but in the more limited context of third-party mediation, is made by Jacob Bercovitch and Allison Houston, "The Study of International Mediation," in *Resolving International Conflicts: The Theory and Practice of Mediation,* ed. Jacob Bercovitch (Boulder, CO: Lynne Rienner Publishers, 1996). A key "context variable" determining the outcome of mediation efforts is "characteristics of the parties," which includes "parties' political context," "parties' power," and "previous relations between the parties." Another key context variable is "the nature of the mediator," which also includes "previous relationship with the parties" (see 20–32).

9. Rubin, *Cases and Strategies for Preventive Action,* also asserts "the primacy of relationships" (20).

10. See John Paul Lederach, "Just Peace—The Challenge of the 21st Century," in *People Building Peace* (Utrecht, Netherlands: European Center for Conflict Prevention, 1999), 29–30.

11. Charles T. Call, building on Terry L. Karl's previous work, argues that "recent studies of democratic transitions have shown that the *process* of negotiation is more important than any specific set of institutions chosen or available." He cites Timothy Sisk to similar effect, that "'getting the institutions right depends less on political "engineering" than on the nature of the transition process.'" Call, *From "Partisan Cleansing" to Power Sharing?: Lessons for Security from Colombia's National Front* (Stanford, CA: Center for International Security and Arms Control, Stanford University, 1995): 30. See also Rubin on "the primacy of relationships," *Cases and Strategies for Preventive Action,* 20.

12. The use of "participatory action research" as a methodology for this purpose is exemplified by the War-torn Societies Project, which has worked in Guatemala, Eritrea, Somalia, and Mozambique. For an overview, see June Kane, *War-torn Societies Project: The First Four Years* (Geneva: WSP, 1999).

13. The importance of security, both actual and perceived, is a consistent theme in Donald Rothchild's work. See David A. Lake and Donald Rothchild, eds., *The International Spread of Ethnic Conflict: Fear, Diffusion and Escalation* (Princeton, NJ: Princeton University Press, 1998).

14. The United Nations Development Program points to some of these elements in its report, *Reconceptualising Governance,* Discussion Paper 2, Bureau for Policy and Programme Support, Management Development and Governance Division (New York: UNDP, 1997), 19.

15. An exercise in political development that has created both the right context as well as the appropriate forms for democratic institutions in a few francophone African countries is the "national conference." First promoted assiduously and successfully by France and by local civil society in Benin in 1990, the exercise has been conducted, with varying levels of success, in several other countries, including some in a state of civil conflict. Yet it has found few takers outside Africa, perhaps given its roots in French liberal and revolutionary tradition. Variations of the exercise might, however, be applicable elsewhere. See Pearl T. Robinson, "The National Conference Phenomenon in Francophone Africa," *Comparative Studies in Society and History* 36, 3 (July 1994): 575–610.

16. Bernard Wood, "Lessons and Guidelines for Donors: Key Points from the Development Assistance Committee's Guidelines on Conflict, Peace, and Development Cooperation," in USAID/CDIE, "After the War Is Over . . . What Comes Next?" report of the Conference on Promoting Democracy, Human Rights, and Reintegration in Postconflict Societies (Washington, D.C., October 30–31, 1997).

17. Thomas M. Franck, "A Holistic Approach to Building Peace," in *Peacemaking and Peacekeeping for the New Century,* ed. Olara A. Otunnu and Michael W. Doyle (Lanham, MD: Rowman and Littlefield, 1998), identifies some of the obstacles to developing coordinated strategies (287–294).

18. See, for example, Alexander L. George and Jane E. Holl, *The Warning-Response Problem and Missed Opportunities in Preventive Diplomacy* (Washington, D.C.: Carnegie Commission on Preventing Deadly Conflict, 1997), 10–12.

19. For analysis of the difficulties faced in gaining U.S. support for multilateral approaches to conflict management, see Charles William Maynes and Richard Williamson, eds., *US Foreign Policy and the United Nations System* (New York: W.W. Norton and Company, 1996), especially the chapter by Edward C. Luck.

20. A key finding of the Aspen Institute Conference on Managing Conflict in the Post–Cold War World: The role of intervention is that "states and orga-

nizations contemplating intervention should know the context (history, culture, local leadership, regional relationships) of both the place and the players." See the report of the conference, held in Aspen, CO, August 2–6, 1995 (5).

21. An important lesson from the UN role in Cambodia implicitly supports this point. According to Doyle, Johnstone, and Orr in "Conclusions and Lessons" (383): "In Cambodia, the electoral component and refugee repatriation seem to have succeeded simply because *they did not depend on the steady and continuous positive support of the four factions* [emphasis added]. Each had an independent sphere of authority and organizational capacity that allowed it to proceed against everything short of active military opposition by the factions."

22. See Michael E. Brown, "Internal Conflict and International Action," in *The International Dimensions of Internal Conflict,* ed. Michael E. Brown (Cambridge, MA: MIT Press, 1996), 613–614.

23. Rubin reaches a similar conclusion in pointing out that "the importance of unofficial actors and civil society must be recognized [because] they are both active themselves on the ground and form important constituencies for (or against) actions by governments." Rubin, *Cases and Strategies for Preventive Action,* 15–16.

24. In fact, in the negotiations leading to South Africa's National Peace Accord, "leaders from civil society, through a joint initiative between the churches and organized business, became the successful mediators and succeeded in facilitating a National Peace Accord . . . Because some components of South Africa's civil society were active and well organized, it was possible to rely on indigenous mediators to both persuade and pressure the main actors to come to terms." See Peter Gastrow, *Bargaining for Peace: South Africa and the National Peace Accord* (Washington, D.C.: United States Institute for Peace Press, 1995), 93.

25. "Somalia as a nation never did really exist," according to Ana Simmons. "Conflict was bound to erupt in the space that has been called Somalia precisely because the state was either incapable of breaking down Somali social organization or creating a nation out of it once irredentism failed." See Simmons, "Somalia: A Regional Security Dilemma," in *Africa in the New International Order: Rethinking State Sovereignty and Regional Security,* ed. Edmond J. Keller and Donald Rothchild (Boulder, CO: Lynne Rienner, 1996), 71–72.

26. Bernard Wood makes this point more generally. However important elections may be as mechanisms for legitimation and however much priority they may therefore receive in a peace agreement, elections "do not in themselves create or sustain democracy. *Democratization must be understood in the broader context of changing relations both within the government and civil society*" [emphasis added]. Wood, "Lessons and Guidelines for Donors: Key Points from the Development Assistance Committee's Guidelines on Conflict, Peace, and Development Cooperation," in USAID/CDIE, "After the War Is Over . . . What Comes Next?"

27. The second head of mission for the OSCE in Bosnia, Robert L. Barry, has let it be known that he thinks elections were held in Bosnia prematurely, largely under U.S. pressure, according to Ann Swardson. The result has been that "the winners from the Bosnian Croat, Serb, and Muslim communities were the same politicians who, for the most part, had been in power during the war." See Swardson, "Bosnia's Reconstruction: A Model for Mistakes," *Washington Post,* July 28, 1999, A17.

28. According to Doyle, Johnstone, and Orr, "Successful contemporary peacebuilding doesn't just change behavior; it also, and perhaps more importantly, transforms identities and institutional contexts. More than reforming play in an old game, it changes the game." *Keeping the Peace,* 382.

29. A dialogue process of this nature, on a small scale, was carried out as a conflict-prevention measure by the Carter Center in Estonia. See Joyce Neu and Vamik Volkan, *Developing a Methodology for Conflict Prevention: The Case of Estonia* (Washington, D.C.: Conflict Resolution Program, The Carter Center, 1999).

30. Pierre M. Atlas and Roy Licklider, "Conflict Among Former Allies After Civil War Settlement: Sudan, Zimbabwe, Chad, and Lebanon," *Journal of Peace Research* 36 (January 1999): 35–54.

31. Roy Licklider, "The Consequences of Negotiated Settlements in Civil Wars, 1945–1993," *American Political Science Review* 89, 3 (September 1995): 681–687.

32. In a statistic now widely quoted, there were fifty-seven civil wars between 1945 and 1993, of which three-fourths ended by victory and one-fourth by negotiation. Of the former, war resumed in 15 percent of them; of the latter, hostilities resumed in 75 percent. Licklider, "Consequences," 684–685.

33. This argument is explicated using game theory in Gerardo L. Munck and Chetan Kumar, "Civil Conflicts and the Conditions for Successful International Intervention: A Comparative Study of Cambodia and El Salvador," *Review of International Studies* 21 (1995): 159–181.

34. John Paul Lederach makes this point: "Peace accords are often seen as a culminating point of a peace process. In the language of the governments and the military, accords are referred to as an end-game scenario . . . In reality the accords are nothing more than opening a door into a whole new labyrinth of rooms that invite us to continue in the process of redefining our relationships." *People Building Peace,* 33.

35. Two disparate cases point toward the importance of participatory and decentralized decisionmaking as an effective conflict management tool. Ohlson and Stedman point out that "when important economic decisions are taken in Botswana, consultation occurs between foreign and domestic economists, between those economists and the bureaucrats who formulate policy, between those bureaucrats and the politicians (both ruling and in opposition) who are accountable for policy and have their own interests, and between those politicians and their constituencies, who ultimately must live with the consequences of government policy . . . *Botswana's greatest policy mistakes have occurred when the government has foregone inquiry and failed to engage all relevant constituencies in debate* [emphasis added]." Thomas Ohlson and Stephen J. Stedman, "State Building for Conflict Resolution in Southern Africa," in *The New Is Not Yet Born: Conflict Resolution in Southern Africa* (Washington, D.C.: Brookings Institution Press, 1994), 229–230. In another example, Salman Khurshid, India's former minister of state for foreign affairs, recognizes in a candid analysis of the Kashmir situation that "there are clearly two separate issues of governance involved—firstly, the legal structure of autonomy *in decision making pertaining to local concerns* [emphasis added]." *Beyond Terrorism: New Hope for Kashmir* (New Delhi: UBS Publishers, 1994), 133.

36. The report of a seminar, "Strengthening Cooperative Approaches to Conflict Prevention: The Role of Regional Organizations and the United Nations," organized by the Department of Foreign Affairs and International Trade and the International Development Research Centre (Ottawa, Ontario,

March 11–13, 1998), identifies "the need to foster a 'culture of dialogue' within a state itself by strengthening the institutions of civil society, particularly those with memberships and affiliations that cut across factional or ethnic lines" as one of the points that "came up repeatedly in the discussion" (2).

37. John L. Hirsch and Robert B. Oakley, *Somalia and Operation Restore Hope: Reflections on Peacemaking and Peacekeeping* (Washington, D.C.: United States Institute of Peace Press, 1995), 150.

38. Hussein M. Adam and Richard Ford, *Mending Rips in the Sky: Options for Somali Communities in the 21st Century* (Lawrenceville, NJ: The Red Sea Press Inc., 1997), 641.

39. Ken Menkhaus makes a similar point. Commenting on the remaining UN and NGO presence in post–UNOSOM Somalia, he writes, "Some have devised innovative ways to support capacity building (enhancing the ability of local governments and communities to take on responsibilities of good governance). *This is the kind of long-term political development that may ultimately make possible the resuscitation of a Central Somali government* [emphasis added]." See Ken Menkhaus, "Stateless Stability," *New Routes* 3, 2 (1998): 24.

40. For examples of international support to indigenously generated peacebuilding initiatives in Africa, see David Smock, ed., *Creative Approaches to Managing Conflict in Africa: Findings from USIP-Funded Projects* (Washington, D.C.: United States Institute of Peace, 1997), 18–19.

41. Gabriel Munuera draws upon Bosnia and other cases in Eastern Europe to offer some specific recommendations on how leaders who manipulate ethnic differences for political purposes can be weakened and more moderate leaderships strengthened, in *Preventing Armed Conflict in Europe: Lessons from Recent Experience* (Brussels: Institute for Security Studies, Western European Union, 1994), 86–88.

42. Some general ideas in this regard can be found in Milton J. Esman, *Can Foreign Aid Moderate Ethnic Conflict?* (Washington, D.C.: United States Institute for Peace, 1997).

43. For a comprehensive review of international attempts to establish, reinforce, or reform public security institutions, see Robert B. Oakley, Michael J. Dziedzic, and Eliot M. Goldberg, eds., *Policing the New World Disorder: Peace Operations and Public Security* (Washington, D.C.: National Defense University Press, 1998).

44. Margaret Thatcher has made an important and historically grounded argument for the role that the resolute use of force "by nation states with a long history of liberty, justice, and democracy" can play in ensuring future peace, even where such use is not bound by multilateral convention but is justified for reasons of self-defense or overwhelming morality. See Thatcher, "Managing Conflict—The Role of International Intervention," in the report of the Aspen Institute Conference on Managing Conflict in the Post–Cold War World.

45. An area of study deserving further expansion is that of the role of religious attitudes and actors in vitiating or reconstructing intergroup relations. A critically acclaimed work in this regard, which sets an agenda for further research, is Douglas Johnston and Cynthia Sampson, eds., *Religion, the Missing Dimension of Statecraft* (Oxford: Oxford University Press, 1994).

46. "None of the UN-created institutions—based on external models of state reconstruction—during the military intervention in Somalia are still standing, with the exception of a few local political councils which themselves have mostly been transformed by local actors to fit local exigencies." John

Prendergast, *Crisis Response: Humanitarian Band-Aids in Sudan and Somalia* (London: Pluto Press; Chicago: Center for Concern, 1997), 150.

47. For discussion of the challenges to as well as opportunities for effective exercise of this office, see Fafo Programme for International Cooperation and Conflict Resolution, "Command from the Saddle: Managing United Nations Peace-Building Missions," Recommendations Report of the Forum on the Special Representative of the Secretary-General: Shaping the UN's Role in Peace Implementation, January 1999.

48. See "Where Do America's Interests Lie?" *Economist,* September 18, 1999, 29–30.

Acronyms

ANKI	National Army of Independent Cambodia
ARENA	National Republican Alliance
ASEAN	Association of Southeast Asian Nations
CARERE	Cambodia Area Rehabilitation and Regeneration (Project)
CARICOM	Caribbean Community
CBI	Caribbean Basin Initiative
CICP	Cambodian Institute for Cooperation Peace
COPAZ	National Commission for the Consolidation of Peace
CPAF	Cambodia People's Armed Forces
CPP	Cambodian Peoples Party
CRIES	Coordinadora Regional de Investigaciones Económicas y Sociales
DHRR	Division for Humanitarian Relief and Rehabilitation
ECCY	European Community Conference on the Former Yugoslavia
FDR	Revolutionary Democratic Front
FMLN	Farabundo Marti National Liberation Front
FUNCINPEC	United Front for a Cooperative, Independent, Peaceful, and Neutral Cambodia
HDZ	Croatian Democratic Union
HNP	Haitian National Police
ICFY	International Conference on the Former Socialist Federal Republic of Yugoslavia
ICORC	International Committee on the Rehabilitation and Reconstruction of Cambodia
ICRC	International Committee of the Red Cross
IEBL	Inter-Entity Boundary Line

IFOR	Implementation Force
ILO	International Labor Organization
IMF	International Monetary Fund
INARA	Haitian government land reform agency
IOM	International Organization for Migration
IPSF	Interim Public Security Force
IPTF	International Police Task Force
JNA	Yugoslav National Army
LAS	League of Arab States
MICIVIH	International Civilian Mission in Haiti
MINUSAL	Mission of the UN in El Salvador
MIPONUH	UN Police Mission in Haiti
MNF	Multinational Force
OAS	Organization of American States
OAU	Organization of African Unity
OIC	Organization of the Islamic Conference
ONUSAL	UN Observer Mission in El Salvador
ONUV	UN Office of Verification in El Salvador
OPL	Lavalas Political Organization
OSCE	Organization for Security and Cooperation in Europe
PIC	Peace Implementation Council
PNC	National Civilian Police
PTT	Land Transfer Program (El Salvador)
QRF	Quick reaction force
RDC	Regional Development Committees
RGC	Royal Government of Cambodia
RRA	Rahanweyn Resistance Army
RRF	Rapid reaction force
SACB	Somalia Aid Coordination Body
SDA	Party of Democratic Action
SDM	Somalia Democratic Movement
SDS	Serbian Democratic Party
SFOR	Stabilization Force
SIF	Social Investment Fund
SNM	Somali National Movement
SOC	State of Cambodia
SRP	Social Rescue Plan
SSDF	Somali Salvation Democratic Front
TNC	Transitional National Council
UNCTAD	UN Conference on Trade and Development

UNDOS	UN Development Office for Somalia
UNDP	United Nations Development Program
UNHCR	UN High Commission for Refugees
UNITAF	United Task Force (Operation Restore Hope)
UNMIBH	UN Mission in Bosnia and Herzegovina
UNMIH	UN Mission in Haiti
UNOSOM	UN Operation in Somalia
UNPA	UN protected area
UNPROFOR	United Nations Protection Force
UNSMIH	UN Support Mission in Haiti
UNTAC	UN Transitional Authority in Cambodia
UNTAES	UN Transitional Administration for Eastern Slavonia, Baranja, and Western Sirmium
UNTMIH	UN Transition Mission in Haiti
USC-SNA	United Somali Congress–Somali National Alliance

Suggested Readings

General

Anstee, Margaret J. "Strengthening the Role of the Department of Political Affairs as Focal Point for Post-Conflict Peace-Building." Internal Report for the Under-Secretary-General for Political Affairs of the United Nations. New York: United Nations, October 30, 1998.

Aspen Institute. "Managing Conflict in the Post–Cold War World: The Role of Intervention." International Conference. Aspen, CO, August 2–6, 1995.

Atlas, Pierre M., and Roy Licklider. "Conflict Among Former Allies After Civil War Settlement: Sudan, Zimbabwe, Chad, and Lebanon." *Journal of Peace Research* 36 (January 1999): 35–54.

Ball, Nicole, ed. *Making Peace Work: The Role of the International Development Community.* Washington, D.C.: Overseas Development Council; Baltimore, MD: Johns Hopkins University Press, 1996.

Bercovitch, Jacob, ed. *Resolving International Conflicts: The Theory and Practice of Mediation.* Boulder, CO: Lynne Rienner Publishers, 1996.

Bertram, Eva. "Reinventing Government: The Promise and Perils of Peacebuilding." *The Journal of Conflict Resolution* 39, 3 (September 1995): 387–418.

Boutros-Ghali, Boutros. *An Agenda for Peace 1995: With the New Supplement and Related UN Documents.* 2nd ed. New York: United Nations, 1995.

Bradbury, Mark. "Behind the Rhetoric of the Relief-to-Development Continuum." Paper prepared for the NGOs in Complex Emergencies Project. CARE Canada, Ottawa, September 1997.

Brown, Michael E., ed. *The International Dimensions of Internal Conflict.* Cambridge, MA: MIT Press, 1996.

———, ed. *Ethnic Conflict and International Security.* Princeton, NJ: Princeton University Press, 1993.

Brown, Michael E., Sean Lynn-Jones, and Steven E. Miller, eds. *Debating the Democratic Peace.* Cambridge, MA: MIT Press, 1996.

Carnegie Commission on Preventing Deadly Conflict. *Final Report, with Executive Summary.* New York: Carnegie Corporation of New York, December 1997.

Chopra, Jarat, ed. *The Politics of Peace Maintenance.* Boulder, CO: Lynne Rienner Publishers, 1998.

Coker, Christopher. "How Wars End." *Millennium: Journal of International Studies* special issue 26, 3 (1997): 615–630.

Cortright, David, ed. *The Price of Peace: Incentives and International Conflict Prevention.* Washington, D.C.: Carnegie Commission on Preventing Deadly Conflict; Lanham, MD: Rowman and Littlefield, 1997.

de Soto, Alvaro. "The Politics of Post-Conflict Reconstruction." In *Making Peace Work: The Role of the International Development Community,* edited by Nicole Ball. Washington, D.C.: Overseas Development Council, 1996.

de Soto, Alvaro, and Graciana del Castillo. "Obstacles to Peacebuilding." *Foreign Policy* 94 (Spring 1994): 69–83.

Doyle, Michael, Ian Johnstone, and Robert Orr, eds. *Keeping the Peace: Multidimensional UN Operations in Cambodia and El Salvador.* New York: Cambridge University Press, 1997.

Doyle, Michael, and Nicholas Sambanis. "Strategies of Peacebuilding: A Theoretical and Quantitative Analysis." September 29, 1999. Manuscript.

Ginifer, Jeremy, ed. "Beyond the Emergency: Development Within UN Peace Missions." *International Peacekeeping* special issue 3, 2 (Summer 1996).

Harris, Peter, and Ben Reilly, eds. *Democracy and Deep-Rooted Conflict: Options for Negotiators.* Stockholm, Sweden: International Institute for Democracy and Electoral Assistance, 1998.

Helman, Gerald B., and Steven R. Ratner. "Saving Failed States." *Foreign Policy* 89 (Winter 1992–1993): 3–20.

Hooper, Rick, and Mark Taylor. "Command from the Saddle: Managing United Nations Peace-Building Missions—Recommendations Report of the Forum on the Special Representative of the Secretary-General: Shaping the UN's Role in Peace Implementation." *Fafo Report 266.* Oslo, Norway: FAFO Institute of Applied Social Science, 1999.

Kühne, Winrich. *Winning the Peace: Concept and Lessons Learned of Post-conflict Peacebuilding.* Ebenhausen, Germany: Research Institute for International Affairs, 1996.

Kühne, Winrich, Cord Meier-Klodt, and Christina Meinecke. *The Transition from Peacekeeping to Peacebuilding: Planning, Coordination and Funding in the Twilight Zone, Berlin Follow-up Workshop: New York, 10 March 1997.* Ebenhausen, Germany: Stiftung Wissenschaft und Politik, 1997.

Kumar, Krishna, ed. *Postconflict Elections, Democratization, and International Assistance.* Boulder, CO: Lynne Rienner Publishers, 1998.

———, ed. *Rebuilding Societies After Civil War: Critical Roles for International Assistance.* Boulder, CO: Lynne Rienner Publishers, 1997.

Lake, David A., and Donald Rothchild. "Ethnic Fears and Global Engagement: The International Spread and Management of Ethnic Conflict." Policy Paper 20. San Diego: University of California Institute on Global Conflict and Cooperation, 1996.

Lewis, Peter M. "Economic Reform and Political Transition in Africa: The Quest for a Politics of Development." *World Politics* 49 (October 1996): 92–129.

Licklider, Roy. "The Consequences of Negotiated Settlements in Civil Wars, 1945–1993." *American Political Science Review* 89, 3 (September 1995): 681–687.

———. *Stopping the Killing: How Civil Wars End.* New York: New York University Press, 1993.

Lund, Michael S. *Preventing Violent Conflicts: A Strategy for Preventive Diplomacy.* Washington, D.C.: United States Institute for Peace Press, 1996.

Munck, Gerardo L., and Chetan Kumar. "Civil Conflicts and the Conditions for Successful International Intervention: A Comparative Study of Cambodia and El Salvador." *Review of International Studies* 21 (1995): 159–181.

Oakley, Robert B., Michael J. Dziedzic, and Eliot M. Goldberg, eds. *Policing the New World Disorder: Peace Operations and Public Security.* Washington, D.C.: National Defense University Press, 1998.

Ohlson, Thomas, and Stephen J. Stedman. *The New Is Not Yet Born: Conflict Resolution in Southern Africa.* Washington, D.C.: The Brookings Institution Press, 1994.

Otunnu, Olara A., and Michael W. Doyle, eds. *Peacemaking and Peacekeeping for the New Century.* Lanham, MD: Rowman and Littlefield, 1998.

Paris, Roland. "Peacebuilding and the Limits of Liberal Internationalism." *International Security* 22, 2 (Fall 1997): 54–89.

Peck, Connie. *Sustainable Peace: The Role of the UN and Regional Organizations in Preventing Conflict.* Washington, D.C.: Carnegie Commission on Preventing Deadly Conflict; Lanham, MD: Rowman and Littlefield, 1998.

People Building Peace: 35 Inspiring Stories from Around the World (Utrecht, Netherlands: European Center for Conflict Prevention, 1999).

Ratner, Steven R. *The New UN Peacekeeping: Building Peace in Lands of Conflict After the Cold War.* New York: St. Martin's Press, 1995.

Rotberg, Robert I., ed. *Vigilance and Vengeance: NGOs Preventing Ethnic Conflict in Divided Societies.* Washington, D.C.: Brooking Institution Press; Cambridge, MA: The World Peace Foundation, 1996.

Sandbrooke, Richard. "Transitions Without Consolidation: Democratization in Six African Cases." *Third World Quarterly* 17, 1 (1996): 69–87.

Sisk, Tim. *Powersharing and International Mediation in Ethnic Conflicts.* Washington, D.C.: U.S. Institute for Peace, 1996.

Stedman, Stephen John. "Spoiler Problems in Peace Processes." *International Security* 22, 2 (Fall 1997): 5–53.

United Nations Department for Development Support and Management Services and United Nations Industrial Development Organization. "Post-Conflict Reconstruction Strategies." International Colloquium sponsored by the Austrian Centre for Peace and Conflict Resolution. Stadt Schlaining, Austria, June 23–24, 1995.

USAID/CDIE. "After the War Is Over . . .What Comes Next?" Report of the Conference on Promoting Democracy, Human Rights, and Reintegration in Postconflict Societies. Washington, D.C., October 30–31, 1997.

Weiss Fagen, Patricia. "After the Conflict: A Review of Selected Sources on Rebuilding War-torn Societies." Occasional Paper No. 1. Geneva: UNRISD, War-torn Societies Project, June 1996.

Bosnia

Bugajski, Janusz, Jonathan S. Landay, John R. Lampe, Charles Lane, and Christine Wallich. "Policy Forum: Bosnia After the Troops Leave." *Washington Quarterly* 19, 3 (Summer 1996): 69–88.

Cousens, Elizabeth M., and Charles K. Cater. *Toward Peace in Bosnia: Implementing the Dayton Accords.* Boulder, CO: Lynne Rienner Publishers, 2000.

Cousens, Elizabeth M., Ameen Jan, and Alison Parker. "Healing the Wounds: Refugees, Reconstruction and Reconciliation." Report of the second conference sponsored jointly by UNHCR and International Peace Academy, June 30–July 1, 1996.

Daalder, Ivo H. "Bosnia After SFOR: Options for Continued US Engagement." *Survival* 39, 4 (Winter 1997–98): 5–28. With Responses from Carl Bildt, Pauline Neville-Jones, and Robert A. Pape.

Gagnon, V. P., Jr. "Ethnic Nationalism and International Conflict: The Case of Serbia." *International Security* 19, 3 (Winter 1994/95): 130–166.

Glenny, Misha. "Decision Time in Bosnia." *New York Times*, September 8, 1996, 17, col. 2.

———. "Yugoslavia: The Great Fall," *The New York Review of Books* 42, 5 (March 23, 1995).

———. *The Fall of Yugoslavia: The Third Balkan War.* New York: Penguin Books, 1993.

Guest, Iain. "Moving Beyond Ethnic Conflict: Community Peace Building in Bosnia and Eastern Slavonia (Croatia)." Paper presented at the USAID conference, Promoting Democracy, Human Rights, and Reintegration in Postconflict Societies. Washington, D.C., October 30–31, 1997.

Holbrooke, Richard C. *To End a War.* New York: Random House, 1998.

International Commission on the Balkans. *Unfinished Peace: Report of the International Commission on the Balkans.* Foreward by Leo Tindemans. Washington, D.C.: The Carnegie Endowment for International Peace, 1996.

International Crisis Group. Bosnia Reports, 1996–present. www.crisisweb.org.

Kaufman, Stuart. "The Irresistible Force and the Imperceptible Object: The Yugoslav Breakup and Western Policy." *Security Studies* 4, 2 (Winter 1994/95): 281–329.

Lane, Charles, and Thom Shanker. "Bosnia: What the CIA Didn't Tell Us." *New York Review of Books* 43, 8 (May 9, 1996).

Malcolm, Noel. *Bosnia: A Short History.* London: Macmillan, 1994.

Owen, David. *Balkan Odyssey.* New York: Harcourt Brace & Company, 1995.

Roberts, Adam. "Communal Conflict as a Challenge to International Organization: The Case of Former Yugoslavia." *Review of International Studies* 21 (1995): 389–410.

Rohde, David. *Endgame: The Betrayal and Fall of Srebrenica, Europe's Worst Massacre Since World War II.* New York: Farrar, Straus and Giroux, 1997.

Rubin, Barney R., ed. *Toward Comprehensive Peace in Southeast Europe: Conflict Prevention in the South Balkans.* Report of the South Balkans Working Group of the Council on Foreign Relations Center for Preventive Action. New York: The Twentieth Century Fund Press, 1996.

Silber, Laura, and Allan Little. *Yugoslavia: Death of a Nation.* New York: TV Books, Inc., 1995.

Szasz, Paul C. "The Protection of Human Rights Through the Dayton/Paris Peace Agreement on Bosnia." *American Journal of International Law* 90, 2 (April 1996): 301–316.

Thompson, Mark. *A Paper House: The Ending of Yugoslavia.* New York: Pantheon Books, 1992.

Ullman, Richard H., ed. *The World and Yugoslavia's Wars.* New York: Council on Foreign Relations, 1996.

Woodward, Susan L. "Implementing Peace in Bosnia and Herzegovina: A Post-Dayton Primer and Memorandum of Warning." Brookings Discussion Papers. Washington, D.C.: Brookings Institution, May 1996.

———. "America's Bosnia Policy: The Work Ahead." Brookings Institution Policy Brief No. 2. Washington D.C.: Brookings Institute, July 1996.

———. *Balkan Tragedy: Chaos and Dissolution After the Cold War.* Washington, D.C.: The Brookings Institution, 1995.

Zimmerman, Warren. *Origins of a Catastrophe: Yugoslavia and Its Destroyers—America's Last Ambassador Tells What Happened and Why.* New York: Times Books, 1996.

Cambodia

Ashley, David. "The Failure of Conflict Resolution in Cambodia." In *Cambodia and the International Community,* edited by Frederick Z. Brown and David Timberman. New York: Asia Society, 1998.

Doyle, Michael. *UN Peacekeeping in Cambodia: UNTAC's Civil Mandate.* International Peace Academy Occasional Paper Series. Boulder, CO: Lynne Rienner Publishers, 1995.

Findlay, Trevor. *The UN in Cambodia.* Stockholm, Sweden: Stockholm International Peace Research Institute, 1995.

Hay, Lao Mong. "Building Democracy in Cambodia." In *Cambodia and the International Community,* edited by Frederick Z. Brown and David Timberman.

Heder, Steven, and Judy Ledgerwood, eds. *Propaganda, Politics and Violence in Cambodia.* Armonk, NY: M.E. Sharpe, 1996.

Heininger, Janet. *Peacekeeping in Transition: The United Nations in Cambodia.* New York: Twentieth Century Fund, 1994.

Kiernan, Ben, and Chantou Boua, eds. *Peasants and Politics in Kampuchea 1942–1981.* London: Zed Press, 1982.

McAndrew, John P. "Aid Infusions, Aid Illusions." Working Paper No. 2, Cambodian Development Resource Institute. Phnom Penh, Cambodia, January 1996.

Moniroth, Aun Porn. "Democracy in Cambodia: Theories and Realities." Trans. by Khieu Mealy. Phnom Penh: Cambodian Institute for Cooperation Peace, 1995.

Muscat, Robert J. "Rebuilding Cambodia: Problems of Governance and Human Resources." In *Rebuilding Cambodia: Human Resources, Human Rights and Law,* edited by Dolores Donovan et al. Washington, D.C.: Foreign Policy Institute, 1993.

Olson, Mancur. "Disorder, Cooperation and Development: A Way of Thinking About Cambodian Development." Phnom Penh, Cambodia: Cambodian Institute for Cooperation and Peace, February 1996.

Peou, Sorpong. "Cambodia in 1998: From Despair to Hope?" *Asian Survey* 39, 1 (Jan./Feb. 1999): 20–26.

Shawcross, William. *Cambodia's New Deal.* Washington, D.C.: Carnegie Endowment for Peace, 1994.
Tith, Naranhkiri. "The Challenge of Sustainable Economic Growth in Cambodia." In *Cambodia and the International Community,* edited by Frederick Z. Brown and David Timberman. New York: Asia Society, 1998.
Vickery, Michael. *Kampuchea: Politics, Economics, and Society.* Boulder, CO: Lynne Rienner Publishers, 1986.

El Salvador

Bollinger, William. "El Salvador." In *Latin American Labor Organizations,* edited by Gerald Michael Greenfield and Sheldon L. Maram. New York: Greenwood Press, 1987.
Boyce, James, ed. *Economic Policy for Building Peace: The Lessons of El Salvador.* Boulder, CO: Lynne Rienner Publishers, 1996.
Child, Jack. *The Central American Peace Process, 1983–1991: Sheathing Swords, Building Confidence.* Boulder, CO: Lynne Rienner Publishers, 1992.
FIS, *Fondo de Inversion Social de El Salvador: Información Básica.* San Salvador: FIS, Julio 1994.
———. *Reporte de Avance No. 37.* San Salvador: FIS, Julio 1994.
Foley, Michael W. *Land, Peace, and Participation: The Development of Post-War Agricultural Policy in El Salvador and the Role of the World Bank.* Washington, D.C.: Washington Office on Latin America, 1997.
Johnstone, Ian. *Rights and Reconciliation: UN Strategies in El Salvador.* IPA Occasional Paper Series. Boulder, CO: Lynne Rienner Publishers, 1995.
North, Lisa. *Bitter Grounds: Roots of Revolt in El Salvador.* Westport, CT: Lawrence-Hill, 1985.
Rosa, Herman. *AID y las Transformaciones Globales en El Salvador: El Papel del la Politica de Asistencia Economica de los Estados Unidos desde 1980.* Managua, Nicaragua: CRIES, 1993.
Schwarz, Benjamin C. *American Counterinsurgency Doctrine and El Salvador: The Frustrations of Reform and the Illusions of Nation Building,* prepared for the Undersecretary of Defense Policy. Santa Monica, CA: Rand Corporation, 1991.
Seligson, Mitchell A. "Thirty Years of Transformation in the Agrarian Structure of El Salvador, 1961–1991." *Latin American Research Review* 30, 3 (1995): 43–74.
Sollis, Peter. "Poverty Alleviation in El Salvador." Washington, D.C.: Washington Office on Latin America, 1993.
Stanley, William, and David Holiday, "Peace Mission Strategy and Domestic Actors: UN Mediation, Verification and Institution-building in El Salvador." *International Peacekeeping* 4, 2 (Summer 1997): 22–49.
United Nations. *United Nations and El Salvador, 1990–1995.* New York: UN Department of Public Information, 1995.
———. *El Salvador Agreements: The Path to Peace.* New York: United Nations, 1992.
World Bank. *The World Bank's Experience with Post-Conflict Reconstruction.* Vol. 3: *El Salvador Case Study,* Report No. 17769. Washington, D.C.: World Bank Operations Evaluation Department, 1998.

Haiti

Ahlquist, Leif. *Cooperation, Command and Control in Peace Support Operations: A Case Study of Haiti.* Stockholm: Swedish National Defense College, 1998.

Bell, Madison Smartt. *All Souls Rising.* New York: Pantheon Books, 1995.

Bentley, David. "Operation Uphold Democracy: Military Support for Democracy in Haiti." Strategic Forum No. 78. Washington, D.C.: Institute for National Strategic Studies, National Defense University, June 1996.

Bentley, David, and Robert Oakley. "Peace Operations: A Comparison of Somalia and Haiti." Strategic Forum No. 30. Washington, D.C.: Institute for National Strategic Studies, National Defense University, May 1995.

Catholic Institute for International Relations. *Haiti—Building Democracy: Comment.* London: CIIR, 1996.

Danticat, Edwidge. *Breath, Eyes, Memory.* New York: Random House, 1998.

Dobbins, James F. "Haiti: A Case Study in Post–Cold War Peacekeeping." *ISD Reports* 2, 1 (October 1995).

Dupuy, Alex. *Haiti in the New World Order: The Limits of the Democratic Revolution.* Boulder, CO: Westview Press, 1997.

Gibbons, Elizabeth. *Sanctions in Haiti: Human Rights and Democracy Under Assault.* Washington, D.C.: The Center for Strategic and International Studies Press, 1999.

Gros, Jean-Germain. "Haiti's Flagging Transition." *Journal of Democracy* 8, 4 (October 1997): 94–109.

Harvard Center for Population and Development Studies. "Sanctions in Haiti: Crisis in Humanitarian Action." Program on Human Security Working Paper Series. Boston, MA: HCPDS, November 1993.

Human Rights Watch/Americas, in collaboration with the National Coalition for Haitian Refugees. "Haiti—Human Rights After President Aristide's Return." New York: Human Rights Watch/Americas, October 1995.

Kumar, Chetan. *Building Peace in Haiti.* Boulder, CO: Lynne Rienner Publishers, 1998.

Lehman, Ingrid. "Public Information Campaigns in Peacekeeping: The UN Experience in Haiti." The Pearson Papers No. 1. Cornwallis Park, Nova Scotia: The Lester B. Pearson Canadian International Peacekeeping Training Centre, 1998.

Maguire, Robert, et al. "Haiti Held Hostage: International Responses to the Quest for Nationhood, 1986 to 1996." Occasional Paper No. 23. Providence, RI: Thomas J. Watson Institute for International Studies, Brown University, and United Nations University, 1996.

Malone, David M. *Decision-Making in the UN Security Council: The Case of Haiti, 1990–1997.* Oxford: Clarendon Press, 1998.

———. "Haiti and the International Community: A Case Study." *Survival* 39, 2 (Summer 1997): 126–145.

Mintz, Sidney. "Can Haiti Change?" *Foreign Affairs* 74, 1 (Jan.-Feb. 1995): 73–86.

Neild, Rachel. *Policing Haiti: Preliminary Assessment of the New Civilian Security Force.* Washington, D.C.: Washington Office on Latin America, 1995.

O'Neill, William G. "Human Rights Monitoring vs. Political Expediency: The Experience of the OAS/UN Mission in Haiti." *Harvard Human Rights Journal* 8 (Spring 1995): 101–128.

Pastor, Robert A. "Mission to Haiti #3: Elections for Parliament and Municipalities, June 23–26, 1995." Working Paper Series. Atlanta, GA: The Carter Center of Emory University, July 1995.
Preeg, Ernest H. *The Haitian Dilemma: A Case Study in Demographics, Development, and US Foreign Policy.* Washington, D.C.: The Center for Strategic and International Studies, 1996.
Reding, Andrew. "Exorcising Haiti's Ghosts," *World Policy Journal* 13, 1 (Spring 1996): 15–35.
Ridgeway, James, ed. *The Haiti Files: Decoding the Crisis.* Washington, D.C.: Essential Books/Azul Editions, 1994.
Rotberg, Robert, ed. *Haiti Renewed: Political and Economic Prospects.* Washington, D.C.: Brookings Institution Press, 1997.
Roumain, Jacques. *Masters of the Dew.* London: Heinemann, 1978 (orig. 1944).
Schulz, Donald E., and Gabriel Marcella. *Reconciling the Irreconcilable: The Troubled Outlook for US Policy Toward Haiti.* Carlisle, PA: U.S. Army War College, Strategic Studies Institute, March 10, 1994.
Shacochis, Bob. *The Immaculate Invasion.* New York: Penguin Books, 1999.
Trouillot, Michel-Rolph. *Haiti—State Against Nation: The Origins and Legacy of Duvalierism.* New York: Monthly Review Press, 1990.
United Nations/Organization of American States. *Haiti—Learning the Hard Way: The UN/OAS Human Rights Monitoring Operation in Haiti, 1993–94.* New York: UN/OAS, 1995.
Watson, Hilbourne A., ed. *The Caribbean in the Global Political Economy.* Boulder, CO: Lynne Rienner Publishers, 1994.
Wilentz, Amy. *The Rainy Season: Haiti Since Duvalier.* New York: Simon and Schuster, 1989.

Somalia

Adam, Hussein M. "Islam and Politics in Somalia." *Journal of Islamic Studies* 6, 2 (July 1995): 189–221.
Adam, Hussein M., and Richard Ford, eds. "Removing Barricades in Somalia: Options for Peace and Rehabilitation." *Peaceworks,* no. 24 (October 1998).
———. *Mending Rips in the Sky: Options for Somali Communities in the 21st Century.* Lawrenceville, NJ: The Red Sea Press, 1997.
African Rights Report. "Somalia: Human Rights Abuses by the United Nations Forces." July 1993.
African Rights Report. "Operation Restore Hope: A Preliminary Assessment." May 1993.
Bolton, John. "Wrong Turn in Somalia." *Foreign Affairs* 73, 1 (Jan./Feb. 1994): 56–66.
Clarke, Walter, and Jeffrey Herbst, eds. *Learning from Somalia: The Lessons of Armed Humanitarian Intervention.* Boulder, CO: Westview Press, 1997.
———. "Somalia and the Future of Humanitarian Intervention." *Foreign Affairs* 75, 2 (March/April 1996): 70–85.
Disarmament and Conflict Resolution Project. "Managing Arms in Peace Processes: Somalia." Geneva: United Nations Institute for Disarmament Research, 1995.
Drysdale, John. *Whatever Happened to Somalia?* London: Haan Associates, 1994.

Friedrich Ebert Stiftung, Life and Peace Institute, Norwegian Institute of International Affairs, in cooperation with the Lessons-Learned Unit of the UN Department of Peacekeeping Operations. "Comprehensive Report on Lessons-Learned from United Nations Operation in Somalia, April 1992–March 1995." Ebenhausen, Germany; Stockholm, Sweden; New York: United Nations, December 1995.

Hirsch, John L., and Robert B. Oakley. *Somalia and Operation Restore Hope: Reflections on Peacemaking and Peacekeeping.* Washington, D.C.: United States Institute of Peace Press, 1995.

Human Rights Watch. "Somalia: A Fight to the Death? Leaving Civilians at the Mercy of Terror and Starvation." Africa Watch Report, February 13, 1992.

Jan, Ameen. "Warlords on the Wane—Will Islam Fill the Political Void?" *Africa Today* 2, 6 (November/December 1996).

Laitin, David D., and Said S. Samatar. *Somalia: Nation in Search of a State.* Boulder, CO: Westview Press; London, Engl.: Gower, 1987.

Lyons, Terence, and Ahmed I. Samatar. *Somalia: State Collapse, Multilateral Intervention, and Strategies for Political Reconstruction.* Washington, D.C.: The Brookings Institution, 1995.

Makinda, Samuel M. *Seeking Peace from Chaos: Humanitarian Intervention in Somalia.* International Peace Academy Occasional Paper Series. Boulder, CO: Lynne Rienner Publishers, 1993.

Marshal, Ronald. "Les *Mooryaan* de Mogadishu: Formes de la violence dans un espace urbain en guerre." *Cahiers d'Etudes Africaines* 33-2, no. 130 (1993): 295–320.

Menkhaus, Ken. "Stateless Stability." *New Routes* 3, 2 (1998). Published by Life and Peace Institute, Uppsala, Sweden.

Prendergast, John. *Crisis Response: Humanitarian Band-Aids in Sudan and Somalia.* London: Pluto Press; Chicago: Center for Concern, 1997.

Sahnoun, Mohamed. *Somalia: The Missed Opportunities.* Washington, D.C.: United States Institute of Peace Press, 1994.

Samatar, Ahmed I., ed. *The Somali Challenge: From Catastrophe to Renewal?* Boulder, CO: Lynne Rienner Publishers, 1994.

The United Nations in Somalia, 1992–1996. New York: United Nations Department of Public Information, 1996.

War-torn Societies Project. "Rebuilding Somalia: The Northeast Somalia Zonal Note." Geneva: United Nations Research Institute for Social Development, June 1998.

The Contributors

Elizabeth M. Cousens is director of research at the International Peace Academy (IPA). Her current research focuses on comparative peace implementation in the context of civil war, with particular attention to Bosnia. Cousens is on leave from IPA, serving with the Office of the UN Special Coordinator for the Middle East Peace Process in Gaza.

Michael W. Doyle is director of the Center of International Studies and professor of politics and international affairs at Princeton University. He has written widely on peacemaking, peacekeeping, and multilateral security issues. His current research interests include the role of transitional authority and administration in peacebuilding.

Ameen Jan was a senior associate at IPA from 1994 to 1999, where he worked on the conflicts in Afghanistan and Somalia and participated in a task force examining the role of the OAU. He worked with the UN Operation in Somalia during 1993–1994. He is currently pursuing a master's degree in business administration at Stanford University.

Chetan Kumar is a program officer in the Office of the Special Representative of the UN Secretary-General for Children and Armed Conflict. Previously, he was a senior associate at IPA and directed IPA's Project on Policy Advocacy and Facilitation in Haiti from 1997 to 1999. The views expressed here are entirely his own, and not those of the UN.

Robert C. Orr is deputy to Ambassador Richard Holbrooke and director of the U.S. Mission to the United Nations Washington office, where he serves on the National Security Council–chaired Deputies Committee. He has conducted extensive research on peacekeeping and democratization, with a particular focus on El Salvador.

Index

About the Book

Although the idea of postconflict peacebuilding appeared to hold great promise after the end of the Cold War, within a very few years the opportunities for peacebuilding seemed to pale beside the obstacles to it. This volume examines the successes and failures of large-scale interventions to build peace in El Salvador, Cambodia, Haiti, Somalia, and Bosnia and Herzegovina.

The authors shed light on the unique conditions for and constraints on peacebuilding in each country and examine the quality and coherence of international responses. Arguing that the defining priority of peacebuilding initiatives should be the development of authoritative, legitimate *political* mechanisms to resolve internal conflicts without violence, they present "peacebuilding as politics" as an effective organizing principle for determining the best range, timing, and priorities of international action.

Elizabeth M. Cousens is director of research at the International Peace Academy. Her current work focuses on comparative peace implementation in the context of civil war. **Chetan Kumar** is a program officer in the UN Office of the Special Representative of the Secretary-General for Children and Armed Conflict. The views expressed in this volume are entirely his own and not those of the United Nations. He is author of *Building Peace in Haiti.* **Karin Wermester** is a program officer in the Research Program at IPA.